D1454447

CINEMETRICS
Architectural Drawing Today

LIVERPOOL JMU LIBRARY

3   1111   01435   0985

Published in Great Britain in 2007 by Wiley-Academy, a division of John Wiley & Sons Ltd

Copyright © 2007   John Wiley & Sons Ltd, The Atrium, Southern Gate, Chichester,
West Sussex PO19 8SQ, England
Telephone   (+44) 1243 779777

Email (for orders and customer service enquiries): cs-books@wiley.co.uk
Visit our Home Page on www.wiley.com

Anniversary Logo Design: Richard Pacifico
All drawings and illustrations © 2007 Brian McGrath, unless otherwise stated

All Rights Reserved. No part of this publication may be reproduced, stored in a retrieval system
or transmitted in any form or by any means, electronic, mechanical, photocopying, recording,
scanning or otherwise, except under the terms of the Copyright, Designs and Patents Act 1988 or
under the terms of a licence issued by the Copyright Licensing Agency Ltd, 90 Tottenham Court
Road, London W1T 4LP, UK, without the permission in writing of the Publisher. Requests to the
Publisher should be addressed to the Permissions Department, John Wiley & Sons Ltd, The Atrium,
Southern Gate, Chichester, West Sussex PO19 8SQ, England, or emailed to permreq@wiley.co.uk,
or faxed to (+44) 1243 770620.

Designations used by companies to distinguish their products are often claimed as trademarks. All
brand names and product names used in this book are trade names, service marks, trademarks or
registered trademarks of their respective owners. The Publisher is not associated with any product
or vendor mentioned in this book.

This publication is designed to provide accurate and authoritative information in regard to the
subject matter covered. It is sold on the understanding that the Publisher is not engaged in
rendering professional services. If professional advice or other expert assistance is required, the
services of a competent professional should be sought.

Other Wiley Editorial Offices

John Wiley & Sons Inc., 111 River Street, Hoboken, NJ 07030, USA
Jossey-Bass, 989 Market Street, San Francisco, CA 94103-1741, USA
Wiley-VCH Verlag GmbH, Boschstr. 12, D-69469 Weinheim, Germany
John Wiley & Sons Australia Ltd, 42 McDougall Street, Milton, Queensland 4064, Australia
John Wiley & Sons (Asia) Pte Ltd, 2 Clementi Loop #02-01, Jin Xing Distripark, Singapore 129809
John Wiley & Sons Canada Ltd, 5353 Dundas Street West, Suite 400, Etobicoke, Ontario M9B 6H8

Wiley also publishes its books in a variety of electronic formats. Some content that appears in
print may not be available in electronic books.

Executive Commissioning Editor: Helen Castle
Content Editor: Louise Porter
Publishing Assistant: Calver Lezama

ISBN   978 0 470 02669 4 (HB)
          978 0 470 02671 7 (PB)

Cover design by aleatoria.

Page design and layouts by aleatoria.

FSC
Mixed Sources
Product group from well-managed
forests and other controlled sources
Cert no. SGS-COC-2953
www.fsc.org
© 1996 Forest Stewardship Council

Brian McGrath Jean Gardner

CINEMETRICS
Architectural Drawing Today

1807
WILEY
2007

WILEY-ACADEMY

CONTENTS

NOW A FEW WORDS FROM THE AUTHORS

'The essence of a thing never appears at the outset, but in the middle, in the course of its development, when its strength is assured.' Gilles Deleuze[1]

Cinemetrics: Architectural Drawing Today brings architectural projection into the 21st century, the age of computer-generated modelling and animation. This illustrated guide introduces a new drawing system not at the outset of computer-generated drawing, but well within its course of development. Now we are ready to discover the essence and strength of drawing digitally. Computer-generated drawing has only recently become more than just an efficient two-dimensional drafting or rendered picture-making tool. It is being recognised as a new way of conceiving architecture multidimensionally in space, movement and time. *Cinemetrics* proposes that today's digital architectural drawing is a way of working, thinking and being in the world, not merely a servo-mechanistic process of simulating objects and illusionary scenes in service of what has become standard building production.

Cinemetrics develops a multi-dimensional method of measuring spatial relationships, movement and time – what is called here **matter-flux** – to replace a two-dimensional geometric projection of static objects. *Cine,* the root of *cinema*, means movement. *Metrics*, as in the word geometry, means to measure. Instead of measuring the earth (*geo*) as a flat plane, we are proposing architectural drawing which measures the movement (*cine*) of architecture in the stream of life. *Cinemetrics* is based within an expanded field of architecture today that includes film, contemporary cultural criticism, philosophy, science and art. Our purpose is to align architectural drawing with the emerging 21st-century paradigm of the cybernetic-organic nature of reality that is replacing the previous mechanistic view of life.

The great outpouring of digitally animated renderings for the rebuilding of Ground Zero and the World Trade Center Memorial Competition showed dramatically that digital modelling and animation have entered the public sphere and imagination. In spite of the enormous expense, labour as well as technologies and talents involved, these presentations were uniformly boring and non-communicative. While momentarily wowing and dizzying audiences, they ultimately confused the public, trivialising and making superficial the complex, controversial and contested architectural and urban design issues surrounding rebuilding and memorialising September 11 2001. It is remarkable that the elaborate presentations lacked any depth of contact with either the robust history of architectural representation techniques, or the power of moving cinematic images, the most universal of contemporary communicative languages.

Cinemetrics fills this gap in knowledge by using as reference Robin Evans' great work on architectural representation: *The Projective Cast,* Gilles Deleuze's two books on cinema: *Cinema 1: The Movement-Image* and *Cinema 2: The Time-Image,* and Charles Sanders Peirce's writings on phanerons and semiosis. Sources for cybernetics include: Gregory Bateson's *Steps to an Ecology of Mind,* Fritjof Capra's *Web of Life,* and Paul Ryan's 'From Video Feedback to the Relational Circuit to Threeing', *Leonardo,* and 'A Sign of Itself', *Video Mind, Earth Mind.* The combination and hybridisation of these thinkers' writings is the basis of the *Cinemetric* methodology. Our approach is a radical inversion of architectural and cinematic education, projection, drawing and design. Evans has demonstrated that architectural drawing or projection is just one node within a networked process of thinking that moves back and forth between the built environment, drawing and cognition. This process follows multiple paths: from the human imagination, to a building, then a drawing, or from a drawing to a building to an inhabitant. Rather than imagining, drawing and building being understood as a linear process, *Cinemetrics* incorporates these three processes into the circuitry of activity compatible with the circuitry structuring your computer.

Deleuze uses cinema to develop a philosophy of the 'new' where movement, time and duration emphasise the importance of imagination and thought – bringing Evans' line of thinking into realm of movement images. While Evans talks about the dynamics of movement between drawing, imagining, building, and perceiving, his book is a comprehensive assessment of architectural drawing before the computer. Deleuze's philosophy of cinema points to the possibilities of not just movement between drawings, observers and buildings, but of *drawings that move*. *Cinemetrics* takes this process one step further by advocating a cybernetic linking of drawing, thinking and building that assists you in developing your own creative imagination, deepens your perception of the world around you and your ability to enrich architectural design work. It is not a training for architects to become film-makers or to make films. It is a methodology for making drawings that generate space as seeds of new worlds in the making.

Cinemetrics begins from within your world of familiar electronic gadgets. The text assumes that you are technologically- and media-sophisticated because electronic tools saturate your life: the internet, mobile phones, digital cameras, video. In contrast, during the 19th and 20th centuries, architects approached drawing by beginning with a blank sheet of paper on a drawing board. Using the empty slate approach, architects then projected an imagined illusionary world, starting with a point and then extending it to line and plane to achieve axonometric and perspective illusions of space. This can lead to a belief in a static illusionary world rather than the current understanding of the physical world as matter-flux that manifests cybernetically.

Cinemetrics will show you how to slow down and stop our fast-paced mediated world in order to lose, instead of make, perspectival illusions. In place of perspective, you will find a methodology for immersive drawing of duration in space-time. The following chapter, *Losing Perspective, Finding Duration* explains how our newly emerging sensori-motor system, stimulated by computer cybernetics, is making us aware of the limitations of beginning on a blank slate. Instead of computer-based reality replicating linear models of the world, this book guides you to use digitally-based imaging to develop analytical reasoning based on cybernetics. Using the computer to think critically can help you to go beyond current architectural practices, in which digital drawings have become fly-throughs of projected buildings with no relation to culture or ecology. The book will supply you with cybernetic techniques of critical visual analysis and perception rather than teach you to use software.

Words in bold are Keywords found on pages 260-265

Acknowledgements

Thanks go to Helen Castle, Commissioning Editor of Wiley-Academy, for helping conceive, edit and produce this book; Louise Porter for seeing the book through production; Karen Willcox for graphic design and Julia Dawson for copyediting. Since 1990, the successive Chairs of the Department of Architecture at Parsons, the New School for Design; Susana Torre, Karen Van Lengen and Peter Wheelwright as well as Lersom Sthapitanonda and Bundit Chulasai at Chulalongkorn University contributed much support for our pedagogical experiments in architectural theory, analysis and representation. Co-teachers Victoria Benetar, Anthony Deen, Ethan Lu, Mark Watkins and Hae Young Yoon all contributed to early pedagogical experiments in digital drawings. Deborah Natsios, Paul Ryan, Sharon Haar, Grahame Shane, Petia Morozov and Mark Robbins gave timely advice, support and criticism. Thanks to Kirin Mishra and Bualong Monchaiyapoom for unwavering support as well. Drawings and modelling were assisted by: Mark Isarangkun na Ayutthaya, Raymond Sih, Stan Gray, Pin Wei (Dylan) Kuo, Steven Hong, Saul Hayutin and Mark Watkins. Manolo Ufer assisted in the selection of the cinema sequences. Shigeru Ban, Bill Brunner and Tomoo Nitta graciously provided drawings of and access to the Photographer's Shutter House, while Sulan Kolatan and William MacDonald provided time and their entire archive of material on the Raybould House. Important support was also received from the Graham Foundation for Advanced Studies in the Fine Arts.

We have been greatly inspired by the writings of Robin Evans, Gilles Deleuze, and Charles Sanders Peirce. We are not, however, scholars of their work. Instead, we have freely made an assemblage of their work in the spirit of the cybernetic regime we describe in Chapter 6. Hopefully, you will join us in "playing" with their ideas in order to draw different worlds in the making.

Illustration assistants:

Introduction: Raymond Sih
Chapter 1: Mark Isarangkun
na Ayutthaya and Stan Gray
Chapter 2: Raymond Sih
Chapter 3: Stan Gray, Pin Wei (Dylan)
Kuo and Mark Isarangkun na Ayutthaya
Chapter 4: Raymond Sih,
Pin Wei Dylan Kuo, Steven Hong
Chapter 5: Stan Gray, Pin Wei (Dylan)
Kuo and Mark Isarangkun na Ayutthaya
Chapter 6: Illustrations provided
by KolMac studio except 6_1, 6_19
and 6_20 with Mark Watkins

1 Deleuze, *Cinema I: The Movement Image,* trans Hugh Tomlinson and Barbara Habberjam, University of Minnesota Press (Minneapolis, MN), 1986, p 3.

INTRODUCTION
LOSING PERSPECTIVE, FINDING DURATION

What happens when architectural drawing leaves the drawing board and moves to the computer screen?

Cinemetrics is your guide to explore architectural drawing after it leaves the drawing board and enters the computer screen. As you proceed through this book, you will learn new skills and concepts for thinking about architecture, not as an isolated object, but as embedded in relationships. The professionalisation of the architect since the 18th century has resulted in a tendency for designers to draw and imagine buildings in isolation from culture and ecology, starting with the ***tabula rasa*** of the drawing board. We continue to suffer from this legacy as even the blank computer screen is most commonly used to reinforce mechanical representational systems detached from real sites as well as material, cultural and ecological processes. The intention of the *Cinemetric* drawing system is to support your own discovery of an architecture responsive to current understandings of the dynamic nature of the world. Rather than starting from a blank slate, *Cinemetrics* starts from an immersion in the fullness of life. Architecture is no longer conceived as an isolated object created through an autonomous set of technical skills. This book and drawing system reveal the possibility of creating open-ended ways of drawing and building in order to live and work within a universe of the continually emerging 'new'. Words in bold are Keywords found on pages 260-265

014 Digital technologies are the everyday experience of today's media-saturated world. This guidebook takes you step by step through a process that helps you 'lose perspective' and its epistemology of certainty, which holds that pictures on a drawing board or computer screen represent reality. Architects have been taught to go from the blank page or screen, to the measurement of points, lines, and planes, to the construction of projected perspectival space. Instead we will endeavour to

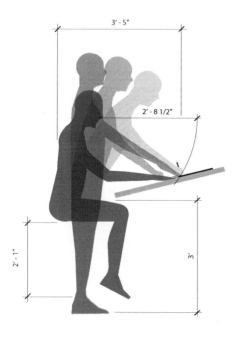

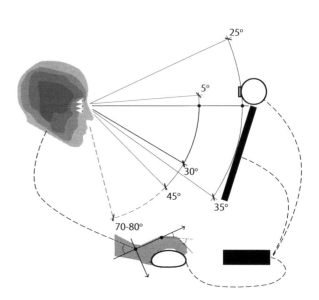

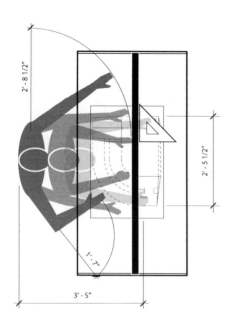

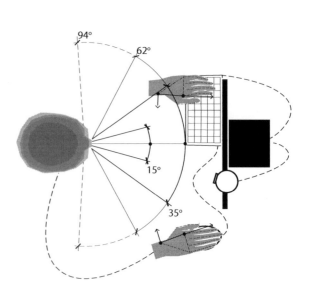

a_From the drawing board to the screen: the act of drawing on a drawing board led to the mechanical architect. Will the act of drawing on the computer screen create a cybernetic architect? Drawings derived from Ramsey, Charles George and John Ray Hoke Jr., *Architectural Graphic Standards*, Tenth Edition, John Wiley and Sons, (Hoboken, NJ) 2000.

'find **duration**' by stopping, sorting and assembling the less certain world of moving images in an open, changing whole.
Aimed at students, teachers, professionals, and the interested public, this book provides an accessible systemic framework
for learning how to position architecture within life-supporting initiatives emerging today in the fields of neurology, biology,
ecology, media and philosophy. Science and philosophy have undergone paradigm shifts away from the certainties of
the Enlightenment. Practitioners in these fields are creating new theories recognising disequilibrium, contingency and
chance. *Cinemetrics,* likewise, represents a paradigm shift away from the traditional habits and certainties of mechanical
architectural drawing.

We begin with the question, 'what happens when architectural drawing moves from the drawing board to the computer
screen?' When you leap from the certainty of a solid table supporting the undeniable physicality of a mechanical drawing to
the changing patterns of polygons and pixels on a computer screen, drawing becomes both a fundamentally different physical
act and artifact. New tools and new drawing systems are transforming the **servo-mechanical** architect of the 19th and 20th
centuries into what could be a cybernetic-organic one for today. If you are eager to start learning the new drawing system of
Cinemetrics, jump ahead to the chapter 1 *Framing.* You can always come back later to read more about *Losing Perspective.*

The question of what happens when architectural drawing moves from the drawing board to the computer screen is central
to the practice of architecture today. How you personally respond to this question affects every aspect of your involvement
with architecture in its expanding field of relations. In particular, your reponse affects what you decide to learn in relation to
both drawing and building, i.e. both the skills and the concepts critical to your practise– what we are calling the **know-how**
and the **know-about** of architecture.[1] But, despite the importance of this fundamental question, there is no agreement and
little discussion about what actually happens to the **sensori-motor system** of the architect in the act of drawing, and to the
drawing itself when the drawing board is abandoned for the computer screen.

Certainly, on the top of any student's list of architectural skills today is the ability to draw using a computer. But what precisely
does knowing how to draw digitally encompass? A place to start is physically experiencing the differences between using a
drawing board and a computer to draw. If you have never used a drawing board, why not give drawing with a mechanical
pencil a try? Having drawn using both a drawing board and a computer gives you the authority of personal experience when
you think about the implications of this book's opening question. Whether you try drawing with pencil and ruler or keyboard
and mouse, remember there is no agreed-on response to the opening question. There is an evolving body of opinions
about it. Your own experiences and thoughts can affect the changes emerging in both the know-how and know-about of
architecture today.

Compare the act of drawing on the drawing board and the computer screen. Instead of moving about with two outstretched
arms over a three by six foot drawing board, we sit, relatively immobile, facing a computer screen. Once we wrestled with
mechanical pencils, graphite, pens and ink using parallel rules, t-squares and triangles over large sheets of paper. Now we
glide and click a mouse or track pad and type on an electronic keyboard, frequently not taking our eyes off the screen for long
periods of time. Our rapid eye movements reassess the effect of our digital inputs rather than the marks we make on paper.
What is your experience of the differences in hand, arm, body, and eye movements using a pencil and electronic tools?

Micro hand movements transmit information through the computer's central processing unit (CPU) to a backlit screen. On
the drawing board we were limited by the size of the sheet of paper to a particular scale of working. The smaller computer
screen usually frames just a detail of the drawing we work on, so we zoom in and out and pan and scroll around a drawing
of a potentially vast breadth of scale and depth of information. How has 'zooming' and 'scrolling' changed what we mean by
drawing? We quickly jump from details to overall drawing and switch layers on and off. The digital act of drawing is marked by
more constrained movements of your body, but an intensification of concentration. When directing the frame of the computer
screen like a camera, we are scanning as well as marking, which stimulates very different responses from us.

LIVERPOOL JOHN MOORES UNIVERSITY
LEARNING SERVICES

016 Just as the act of drawing has fundamentally changed, the digital drawing produced is no longer a single crafted artifact, but a body of data from which innumerable drawings can be electronically transmitted, projected or reproduced. Rarely is a drawing constructed by a single hand, rather it is passed on between collaborators, consultants and team members. Information processing and data management has replaced crafted picture-making and the collaborative team has replaced the master draftsman. Also, while the drafted drawing could be mechanically blueprinted, the digital drawing can be viewed at various scales with varying combinations of layers of information, depicted in multiple projections, e-mailed around the world, and even animated. The digitally produced drawing does not exist as an artifact but is a dynamic stored **set of information** that can be altered and continually updated electronically.

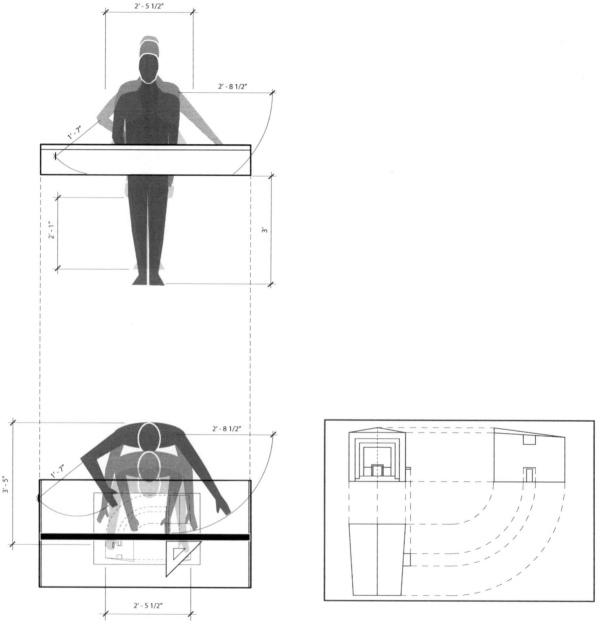

b_The act of drawing on the drawing board consists of measuring, scaling and projecting. The size of the paper and mechanical drawing projection require considerable bodily movement around the drawing board. These sensori-motor acts of drawing produce things: drawings on paper, which can then be mechanically reproduced. Orthographic projection drawn from Evans, Robin. *The Projective Cast: Architecture and Its Three Geometries*, MIT Press, (Cambridge, Mass.) 1995.

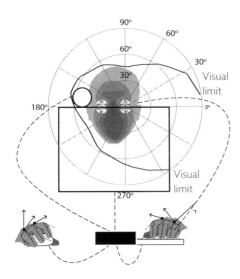

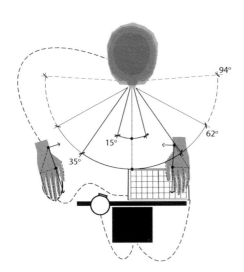

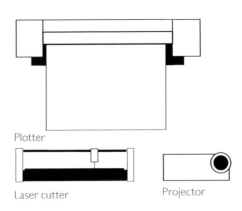

Plotter

Laser cutter

Projector

c_The act of drawing on the computer screen consists of micro movements of the hands and eyes, but very limited movement of the body. The 'drawing' produced exists first as bits of information which can be laser cut or moulded as a physical model, plotted as lines and tones by digital printers producing mechanical drawings, projected on a screen as stills images or animations, but also can be transmitted electronically via the internet.

Development of Digital Tools

The first computer-aided design software (CAD) moved architectural drawing directly from the drawing board to the computer screen by providing a familiar interface with which the architect virtually 'drafts' construction documents in an accurate, time-saving way. This approach to architectural **know-how** defined and dominated architectural production during the 1980s and few offices can operate without these tools. CAD demanded new skills from architectural school graduates and provided new efficiencies and accuracy in the workplace, but did not acknowledge the differences between the computer and the drawing board or the new **know-about** of architecture that could emerge in relation to the computer.

The arrival of personal computers and the first three-dimensional modelling software in the early 1990s brought a new virtual environment to architects and designers: a multi-dimensional drawing space that could reposition 3D objects from top to side to bottom, revealing the six sides of any three-dimensional cubic space, or even rotate in an infinite number of intermediate positions. Pioneering software simulated the Cartesian x, y, z space of physical model-making in a digital environment. While traditional physical models moved from drafted plans to extruded three-dimensional volumes uniformly in the z axis, the computer's new 3D interface could be used to draw and design in a gravity-free virtual space perceived gyroscopically and synoptically rather than as an extrusion or projection off a flat drawing. A new know-how for architectural drawing was being initiated based on new sensori-motor knowledge developed in using the computer.

In the 1990s, architects began abandoning the simulated architectural know-how of drafting tools and Cartesian space. Instead, they grew interested in software suited to making moving images and animate form. These applications were initially intended for making background scenes and characters for cinema rather than for designing buildings. Instead of **Euclidean** based regular geometries, and the linear extrusion of point, line and plane in gridded x, y, z Cartesian space, these new programs introduced splines, patches and meshes. New complex forms and **topologies** were created and manipulated through given parameters, which affected the form and space of buildings in unexpected ways. Architects had begun to use computers to explore topological invariants rather than orthogonally extruded Euclidean form and space. Computerised movement and animation had become critical design tools rather than just means of efficient production or slick representation. By the turn of the new millennium, it was clear that finally a new know-how for drawing architecture was emerging..

Shifting from Linear Thinking

The pinnacle of mechanical architectural drawing know-how on the drawing board was the construction of perspective images. For decades, students of architecture learned to draft points and lines to form plans and elevations, and then, as their skills developed, parallel line and finally perspective projections. Perspective is a graphic method of systematising architectural projection on a two-dimensional surface so what one eye sees is replicated in a picture-like image. As architectural historian Robin Evans has noted, perspective has been vigorously criticised as a drawing system, yet it continues to be more pervasive than ever because of its continuing power to provide striking likenesses in photographs, films, and videos – and now in computer-generated images.

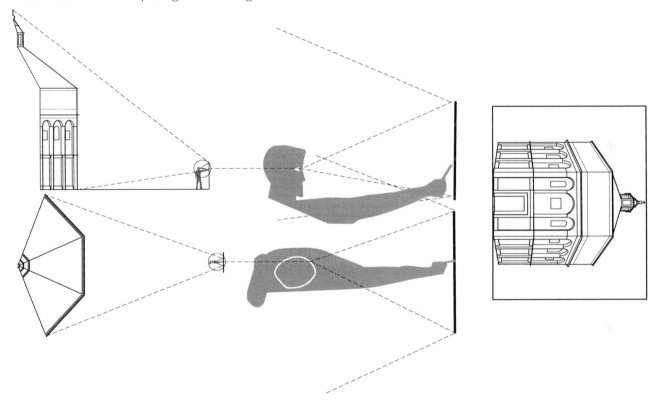

d_Filippo Brunelleschi developed the mechanical drawing when he turned his back to the Baptistery in Florence and held up a mirror to its reflection. He then traced the image of the building on the mirror, leaving the sky reflected in the background. This system only works on a symmetrical building, because it results in a backwards reflection of the original. To prove the accuracy of his tracing, Brunelleschi used a second mirror, which created a reflection of a reflection that could be read correctly. Redrawn from Dubery, Fred and John Willats, Dubery, Fred and John Willats. *Perspective and other drawing systems*, Van Nostrand Reinhold Company, (New York) 1972 To prove the accuracy of his tracing, Brunelleschi used a second mirror, which created a reflection of a reflection that could be read correctly.

The architect and mechanical engineer Filippo Brunelleschi demonstrated the geometrical method of perspective in 1415 at a time when the emerging civic and collaborative culture of Florence, Italy was reshaping medieval thinking. Perspective, first optically defined by the Arabian mathematician and philosopher Alhazen, contributed significantly to what later was called the European Renaissance and Enlightenment. According to Antonio Manetti, Brunelleschi's biographer, Filippo stood in front of the Florentine Baptistery and traced its reflection on a mirror in order to record what his eye saw. Analysing this experiment mathematically, Brunelleschi developed a method that anyone could repeat – a **know-how** – to transfer objects in three dimensions to a two-dimensional surface. Implicit in Brunelleschi's action is the belief that the eye is a dependable and accurate source of truth and that visual perception is able to recover the pre-given properties of the world. This new **know-about** opposed the one prevalent at that time in Europe when God was considered the source of truth.

020   Perspective developed within the cultural context of Renaissance Italy as drawing and printing shifted from hand-manipulated to mechanical devices. In particular, Johannes Gutenberg's invention of the printing press in the 1440s helped spread familiarity with and the use of perspective. Both of these inventions – perspective and the printing press – share a similar mindset in which the standardising and codifying of once diverse communication tools dominates. The cultural impact of the printing press and perspective is comparable to that of the invention of writing and the alphabet. We now live in a cultural context that is changing from mechanical to **cybernetic** instruments, of which the invention of the electronic computer is a prime example. Yet the most public display of computer-generated drawings today remains invariably perspectival renderings and perspective-based animated walk-throughs. Why has this 15th-century drawing system remained so pervasive?

The Florentine cultural context nurtured the emerging belief in linear scientific thinking as the source of truth. The eye and its extension, the mirror, led Brunelleschi to certain actions, in particular tracing, from which in turn emerged a method and theory of perspective. During the ensuing centuries of the European Renaissance and the Enlightenment, the act of drawing or painting using the system of perspective was widely believed to do what Brunelleschi thought he had achieved by tracing the Baptistery's reflection on a mirror: recording accurately the pre-given properties of the physical world.

Leon Battista Alberti codified a mechanical process of perspective drawing in his treatise on painting. Instead of utilising a mechanism to capture the real world, Alberti codified a method of transferring this abstract visual system onto the drawing

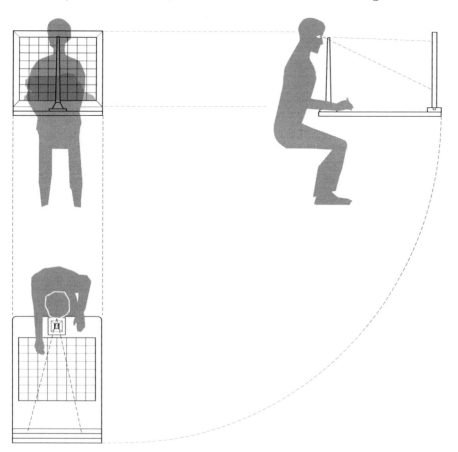

f_William Ware taught perspective drawing at Columbia University for many years at the beginning of the 20th century. His treatise on *Modern Perspective* (1905) explained that it was the architect's role to impose an ideal perspectival image on an unruly natural world. Perspective drawing is ' … free from most of the perplexities that constantly annoy the student of nature'. Architectural drawing continues to be taught as a closed illusionary system in the service of filtering out the messy reality of nature. (William Ware, *Modern Perspective: A Treatise upon the Principles and Practice of Plane and Cylindrical Perspective*, The MacMillan Company (New York), 1905, p.v.)

board as a virtual world. Four hundred years later this method had become the basis of the role of the Enlightenment architect – that magician who could conjure a perfect ordered world out of his imagination. From William Ware, founder of the schools of architecture at the Massachusetts Institute of Technology and Columbia University, to Francis Ching, author of many books on architectural drawing, architects were schooled to use perspective as the ultimate tool for organising both images of architecture and architecture itself. Buildings inevitably became a kind of set design. They defined a closed world of points, lines and planes, conceived through a static single eye and marked on a blank slate or *tabula rasa*. The architect, drawing on this utopian, empty sheet of paper, developed buildings as ideal forms without considering the complexities of human history, context and ecology.

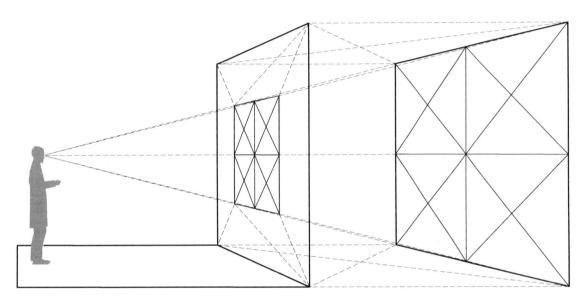

e_Albrecht Dürer printed a woodcut view of a mechanical device which consisted of a gridded screen between him and a reclining figure in 1536. He closed one eye and used another optical device to steady his open eye in a fixed position. He could then transfer the three-dimensional information behind the screen to a flat gridded, drawing board – only if his model remained in a frozen position. **Redrawn from** Dubery, Fred and John Willats, Dubery, Fred and John Willats. Perspective and other drawing systems, Van Nostrand Reinhold Company, (New York) 1972.

In his book, *The Projective Cast*, Robin Evans repeatedly demonstrates the gap between the architect's imagined projected world rendered in perspective and the spaces experienced by a mobile perceiving subject. Evans suggests we should consider ten transitive spaces between orthographic and perspectival drawing, building and the human observer. The final diagram in his book (illus g) provides numerous ways to move between drawing, building and observing. Finally, Evans alerts us to the limits of all modes of representation, as well as human perception and imagination. While Evans' diagram appears at the end of his book in summation of his observations on 'architecture and its three geometries', for us this diagram is only the beginning of exploring the potential of architectural drawing today. For Evans, the three geometries of architecture – compositional geometry, projective geometry, and symbolic geometry – form a network of possible relational ways to compose, observe and think about architecture today.[2]

The infusion of digital technology into architectural representation affords the opportunity to explore and expand Evans' diagram in multiple ways. The three architectural examples presented in *Cinemetrics* occupy very different routes through Evans' diagram. The first example, Shigeru Ban's Photographer's Shutter House, follows the most conventional process in modern architecture: a building is designed and drawn in orthographic projection (and physical models in this case). The building is built from orthographic construction documents, and then photographed (perspectival projection through the camera) after it is built. As a private house, it is through these plans and photographs that we must come to understand it.

The second example, Casa Malaparte, represents a break in this route, since the building as constructed differs substantially from the plans drawn by the architect Adalberto Libera. We will examine this building as it was filmed by Jean-Luc Godard in the film *Contempt*. It was only during its renovation in the 1980s that accurate orthographic survey drawings were done of the house. Finally, the third example, KolMac Studio's Raybould House, is an example of building construction that can proceed directly from computer models through new techniques such as computer numerically controlled cutting of materials.

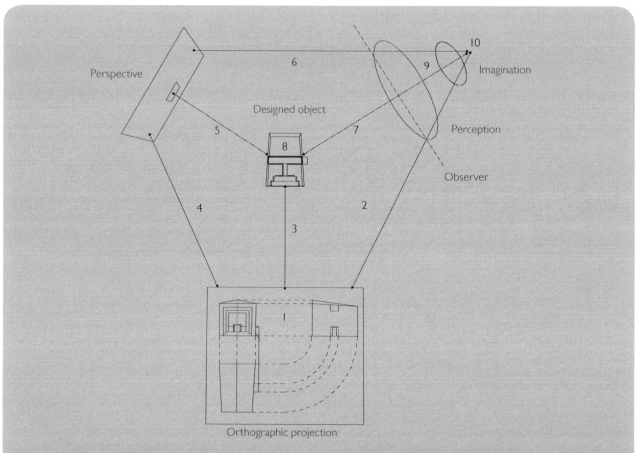

g_Robin Evans' *Projective Cast* demonstrates that architectural projection is a system consisting of ten transitive spaces between building, orthographic projection, perspectival projection, and the perception and imagination of the observer. While architectural graphics has traditionally taught a linear mechanical system from point to line to plane, and from drawing to building, in Evans' system the ten transitive spaces go in both directions in the service of architecture and its three geometries: geometric, projective and symbolic. Redrawn from Evans, Robin. *The Projective Cast: Architecture and Its Three Geometries*, MIT Press, (Cambridge, Mass.) 1995.

1_ The scalar geometric coordination between two dimensional plans, elevations and sections in multi-view orthographic projection.

2_ The route from the human subject as perceiving, mobile author making the drawing and the route from the drawing to a perceiving, mobile observer.

3_ The two routes between orthographic drawing and building: from drawing plans to building construction - the standard practice in architecture, and the reversed direction from building to orthographic projection of measured survey drawings.

4_ The constructed projection of a perspective from orthographic drawings, or the derivation of plans and elevations from an already constructed perspective or photograph.

5_ The taking a picture or making a drawing of a building, or the reconstruction of a building from a photograph or perspectival drawing.

6_ The making of perspectival drawings from our imagination, or the reading of a photograph or perspectival drawing such as in a magazine or architectural monograph.

7_ The perspectival space of a perceiving, mobile subject in the built environment and the impact or presence of that building on us.

8_ There is a distorted, collapsed or distorted perception of space within the built object.

9_ and 10_ The pictorial space of and between perception and imagination.

Cybernetics: Thinking in Circuits

How can architecture and architectural drawing change if the mechanical tools of drawing board **know-how** are still used when drawing on a computer? The medium of the computer with its electronic circuits is fundamentally different from the medium of the drawing board with its mechanical tools and methods, from pencils and paper through perspective constructions. Perspectival projections and cybernetic circuits organise thoughts and images in intrinsically different ways. Perspectival projections emphasise static parts in a linear configuration constructed from a **tabula rasa.** Cybernetic systems organise relational information-processes in circuits where differences make a difference, while perspective emphasises similarities. Fundamental to the *Cinemetric* drawing system is knowing that electronic drawings are bits of information in cybernetic circuits rather than computer-assisted picture-making.

Cybernetics takes as its domain the discovery, design, and application of principles of regulation and communication. It has been described as 'the science of effective organisation' as well as 'the art of ensuring the efficacy of action'. Noted anthropologist Gregory Bateson described it as 'the biggest bite out of the fruit of the Tree of Knowledge that mankind has taken in the last 2000 years'. W Ross Ashby, one its originators, defined it as 'the art of steersmanship'. Norbert Wiener coined the term 'cybernetic' from the Greek *kybernetes*, meaning pilot or steersman, which gives us an image for our own

CPU Board: Analogue Input Circuit

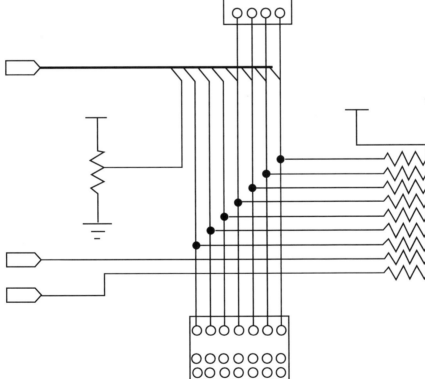

Analogue Inputs

h_Fred Martin's design for a computer's processing unit is redrawn here to show the non-linear inner workings of the computer. Cybernetic thinking led to a tool that relies on networking inputs, memory and circuits. This drawing is used analogously as inspiration for the *Cinemetric* drawings that begin on page 43. Redrawn from Fred Martin, MIT Media Lab, 1995. http://www.utdallas.edu/~axc018100/index_files/hbsch12.pdf, site checked on 02/19/2007

efforts to work cybernetically. Whether we are in a stream of water, stream of cars, people, or drawing, we may have a predetermined destination but cannot predict the behaviour of the stream. We must respond constantly to the changing context of our efforts in order to reach our goal. We focus on our relationship to the stream rather than blindly following a fixed pattern of movement. Cybernetics, which is a dynamic set of ideas, differs from linear thinking in the following ways:

1   A shift from considering parts to regarding the whole: cybernetics maintains that the whole is more than the sum of its parts;

2   A shift from objects to relationships: cybernetics is thinking in terms of relationships, not isolated parts;

3   A shift from measuring to mapping: parts are weighed and measured. Relationships are mapped;

4   A shift from contents to patterns: when we map relationships, we find certain configurations occur repeatedly. This is pattern. Patterns are configurations of relationships that appear again and again;

5   A shift from quantitative to qualitative: cybernetics focuses on the essential identifying nature of patterns rather than numbers of isolated parts in a pattern;

6   A shift from linear arrangements to feedback loops: feedback involves information about actions that make a difference. In cybernetics, feedback is a process whereby some feature of the output signal of a system returns to the system and changes its behaviour – a difference that makes a difference. Continuous feedback in a system is called a feedback loop. When what is fed back changes the system's behaviour by adjusting it to the output, we call the feedback 'negative'. When the feedback intensifies, rather than changes, the original behaviour of the system – creating a run-away system – we call it 'positive' feedback. Feedback is observed or used in various areas dealing with complex systems, such as engineering, economics, biology, and ecology;

7   A shift from thinking about isolated parts to contextual thinking: when we study relationships between a sub-system and a larger system to which it relates, we are thinking about context.[3]

Computers result from applied cybernetics. Designing digital interfaces and software as if they were the same as desktops and drawing boards is similar to designing cars with the look of horse-drawn carriages, which is exactly what Ford Motor Company did in its early years. The outward design masks the internal changes. We are currently witnessing the shift from perspectival linear thinking to cybernetic circuit thinking. Yet the potential for computers to develop architecture as an open process in a field of relations is ignored if we continue to use drawing-board tools manipulated through keyboards to produce static images of architecture. So the answer to the question of 'what happens when we move from drawing board to computer screen' is incomplete and inconclusive. On the one hand, up to now, a confused mix of tools for the know-how of architecture has been developed which support an increase in efficiency in the making of images for a mechanical worldview. On the other hand, recent thinking and experiments consider computer-generated architecture as process-images for a cybernetic worldview. Which worldview do you hold?

Early 19th-century studies of how the human sensori-motor schema functions helped to undermine the authority of perspective. This research disputed previous explanations of the eye as a transparent device registering the world around it. Instead, vision proved to be incomplete.[4] As a result of this two hundred year old research into the human sensori-motor system, we can make the following observation about the opening question concerned with the impact of architectural drawing using the computer:

If we draw on the computer, using drawing-board tools based on 600 year-old questionable concepts about how the human eye works, we cannot grasp the significant changes that the cybernetic computer has set in motion.

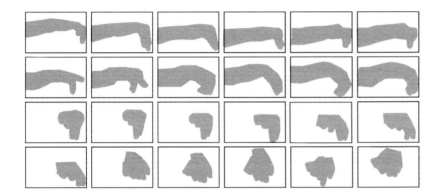 

i_The British photographer Eadweard Muybridge (1830–1904) created novel serial photographs that stilled the complexity of body movements into isolated frames. Here, a series of close-up photographs depict the micro movements of a hand from both side and front points of view. The mechanical production of images through photography offered the promise of an expanded vision, isolating moments which often pass too quickly for an unaided human eye to catch. Redrawn from Eadweard Mubridge, "Movement of the Hand, Drawing a Circle" *Animal Locomotion* Plate 532, 1887 http://americanhistory.si.edu/muybridge/index.htm site checked on 02/19/2007

Modern architects inspired by the revolutionary art movements of De Stijl, Cubism, Constructivism and Futurism also rejected static perspectival representations and revealed the complexity of form afforded by shifting frames and figures. El Lissitzky's famous *Proun* drawings are remarkable in that they are axonometric drawings and are meant to be viewed by turning the paper and looking at the drawing from each side. European modernists – in revolutionary Russia and the Bauhaus – likewise rejected pictorial perspective projections. Their drawing methods allowed detached examinations of three-dimensional compositions of form and space from disembodied vantage points.

The painter David Hockney, criticized the standard still image with his photographic experiments. He censured conventional photography as being devoid of time when compared to manual drawing that has a duration – the length of time it takes to construct an image by hand as opposed to the instantaneous moment of the click of a camera. His 'joiners' – Polaroid snapshots of the same figure or objects joined in grids – are like Cubist drawings of space, constantly repositioning the point of view or capturing the movement of figures. While Albrecht Dürer's grid was painstakingly static to create a seamless image (illus e), Hockney's celebrates the figurative disjunction created by movement and time. Hockney uses a camera as a moving drawing rather than a static picture-making tool (illus l).

Communication Professor Brian Massumi's research in bodily spatial orientation suggests '… the body is inseparable from dimensions of lived abstractness that cannot be conceptualized in other than topological terms'. This research suggests that

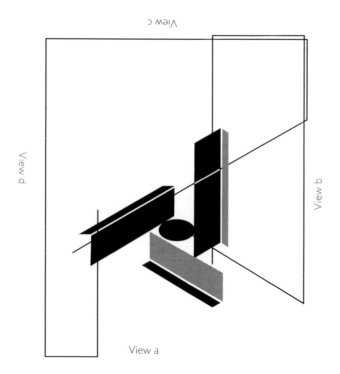

View c

View d

View b

View a

j_El Lissitzky's *Proun* drawings are an affront against the spatial limitations of perspective. He drew on the ambiguity of axonometry to develop drawings which can be looked at from any of the four sides. Turn the page of this book around and look at his drawing from the top, sides and bottom. Redrawn from Proun #69, gouache and crayon, 1924, Rubniger, Krystyna, *El Lissitsky* Catalogue from the exhibition from April 9 through the end of June, 1976, Gallerie Gmurzynska, Cologne, Germany, 1976.

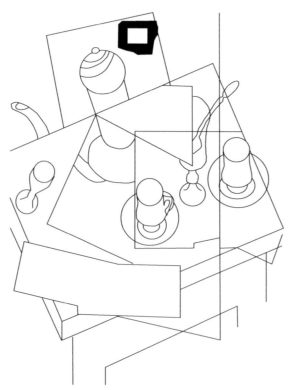

k_Juan Gris' still-life painting *Breakfast* (1914) shows simultaneously several layered views of a café tabletop. The table and the objects on it, shown from different angles, are necessarily viewed at different moments of time – the essence of Cubism. Drawing adapted from Fred Dubery and John Willats, *Perspective and Other Drawing Systems*, Van Nostrand Reinhold Company (New York), 1972, pp 113–14.

we have been operating on two different systems of reference: 'a predominantly **proprioceptive** system of self reference … and a predominantly visual system of reference for the vistas outside'.[5] Research into moving topological architectural forms suggests that as architects are developing new computer tools suited to the computer, these new tools are, in turn, supporting the emergence of new concepts based in a new **sensori-motor schema** – in new relationships between how we sense and how we act. *Cinemetrics* introduces you to this new sensori-motor schema, the tools and practices emerging from the schema and its relation to the expanding field of architecture.

By thinking cybernetically, video artist Paul Ryan created a topological form he calls the Relational Circuit based on the differences between seeing himself in a mirror and seeing himself on video. He first mapped the feedback loops of seeing himself on video onto a Möbius strip in the 1960s. This led to the creation of the Relational Circuit as a cybernetic and topological tool for understanding complex cultural and ecological relationships.

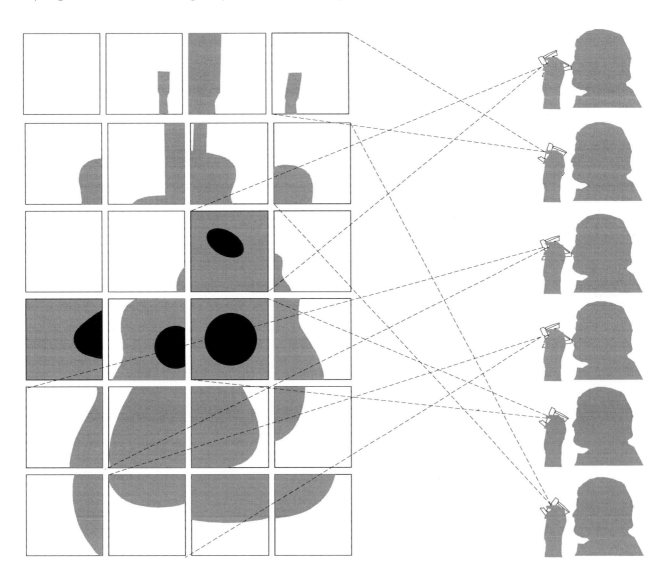

1_British artist David Hockney moved his Polaroid camera around still and moving objects creating Cubist-like compositions with photography. He argued that the camera image was dead – it lacked time. He called his photo montages 'joiners' that created an image, which like drawing or painting contained time and movement, David Hockney, *Photographs*, International Exhibitions Foundation (Washington, DC), 1986, pp 29–39.

028 Our newly forming sensori-motor system is affecting what we sense in general, which, in turn, influences what and how we draw and eventually the architecture that we build. Our emerging sensori-motor system is also changing our behaviour off the computer as well as our culture in general. Media critic Marshall McLuhan alerted us to the cultural effects of all media, including electronic devices, in his memorable phrase: 'The Medium is the Message'. 'In a culture like ours ... it is sometimes a bit of a shock to be reminded that ... the medium is the message. This is merely to say that ... personal and social consequences ... result from ... any new technology.' McLuhan argued that the greatest impact of any medium is in the cultural changes the medium triggers rather than in any particular content it communicates. In *Understanding Media*, McLuhan recounted how all media extend our bodies, creating new systems that have effects that return to us. This feedback loop ultimately alters us, potentially making us into **servo-mechanisms**. This individual process then changes our cultural context.[6]

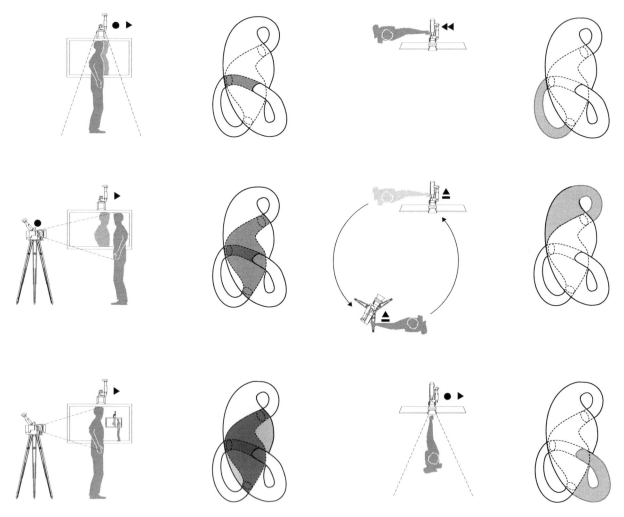

m_Paul Ryan developed the Relational Circuit (seen in the second and fourth columns) as a topological figure that grew out of a 1969 video art installation – Everyman's Moebius Strip. The figure maps the feedback loop between a person, a camera, a monitor, a second camera, and the ability of the videotape to be rewound and reviewed in real time (seen in the first and third columns). There are three main positions in Ryan's recursive video circuit: firstness, a spontaneous recording of himself on video (left, top); secondness, a recording of his reaction to the first tape being replayed (left, middle); and thirdness, a third recording of his commentary on his taped reaction to the first spontaneous tape. In between these three positions within the Relational Circuit are uncontained loops that include rewinding the first tape (between firstness and secondness as seen in the top right figure); exchanging tape one for tape two (between secondness and thirdness as seen in middle right figure); and starting the process all over again by completing the loop (between thirdness and firstness as send in the bottom right figure). Redrawn from Ryan, Paul. *Video Mind, Earth Mind: Art , Communication and Ecology*. New York: Peter Lang, 1993.

Finding Duration

At the turn of the 20th century, Bergson responded to the proposition that humans are predictable with an opposing view. He worked amid the mounting distractions of urban life that placed multiple, conflicting demands on human attention. Bergson challenged the increasing instrumentalising of life based on deterministic explanations of the body, its perceptions and its actions. He argued that having control over our sensori-motor system – over what our senses perceive and what our actions are – is not only possible but can even liberate us from the control of these modern demands. Opposed to mechanistic determinism, Bergson presented a more creative and more hopeful understanding of the know-about of humanity and its relation to the world in general.

To develop an appropriate **know-how** and **know-about** for an architecture of '**newness**' when architectural drawing has left the drawing board and moved to the computer screen, the thinking of French philosophers Henri Bergson (1859-1941) and Gilles Deleuze (1925–95) will guide us. Their work illustrates the ways in which new sensori-motor relationships lead to new conceptual knowledge. In many of Bergson's writings and Deleuze's two books on *Cinema*, these authors used film with its moving images to explain their concepts.[7] The architectural drawing system of *Cinemetrics* applies Bergson's and Deleuze's ideas to architecture.

Deleuze's approach to cinema derives in part from the work of Bergson, in particular, his two books, *Matter and Memory* and *Creative Evolution*. Bergson's experience of space and time informs Deleuze's ideas about cinema. Deleuze contends that what most of us call space and time are not what Bergson meant when he used these words. Bergson held that space and time are the 'extremes of a contracting and dilation of a single *duree'* or **duration**. The universe for Bergson is an open vibrational whole, a flow of matter-movement that contracts to form the fixed and discrete entities of the spatial world and dilates to form the temporal dimension of a universal past surging through the present and into the future.[8]

Bergson argued in *Matter and Memory* that the world of matter-movement is made up of images. Bergson used the word **image** to signify 'an existence placed halfway between the "thing" and the "representation"'.[9] 'In this world of images, non-living entities are images that interact with surrounding images like so many billiard balls, whereas living entities are images that function as **centers of indeterminacy**, pausing before reacting to a collision with another image.' Bergson explained that 'living images gain autonomy from surrounding images by mastering space and time – by perceiving impending encounters with other images, predicting their movements, planning counter-movements, and so forth.' Bergson held that 'a "**sensori-motor schema**" organises and coordinates the perceptions, feelings, and actions of each living image and from that schema issues a particular configuration of the world centered on that given image.'[10] Bergson's philosophy about the nature of space and time held that the universe is a vibratory whole in which the creation of the 'new' is a constant.

The research of American pragmatists – such as philosopher Charles Sanders Peirce – likewise supports life as open to the creation of 'newness'. The more recent researches of British anthropologist, social scientist, linguist and cyberneticist Gregory Bateson as well as of Chilean scientists and philosophers Humberto Maturana and Francisco Varela and of the French philosopher Gilles Deleuze, have all strengthened Bergson's position on the conceptual understanding of our world as an open vibratory whole.

Of particular note are the studies of biologist Francisco Varela, which confirm earlier research of Bergson, Dewey, and Bateson. For Varela, reality is not a given, as it was for Brunelleschi. In *The Tree of Knowledge: The Biological Roots of Human Understanding* (1987), Varela and Maturana demonstrate that what counts as relevant in the world is inseparable from our lived experience of that world. We, in effect, create our world – a process they named **autopoiesis**. Drawing on his and Maturana's research into the biology of human understanding, Varela contended that our ideas emerge from the recurrent patterns created by the particular ways our nervous systems link sensory and motor surfaces. As we have reviewed, these patterns are altered when we change our tools, and as a result, our concepts transform.[11]

You may be wondering how these studies have an impact on the tools and concepts of architectural drawing when it leaves the drawing board for the computer screen. In the body of this book, we will guide your discovery of a new know-how and know-about for an architecture responsive to the revolutionary changes in our understanding of the world today. We will discuss architecture, not as an autonomous object, but as a field of relations within the open-whole of **duration** – an architecture which creates 'newness'.

Realising that the universe is a vibrational whole – a duration – opens up new conceptual territories for architecture in the 21st century. But despite Bergson, despite Bateson, despite Maturana and Varela – despite the enormous potential of computer-generated cybernetic architectural projections, most of the current practice of architecture remains a 19th-century Beaux-Arts discipline. It utilises simulated tools that developed over the last five centuries for a different know-how of drawing and know-about the world. What is at stake when architectural drawing leaves the drawing board and enters the computer screen is the opportunity to transform the practice of architecture. The combination of our newly forming sensori-motor schema, new tools, and new concepts can produce a radical new art form and revolutionise architectural production. This combination of art form and production has the potential to engage broad popular imagination and participation in the making of architecture. This is the promise of *Cinemetrics,* which demonstrates that once you lose perspective and find duration, you can begin the process of thinking cybernetically in order to model a critically conceived, systemic architecture that addresses the unprecedented opportunities of the 21st century.

Book Organisation

The six main chapters of the book, which flip between film and building analysis, explore *Cinemetrics* as an alternative to standard drawing methods. Instead of beginning with the *tabula rasa* of the drawing board, we begin with the richness of life and the ability of the computer – a tool based on cybernetics – to store and access information. From there we progress to how how computer cybernetics relates to drawing systemically. The three film and building examples are located between cinematic and architectural modes of representation and thought. The films are examined both spatially and temporally through architecturally-based drawing and the buildings are examined through moving images. The juxtaposition of film and building examples provides ample evidence of the social and ecological contingencies architecture must embrace if conceived of as part of a world of relationships. The result is a way of imagining architecture not as isolated objects on a drawing board but instead as a field of relations within the **open whole** of life where the 'new' continually emerges.

We begin from within matter-flux by selecting **sets of information** that emerge through **framing** moving images in Yasujiro Ozu's film *Early Spring* (1956). Framing as a technique and as a way of examining architecture as flowing **matter-flux** is then applied to an example of architecture: Shigeru Ban's Photographer's Shutter House (2002–3). Together these two initial examples explore the tendencies of framing from a still camera in cinema and architectural drawing to 'slice' through flowing matter-flux as **immobile cuts**.

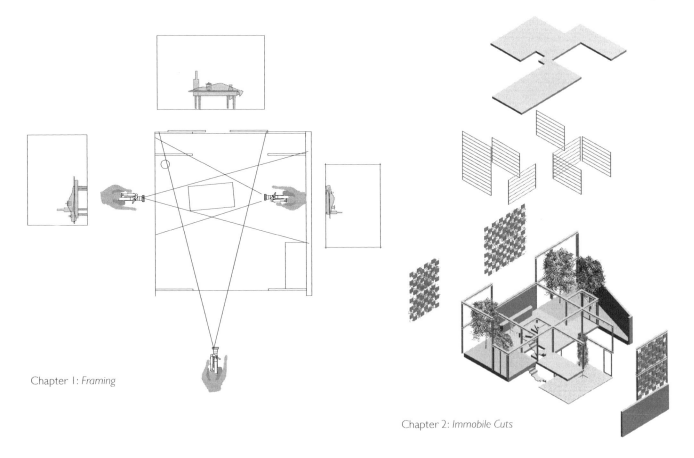

Chapter 1: *Framing*

Chapter 2: *Immobile Cuts*

n_Chapter 1 *Framing* examines Yasujiro Ozu's filming technique. He used a fixed camera on a low, floor level tripod. In his film *Early Spring*, he moved his camera in a 360-degree movement around his simple studio sets, carefully observing objects and characters in his films repeatedly. Chapter 2 *Immobile Cuts* applies Ozu's cinema style in analysing Shigeru Ban's Photographer's Shutter House in Tokyo, Japan.

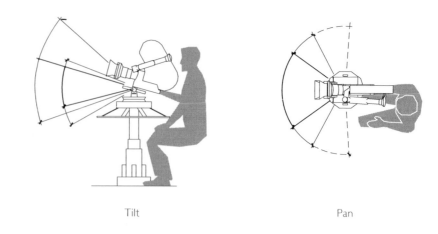

Tilt   Pan

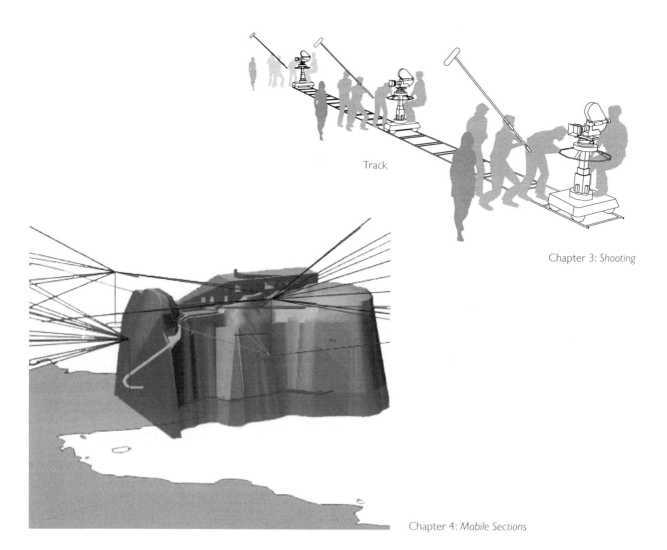

Track

Chapter 3: *Shooting*

Chapter 4: *Mobile Sections*

o_Chapter 3 *Shooting* follows Jean-Luc Godard's panning, tilting and tracking camera in the film *Contempt.* His shooting style comes from a detached, mechanical camera eye, distinct from the movement of the characters in his film. Chapter 4 *Mobile Sections* follows Godard as he takes his shooting style to analyse Casa Malaparte on the island of Capri off the coast of Italy.

The second pair of examples is Jean-Luc Godard's film *Contempt* (1963) and Curzio Malaparte's house on Capri (1938–41).
Contempt provides examples of **shooting** from a mechanically panning, tilting and tracking camera in the film. The mobility of the camera adds a dynamic to the shot not present in the example of Ozu. What happens when we view architectural constructions through **mobile sections** rather than static architectural drawing? When we move planes vertically and horizontally through architecture, much like a CAT scan, we sense a living organism rather than dissecting an inanimate object. The virtual camera can provide a non-human eye lens for architecture: transparent and able to cut through solid matter. Shooting and the mobile section will be examined not just as a representational technique, but as a new drawing tool and as a means of generating space.

Finally, John Cassavetes' hand-held camera in the film *Faces* (1968) results in cinematic frames and shots that through **assembling** produce a time image. His film breaks the **sensori-motor schema** of the action image, resulting in the appearance of pure optical and sound images. *Faces* is paired with KolMac Studio's project for the Raybould House (1998), a parametrically derived design that demonstrates the generative possibility of computer-based design, and is seen as a seed project for a cybernetic architecture in an expanded field.

We will consider just one domestic scene in each film as examples of framing, shooting and assembling images of flowing matter-flux. The digitisation of cinema – in digital video formats of old and new films and digital video editing software – allows us to understand cinema as an information system rather than ninety minutes of escape and entertainment. Now we can freeze the moving image and index carefully how different kinds of moving images are constructed as a critical tool in understanding the possibilities of architectural drawing today.

Inversely, the three houses are examined as sets for movement and time images as a basis for understanding architecture as a dynamic field of space-time and time-space relations within particular cultural and ecological contexts ranging in scale from the room to the house to site relationships. This narrowing of the range of examples allows for a close-up and detailed account of the nuances of architecture, cinema and representation, which is currently missing in both architectural and drawing discourses. In the final chapter we present a generative and de-generative drawing system based on the **semiosis** of Charles Sanders Peirce. This system is based on the continual recombination of signs and images as a continuous process of the discovery of the new, both as an analytical tool to understand contemporary architecture, and as a way to generate new architectural forms, processes and relations to an open whole.

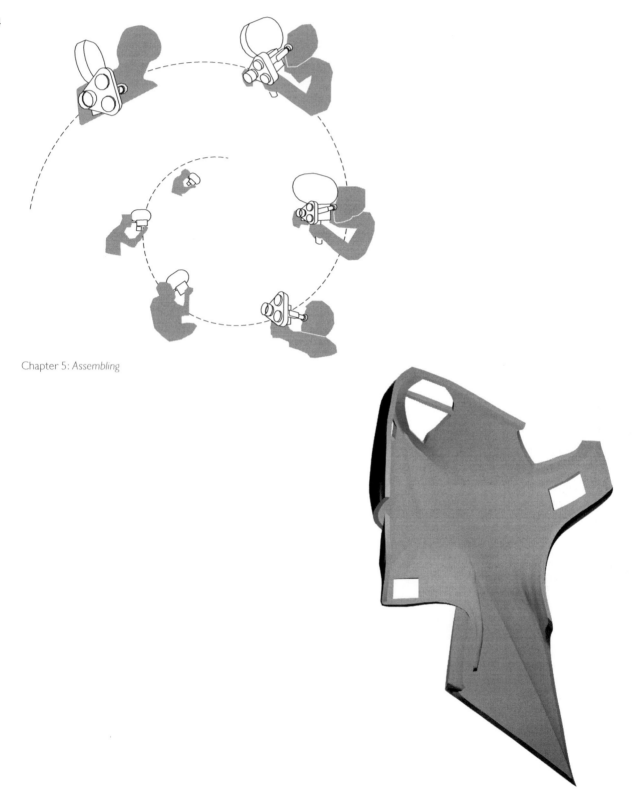

Chapter 5: *Assembling*

Chapter 6: *Cybernetic Seeds*

p_Chapter 5 *Assembling* presents John Cassavetes' use of the hand-held camera where he achieves maximum spontaneity and intimacy in shooting the moving bodies of his actors within his scripted films. Chapter 6 *Cybernetic Seeds* looks at how computer-generated processes can produce form and space with an examination of the Raybould House by KolMac Studio.

1 John Dewey, *Experience and Nature*, Open Court Publishing Co (Chicago), 1925.

2 Robin Evans, *The Projective Cast: Architecture and its Three Geometries*, MIT Press (Cambridge, MA), 2000, pp 366–70.

3 Based on Fritjof Capra, *The Web of Life: A New Scientific Understanding of Living Systems*, Anchor Books, Doubleday (New York), 1996.

4 Jonathan Crary, *Techniques of the Observer: On Vision and Modernity in the Nineteenth Century*, An October Book, MIT Press (Cambridge, MA), 1990, p 73.

5 Brian Massumi, *Parables for the Virtual: Movement, Affect and Sensation*, Duke University Press (Durham, NC), 2002, p 179.

6 Marshall McLuhan, *Understanding Media: The Extensions of Man*, Penguin Group (New York), 1964.

7 Henri Bergson, *Matter and Memory*, Zone Books (New York), 1988 (originally published in 1896) and *Creative Evolution*, University Press of America (Lanham, MD), 1983. Gilles Deleuze, *Cinema 1: the Movement Image*, trans Hugh Tomlinson and Barbara Habberjam, University of Minnesota Press (Minneapolis, MN), 1986 and *Cinema 2: the Time-Image*, trans Hugh Tomlinson and Robert Galeta, University of Minnesota Press (Minneapolis, MN), 1989.

8 Ronald Bogue, *Deleuze on Cinema*, Routledge (New York), 2003, p 3.

9 Henri Bergson, *Matter and Memory*, pp 9–10.

10 Bogue, *Deleuze on Cinema*, p 4.

11 Humberto Maturana and Francisco Varela, *The Tree of Knowledge: The Biological Roots of Human Understanding*, Shambhala Publications (Boston, MA), 1987.

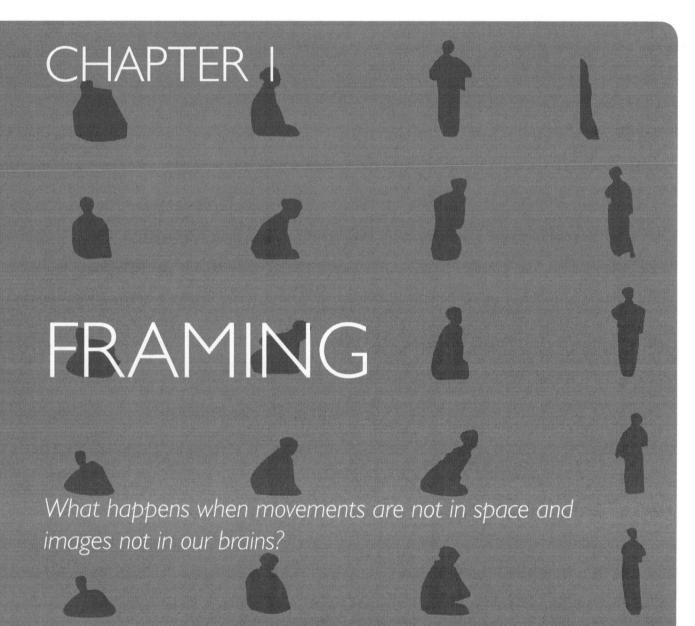

CHAPTER 1

FRAMING

What happens when movements are not in space and images not in our brains?

When we wake up in the morning, we open our eyes. Perhaps we look around our room, then stretch, maybe roll over and pretend we have not heard the alarm. Eventually, we get up and get ready for our day. As we get out of bed, we see our room. Where do we locate these images of the room? For that matter, where do the images of ourselves as we wash, get dressed and eat originate? Are they in our brains? If that's what you answered – that images are in our brains – that is what most of us believe. And what about your body's experience of movement? Where do you think movement is located? The common response is in the space of your bed and then, later, in the space of the room. Is that what you thought as well?

Words in bold are Keywords found on pages 260-265

038 Believe it or not, this is not what scientific research indicates. The images we see cannot be found in our brains and the movements we make are not limited to our changing positions in space. Instead, the images we perceive and the movements we experience both materialise out of **matter-flux**, where there are no edges, no up or down, no right or left, no in or out. We can frame or select images out of the enormous possibilities of sensations, and we can experience movement as a qualitative transformation in time rather than a measurable translation of a body in space. Modern science and philosophy both hold that there is absolutely nothing for us to use as an anchor for all that we are familiar with. There is only 'universal variation … universal undulation, universal rippling'.[1]

Science and philosophy also propose that the universal vibrations of matter-flux are the matrix of everything – the medium from which all movement, images, thoughts, and matter generate. Matter-flux is the **whole**. Matter-flux is probably not what you expected as the source of your images and your movements, let alone what you think about when you wake up in the morning. How can you adjust your perceptions to these discoveries so that you don't continue to put movements in space and images in your brain? Changing your preconceptions about images and movements is a critical step in learning the central lesson of this book: *how to develop moving drawings of architecture as a field of relations within matter-movement so you can design within an expanded domain of architecture.*

Exercise 1.1: *Thought experiment*

Let's try this experiment to help you change your preconceptions and thus your perceptions about images and movement. Next time you wake up, make an effort to experience matter-flux. Even before opening your eyes, let yourself become aware of your senses. What are you hearing? Perhaps noises from the street. What do you smell? Perhaps a whiff of coffee even though there is none brewing? And then an imagined taste of your favourite muffin makes your stomach growl. Your body is tangled in the bedcovers; your feet feel cold. As you start to move around, your muscles and joints tingle. In this heightened state of sensory awareness, rather than leaping into action, try something different. Suspend the movements that your sensory input is propelling you to make. Instead, remain still. Consider what else you might do instead. Why not find out more about the relation between your senses and your actions by turning your attention to your body? Understanding the relation between your senses and your actions – your **sensori-motor system** – can help you understand through direct experience where movements of your body and the images you see are located.

As a place to start, try this: see if you can find the gap between sensory input and immediate action output. There is such an **interval**, no matter how small, that has perception on one side and action on the other. By slowing down your habitual pattern of immediate motor reactions to sensory intakes, you can become aware of this tiny gap. It may take several tries to discover it. One way to find it is to take a deep breath in and pause. Then after exhaling, pause again, holding your breath out. These pauses are the intervals you are looking for. Next try to feel the involuntary pulsing of your own body in the stillness of pausing between breaths. What you are aware of when you come into contact with involuntary body pulse-movements is vibrating matter. The more you become aware of your own body pulsations, the closer you come to feeling the matter-flow from which images and space emerge. No need for special equipment to observe matter-movement, you already have the tools necessary: your body as a sensorial medium capable of detecting universal vibrations.

You may not experience matter-flux on the first few tries or even your pulse. But keep trying. This exercise helps you learn to develop moving images of architecture as a field of relations within matter-flux. So continue trying to observe the pause between breaths and when you do find it, increase its **duration**. But even before your experience matter-flux, by just attempting this exercise, you have begun changing your automatic preconceptions – the immediate goal and the first step in transforming the way we use computers to make architectural drawings today.

How has that happened – that you have already begun to change your preconceptions? Remember when you noticed yourself waking, hearing, smelling, tasting, feeling, seeing, and then pausing. These everyday physical states of your body – stretching, yawning, feeling hungry – themselves relate to matter-flux. They emerge from it. Also recall that your movements are not in your room and your images not in your brain but in matter-flux. You literally make your everyday physical states, usually instinctually or out of habit, by selecting blocks or **frames of space-time** from the undulating whole. When you consciously chose your physical state, you first pause to observe and then you select by framing space-time. This procedure of consciously framing space-time is exactly what you will do when you make moving images of architecture.

By pausing and considering what to do next – by making choices – you discovered that you are a **center of indeterminacy** within an acentered world of matter-flux and that you can consciously frame your sensations and actions from it. In effect, by finding the **interval**, the pause with sensory input on one side and action output on the other, you have become conscious of how you brought yourself into being. The act of drawing will help you to separate and layer these frames and to make that act conscious. How? As you select what to draw, you can become conscious that you are also selecting what you perceive. With this awareness, you become a **living image** - no longer a creature of habit but a conscious being choosing your actions.[2]

Understanding your indeterminacy is critical in working creatively with the opportunity provided by the shift in our **sensori-motor** relations when you use digital technology. You are not an unconscious **servo-mechanism** to your computer. You don't have to just sit there and react robotically to its directives. Realizing you have choices within a world of matter-flux is just as important in making moving images as understanding that those images don't exist in your mind, just as movements don't exist in space. All of these insights help you learn one of the central lessons of this book: *moving images of architecture are a field of relations within matter-flux.* The next step in your process of making such images is investigating in more detail what is involved as you live your day by framing blocks of space-time because, as you will discover, this is the same process you use when making moving drawings.

Framing Matter-Flux

As an experiential context for your next *Cinemetric* exercise, let's examine the process of framing your day more closely. There are mornings when, as you look over the top of the bedcovers at your room, you zoom-in on your computer. You don't notice the weather or that your clock indicates you overslept. Your attention is solely on your computer because you are excited about the project you are working on. What you have just done is frame a particular set of elements from the matrix of **matter-flux**. You disregarded everything else because it didn't seem to affect you right now. You then react to the initially selected **set of information** by choosing data from it that you think important, creating a new frame. You jump out of bed and start clicking through the drawings. All your actions leading up to this moment are a series of blocks or **frames** of space-time that you selected. They are not predetermined, only set off by the habits of your particular sensori-motor schema.

The analogy between consciously selecting the frames of space-time that compose your day and the framing of shots in a film is not far-fetched. It can help you understand *Cinemetrics,* the new system of drawing described in this book. Here's how. The frames you observe and select when you perceive and act are to the universal rippling of the **open whole** of matter-flux as film frames are to the world in which they are made. We understand that a single film is not the entire world; it is only an assemblage of framed moving segments from a larger whole. Likewise, your day is a framed moving section from the whole of matter-flux. That building you want to draw digitally for your project, it also is a framed moving segment from the whole of matter-flux. Your day, a film, a building, a moving drawing: they are all framed moving portions drawn from matter-flux.

Cinemetrics maintains that by studying cinema, which is composed of thousands of single images that appear to move, we begin to understand how to frame moving architectural images drawn on the computer. Examining film closely also introduces us to the people and systems that the built environment interacts with, which are often missing when we study the history of architecture as a series of isolated objects. In the case of Yasujiro Ozu's *Early Spring,* we witness, within the architecture of home and office, the impact on domestic life of the shift to salaried work in Japan. Ozu's film gives us insights into a particular field of relations in which the architecture is a critical player. This is how exploring film helps you to appreciate that architecture is not an autonomous object but instead a field of relations within the open vibrational whole of matter-flux. The study of film also helps you to begin to experience the universal rippling before opening your eyes in the morning by deepening your understanding of matter-flux. The study of film can thus inform your efforts to experience your own sensori-motor schema within a field of relations. In addition, it can also expand your understanding of the new *Cinemetric* drawing system.

Exercise 1.2: *Framing different kinds of movement images*

In exercise 1.2, record your daily routine of getting up in the morning with a digital camera. This exercise will gain resonance if you persist in sharpening your attention through repetition. You are now collecting data, which can be stored in your computer for comparative analysis. The key concept is the notion that a framed image is a provisionally closed set of information within an open whole of matter-flux. We are incapable of perceiving, never mind remembering all the sensory information that bombards us daily. The framing technique is a selection process, a matter of choosing what to focus on and what to disregard. This selection process is one we constantly make in architectural design. What this technique provides, though, is a way to consider those choices not as permanent closures but as moving images within the **open whole.**

It may seem counterintuitive that to understand the movement of matter-flux you must slow down, pause and stop, but this is the key to the first *Cinemetric* exercises. We start with the idea of framing matter-flux as **intervals**. Your first tool is your body, the second will be a camera as a drawing tool. How can you draw or represent the spatial field of your experiences of

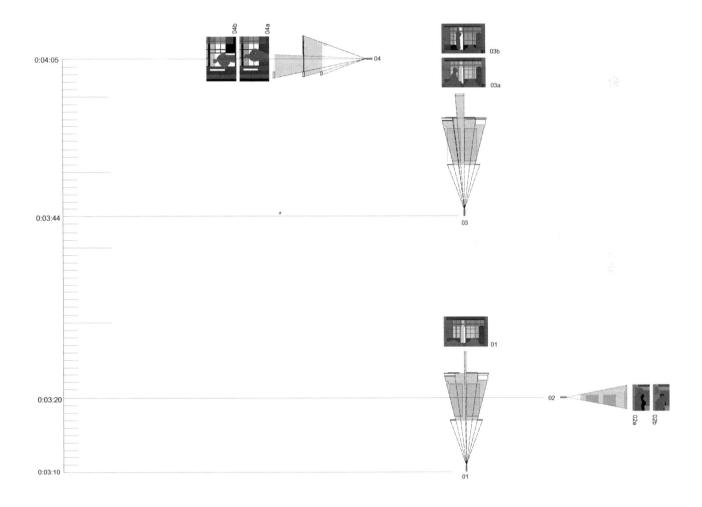

1_02 The first four shots of *Early Spring* show the wife getting up in the morning from three frames positioned at right angles. The camera in each shot remains stationary, but when assembled together they encompass a 270-degree description of three sides of the couple's bedroom, the first set of the movie. The movement of the camera between the shots gradually unfolds the interior of the couple's house, as each shot adjusts the distance between the space, characters and action and the camera. In the following diagrams a plan shows the cone of vision of the camera with a film still redrawn above or along side it. All film frames are repositioned according to the angle of framing in plan. The cones show the direction of the shot. The graph on the left marks the duration of each framed shot in seconds.

these awakening sensations? You can start by following the examples of Ozu's opening scene of the film *Early Spring,* shown here. In this scene we can use his filming of a couple waking up in the morning as an example. Notice how Ozu uses a strictly limited cinematic vocabulary. His camera never moves in a shot, and he films the space and the action of the couple waking up from only three 90-degree camera angles. This strict orthogonality resembles the way architects begin to draw three-dimensional space, drawing one side and then another of a volume. Picture-taking, as we have seen in the example of Hockney in the chapter on *Losing Perspective,* can be a form of drawing. You can map moments of heightened states of sensory awareness as **immobile cuts**, the creation of what Robin Evans calls the 'arrested image', a freezing of one moment in space flow.

Record your moments of awareness while waking up in a manner similar to Ozu by framing matter-flux. How is space formed by the movement of bodies within architectural frames? What are the ways to frame matter, space and flows? Ozu's technique is to begin with simple, clear static frames, which make us aware of slight changes within the frame. It is only by freezing the movement of the observer that he brings awareness of the flow of matter-flux.

In the cybernetic drawing language we are developing, two tools are fundamental: the camera's eye, and your body here as both a locus of experiencing and observing. Architectural drawing usually begins with orthographic projection. Survey your room with a measuring tape, determining the dimensions of the floor and four walls. Compare the orthographic drawings with the photographs or drawings you produced as you were waking up. Trace the movements of your body as you move through the space of your bedroom. Sketch in your movement on the plan and the photographs. Can you begin to convert these photo diaries to a drawing system which combines photography, motion mapping and orthographic projection, using the illustrations in this chapter as a guide? It is in the computer that you can begin to combine these very different representational methods, transforming them into a new **know-how** for computer drawing. Some of these tools originate in a context different from **cybernetics**, but digital technology allows us to combine them in a fully electronic system that helps us understand them cybernetically.

These sets of information form images that we can distinguish, following Deleuze and Bergson, as perception, affection, and action movement images. Deleuze was inspired by the work of Charles Sanders Peirce, although Deleuze had only limited access to Peirce's voluminous writings through secondary sources.[3] Deleuze related his movement images to Peirce's scrutiny of '"direct appearances" as they pop into the mind'.[4] Peirce's scrutiny involves observing our bodily process of becoming conscious. Peirce's three categories frame Deleuze's images in a system of direct observations of self, just as you did by observing yourself waking up. Peirce distinguished three categories of direct appearances, which never sever their relations to each other. These relations are all always present, which he articulated in his system of **semiosis** that we will examine in detail when we discuss *Mobile Sections*. For now, we will explore his three basic categories in order to understand the movement images that you will be using to make moving architectural drawings.

Peirce argued that when we scrutinise qualities of direct appearances, such as colour, texture, smell, we are in **firstness**. When we scrutinise facts – the specifics of the physical world – we are in **secondness**. When we scrutinise patterns and context, observing the whole, laws or theories, we move to **thirdness**.[5]

Deleuze called the images we make when we are observing what appears in firstness, **affect images**, those we make in secondness, **action images**. He did not find a counterpart to his **perception image** in the secondary sources describing Peirce's philosophy that he was reading. In the next chapter we will see that Deleuze called the images we make in thirdness, **relation images**. We will also review two more movement images that Deleuze added to these four – the **impulse image** and the **reflection image**.

Perception Image

Ozu begins the first scene of *Early Spring* with a shot that presents a 'total, objective perception which is indistinguishable from the thing'.[6] Ozu's camera impossibly intrudes into the bedroom of a sleeping couple, but looks straight ahead, over them, and not at them. The dim morning light seeps in from behind a gridded screen facing the camera. Here is a room frontally and fully presented. A soft glow emanates from the middle right of the background, and gradually fades to black at the edges. A curtain, slightly drawn, is in front of the square-paned screen. The lower left edge of the frame contains a sleeping woman, her face lit from behind, her feet towards the camera. There is another obscured person next to her on the right side of the frame. The composition is frontal, slightly off-centre. Neither the camera – which is positioned at the level of a viewer sitting on the floor – nor the couple moves.

As a studio film director, Ozu presents us with an image of a stage set that is impossible to tell apart from an actual Japanese bedroom. The Japanese have a name for this – '*mono no aware,* which [is] … the capacity to experience the objective world in a direct and unmediated fashion, to understand sympathetically the objects and the natural world around one without resorting to language or other mediators'.[7] This capacity to experience the objective world in a direct and unmediated fashion is something you might want to experience in the drawing system of your day. A world as unmediated as possible is also what you might want to show when drawing a building. Such an image of a building is what we are calling a **perception image**.

Images that attempt to be as similar as possible to the thing itself make legible all of the important features of what is being considered. In Ozu's frame (illus I_03 and I_04), we become aware of the proportions of the 'room' and the bed within it because we sense the floor, the ceiling, and see the gridded screen. We intuit where the other three walls are in relation to these elements in the **framed set of information**. The morning light filtering into the 'room' we assume is coming from the east. Thus, this 'image that attempts to be indistinguishable from the thing itself' has given us shapes of room and furniture, the proportions of these, room orientation, sources of light, and furniture, all of which define the interior, just as you need to do when making an architectural interior drawing.

To create the first shot for *Early Spring,* Ozu frames **blocks** of space-time. Similarly, when we live our day or when we make digital drawings, we are framing blocks of space-time out of the whole of **matter-flux**. What we are doing when we select blocks of space-time is framing sets of information. We can cause a set of information to emerge as a perception image from flowing matter in one of three possible spatial conditions: in a gaseous state, in a liquid phase, or as solid objects. Here again may be something that you never thought about before in relation to yourself or to architectural drawing – that you can choose a spatial condition to live within or to draw. You probably just always habitually live and draw in a space that contains solid physical objects. But you can choose instead the liquid phase of space or the gaseous one. Physicists work with these spaces. Artists often choose the liquid or gaseous spaces over the more familiar one of solid objects.

Exercise 1.3: *Framing perception images.*

Using a camera as Ozu does, try repeating your *Cinemetric* drawings moving from gaseous, liquid to solid states of perception.

A possible way to understand directly these three spatial perceptions that you can draw from the whole is to remember that you have seen water in gaseous, liquid, and solid states – as steam, rain, and ice. Then try imagining your room as being in a gaseous, then in a liquid condition, and then in the customary solid state. Here again, don't expect stunning results the first few times you attempt this experiment. Practice is needed to develop the skill of perceiving directly space in its varying

046 conditions. Now return to drawing with solid objects. Note how your perceptions of space with solid objects may have changed by perceiving the gaseous and liquid spaces from which the solid object space emerges.

The Ozu film sequence that we just described eventually shows us a set of information as a room of solid objects, but it begins in a gaseous state of low light level where we have to adjust our eyes to make out the elements of the set. The image gradually composes the familiar world of matter that we are used to seeing in our room or as the future physical buildings we want to draw.

The process that we go through when we perceive sets of information in gaseous, liquid or solid states also eliminates information that we decide is not useful. Let's look at this procedure more closely. We have seen that because we are indeterminate, we allow external influences to which we are indifferent to pass through us, others that we consider important we isolate and keep. The resulting frames of space-time become our perceptions. This detaching of sets of information from matter-flux to make **movement images** is what film-makers do when they focus their cameras and what architects do when they draw using the computer camera. The virtual camera becomes a drawing tool for architects working digitally because it can zoom in and out, change points of view, and turn on and off layers by continually framing sets of information as images, thus directing our attention to them. Rendering techniques and pixel manipulation can change the perceived state of images as well. Note the differences in drawing with a pencil as a marking tool and drawing with a digital camera as a light sensitive tool for framing, selecting, receiving, and digitally manipulating.

We call perception images that are indistinguishable from the thing itself **objective** because they attempt to create an image in an unmediated fashion. Objective perception is from a point of view outside the information set in the image. The image you created of your room when you looked over the bedcovers and focused in on your computer was not objective. Your reaction to seeing the computer was so strong that you didn't realise it was raining or that you were late. All you knew was that the computer held drawings that you were eager to work on. If you drew the image of the room you reacted to by leaping out of bed, you would leave the rain and the clock out. The resulting image is a **subjective** perception image because it is distinguishable from your physical room. A subjective perception is from a point of view within the objective information set.

1_03 Ozu's camera frames a set of elements which include the threshold of the bedroom in the foreground, the two futons in the middle ground and various layers of curtains, screens and sliding doors emitting a low early morning light in the background.

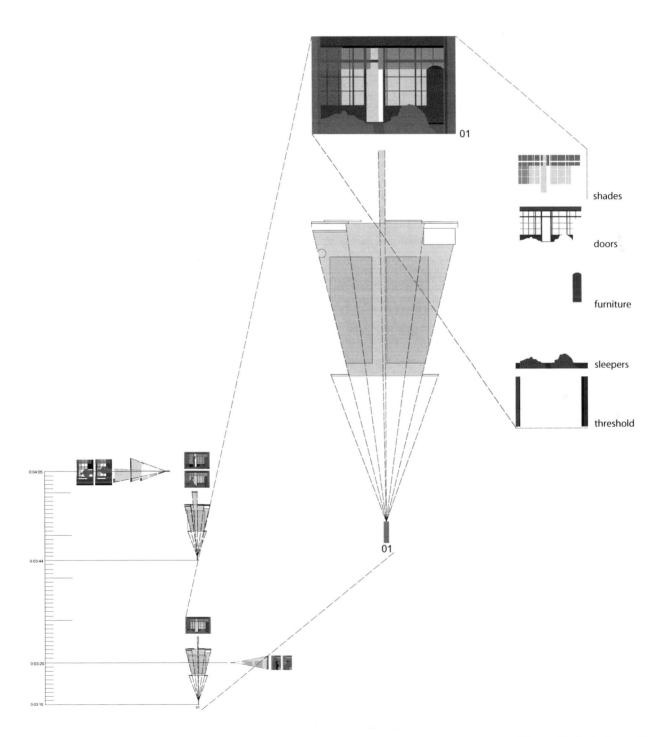

shades

doors

furniture

sleepers

threshold

01

01

0:04:05

0:03:44

0:03:20

0:03:10

I_04 Shot I frames a set of elements from a camera frontally positioned on a low tripod placed respectfully outside the bedroom. The view presents a classical one-point perspective composition where the camera is parallel with the back wall of the bedroom. The still camera reinforces the stillness of the sleeping couple and is held for a long 10 seconds.

Affection Image

In the second shot we see the sleeping wife close-up and in profile. The frame is full of feeling – a subjective **affection image**. In this frame the camera has moved 90 degrees to the left of the establishing perception shot, creating an affection image rarefied with little data. We observe intimately the sleeping wife in profile in this close-up information set. Her head is resting on a neat flattened pillow, her arms folded across her chest on top of a blanket. It feels as if we are sitting on the floor next to her, watching her. Because sleeping is such a familiar experience, an uncanny quality of observing one's self permeates this image. We are in the **interval** between receiving sensory input and before acting. We are suspended, nothing actively is happening. In this frame, Ozu creates an image of a quality, an affection image that is a lived state of subjectivity.[8]

In this frame, Ozu has shown us how to create a field of relations within **matter-flux** that includes ourselves. This is what you can do when you draw by framing movement images that include the viewer within the qualities you create. We experience ourselves, not as extraneous to the image, but as sitting on the floor next to the wife. This experience is possible because movements are not in space and images not in our brains but in matter-flux, a portion of which the image frames in a way that reveals qualities of the data. We will see later that these film techniques are fully applicable to making moving drawings of architecture.

I_05 The shot is abruptly cut when the wife's head begins to move outside the top edge of the restricted close-up camera frame.

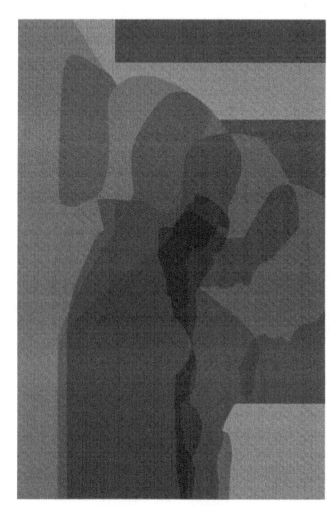

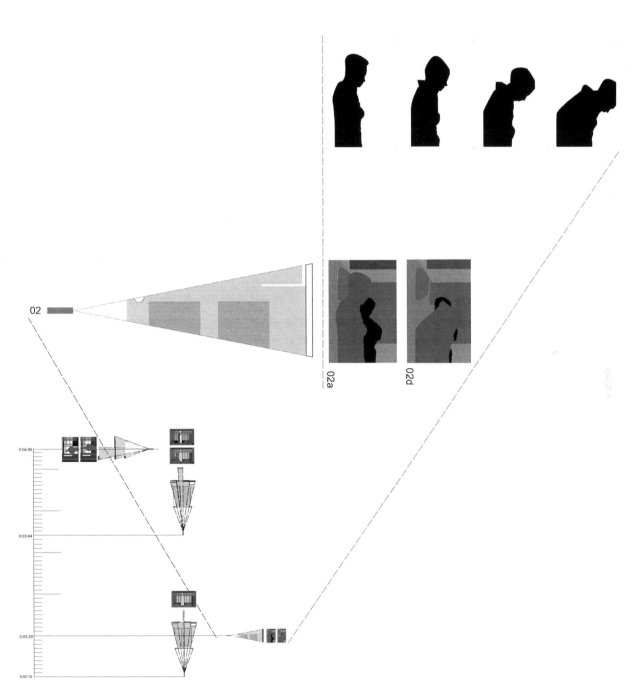

02

02a

02d

0:04:05

0:03:44

0:03:20

0:03:10

I_06 The second shot frames a close-up view of the sleeping wife in profile from a camera which has moved left 90 degrees clockwise from the first shot. During this 24 second shot, the alarm clock goes off, the husband turns over and covers his head with his blanket, and the wife moves to sit up in bed.

050 In the third shot, Ozu positions the wife again in profile but from the angle of the initial establishing perception image shot. Now, in contrast to that opening shot where she was sleeping with her head illuminated, she is awake but her head is in darkness. She turns to face the right, kneeling in the process of getting out of bed. Perhaps she is outwardly regarding her motionless husband or inwardly contemplating him. Like you, she takes a deep breath before she gets up. We don't know what she is experiencing. What we experience is her quiet, reinforced by the stability of her pyramidal shape. In this image, Ozu has linked the two previous images to this one, creating continuity between the frontal view of the room and the side view showing the sleeping wife in profile. But in the process he has transformed the objective perception image established by the opening shot into a subjective affection image, even though we view the room from almost the same position as the opening shot.

Shot 3 is subjective because the frontal view is now infused with information selected from the close-up of the sleeping wife. Even our perception of the architecture has changed. Now, in contrast to the opening shot, the translucent curtains, which diffuse the light in both of the frontal frames, are an element in creating an image where both the architecture and its inhabitants are veiled. Although we view the room from almost the same angle as the opening frame, we now have, rather than an objective perception image, a subjective affection image. This is a technique that you can use in your moving drawings to communicate qualities of the space.

Exercise 1.4: *Framing affection images*

Get your camera as close as you can to your subjects, objects and surfaces in order to frame affection images that you notice during intervals in your daily routine of getting up in the morning.

1_07 The wife twists her body into a standing position, turning her back to the camera. She opens the curtain slightly, and turns to leave the frame on the left.

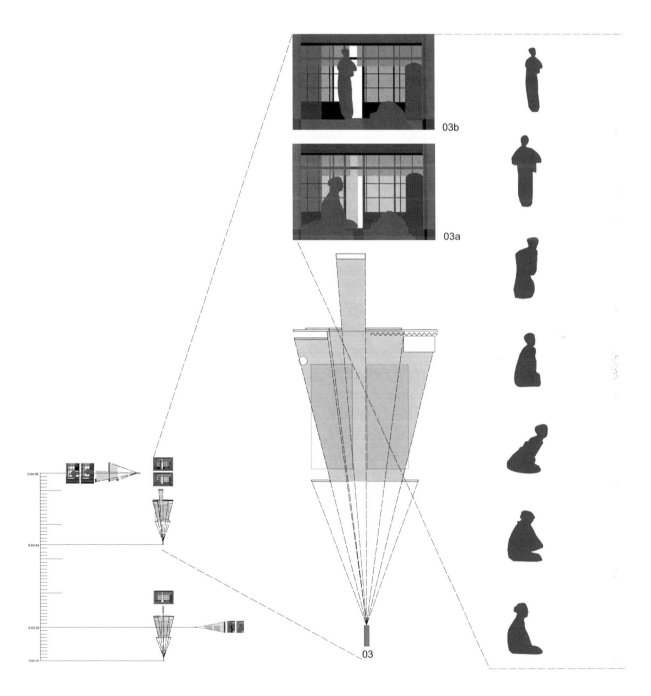

03b

03a

03

I_08 Shot 03 returns to the same position as the first frontal shot. The woman, now viewed in the act of getting up, turns to a kneeling position in profile.

Action Image

In the fourth **shot,** Ozu has selected a set of information that forms a medium distance action image. Here the wife has her back to us, which continues the feeling of something unseen experienced in the earlier images. The preceding sequence of shots also contained action images when we witnessed the physical movements of her waking, getting up by kneeling on the bed, and then facing her husband who pulls the covers over his head as he turns over rather than getting up. Now the wife has almost left their room, raising a translucent blind that closes the opening and modulates the concealing interior light. The lane she enters is bathed in a sharper light, seen through the screen. The exterior light illuminates her forehead and more strongly reveals, than the interior light did, her body as well as the pattern of her kimono, wrapped snugly around her moving figure.

I_09 If the opening frame was from a respectful distance outside the bedroom (**perception image**), and the second shot was framed in close-up (**affection image**), this shot is at a medium distance, where there is less information on the spatial context, but more on the woman's gestures and movements (**action image**).

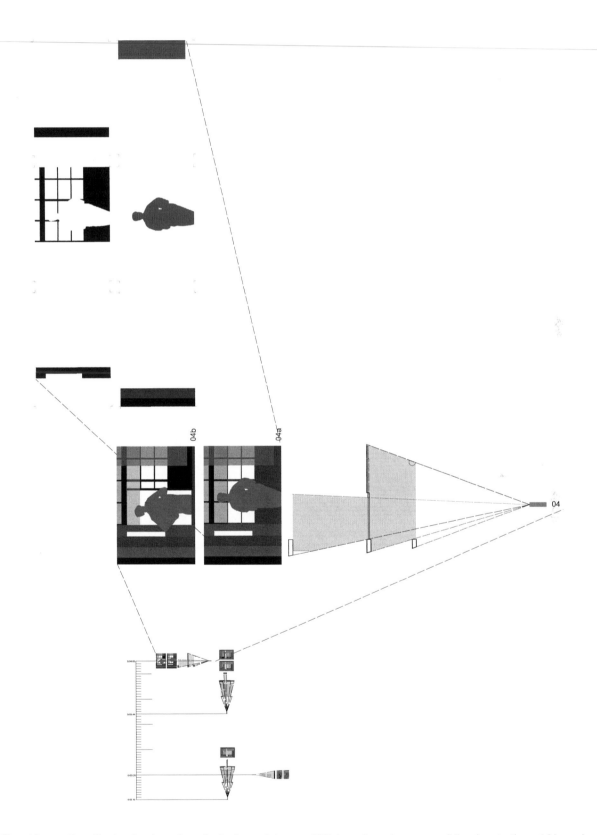

I_10 Shot 4 frames the wife stepping down from the bedroom into a small kitchen where she opens a sliding door to the outside, again with her back to the camera.

The action image of the wife leaving the bedroom is not an image showing her immediate reaction to waking up. What is made legible here is a delayed reaction that relates movement to a conscious end rather than a habitual one. Ozu interrupts the wife's waking movements with an **interval** as she kneels on the bed, thus creating the affection image we previously studied. We experience her in that image as a **centre of indeterminacy** – an **image arrested** between perception and action. This experience is similar to our own when, if instead of leaping out of bed to look at our computer drawings, we pause to consider what to do next. The actions of the retreating wife in this image, as our own when we finally get up, are thus filled with qualities permeating the experience of the interval between perceiving and acting. The retreating wife is now actually an **assemblage** of the three images we have explored – **perception, affection,** and **action** – with the action image predominating in this frame. Likewise, our architectural drawings and the moving drawing of our day are assemblages of image types when we pause to consider how to best draw matter-flux as moving images.

Exercise 1.5: *Framing action images*

Place your camera at a medium distance so you can observe the movements of your subjects in their daily routine of getting up in the morning. Are there other movements or actions such as vehicles, tools, television or computer screens, wind, light, an oscillating fan or the hands of a clock, that also form action images?

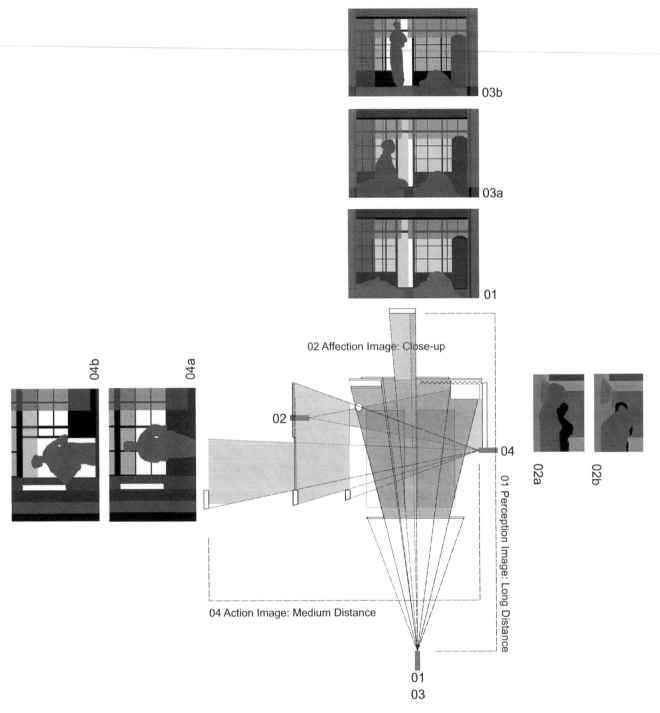

03b

03a

01

02 Affection Image: Close-up

04b

04a

02

04

02a

02b

01 Perception Image: Long Distance

04 Action Image: Medium Distance

01
03

I_II These first four shots frame three elevations of the couple's bedroom, unfolding the room like a multi-view orthographic architectural projection. But they also frame the act of the wife's routine as she first wakes up in the morning. The camera seems to both anticipate her movement, but to always be too late as she continually turns her back or leaves the frame of the camera. Her fluid movement is in contrast to the stability of the camera and the architectural set. If Ozu's 90-degree camera movement unfolds three of the six sides of the cubic bedroom, much like orthographic drawing, his framing of the wife's movement engages the six spaces of the cinematic frame: the top, right side, bottom, left side of the frame, behind the set and behind the camera. This diagram also reveals the changing depth of field of the shots. The first and third shots reveal three layers of space and give a perception image through a relatively long shot. The second shot is a close-up which creates an affection image, focusing on the face of the wife. The fourth medium-distant shot is an action image showing the wife leaving the house.

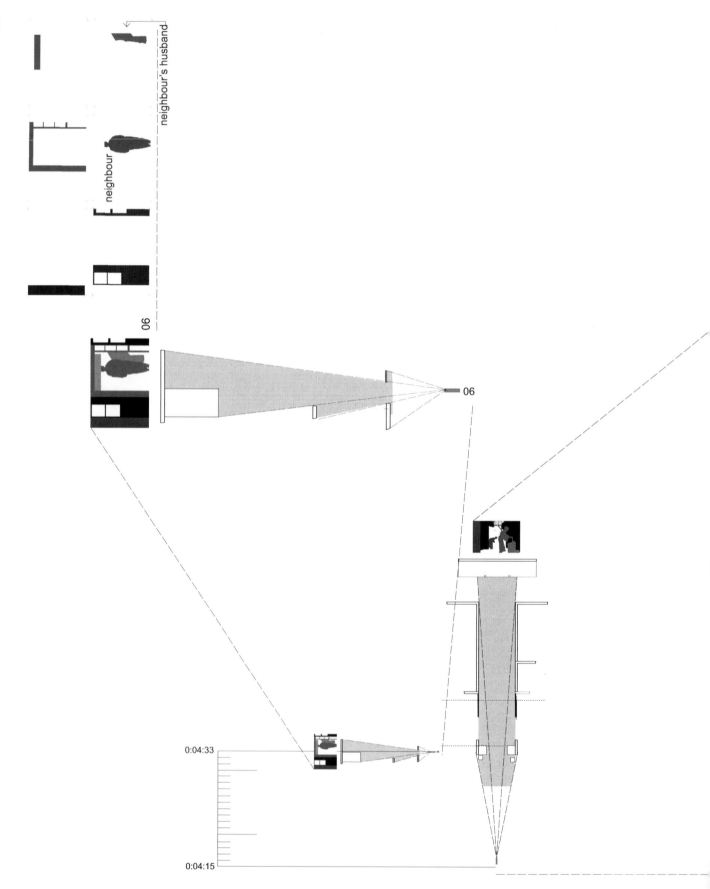

neighbour

neighbour's husband

06

06

0:04:33

0:04:15

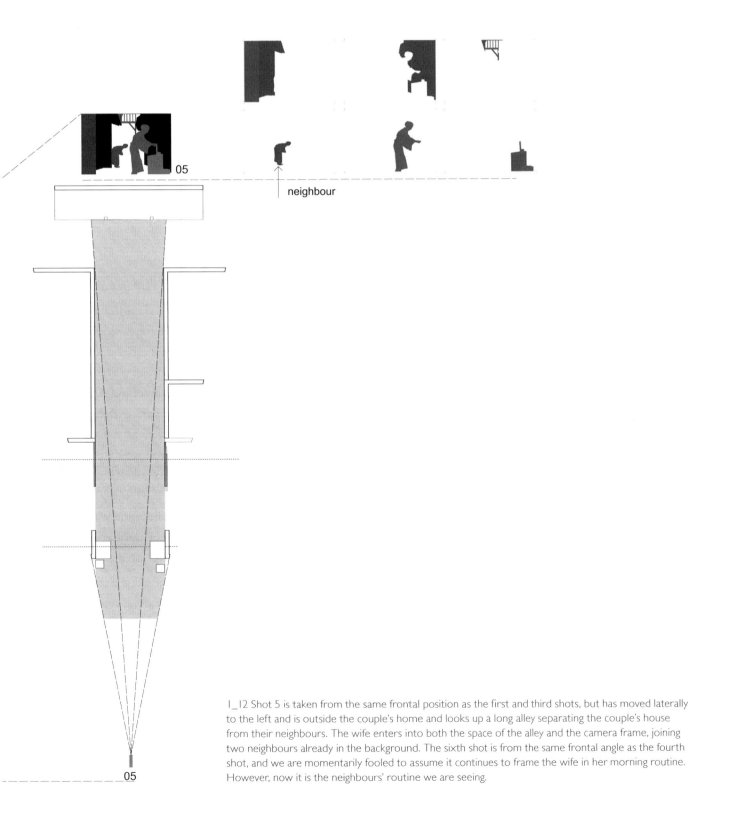

05

neighbour

05

I_12 Shot 5 is taken from the same frontal position as the first and third shots, but has moved laterally to the left and is outside the couple's home and looks up a long alley separating the couple's house from their neighbours. The wife enters into both the space of the alley and the camera frame, joining two neighbours already in the background. The sixth shot is from the same frontal angle as the fourth shot, and we are momentarily fooled to assume it continues to frame the wife in her morning routine. However, now it is the neighbours' routine we are seeing.

In the fifth shot, the camera, and ourselves as viewers of the scene, are positioned just outside the front edge of the image, looking at the wife in the lane next to her home. Ozu used this angle of framing to create a long shot, which establishes an extended field, showing the particulars of the passageway between the couple's and their neighbours' homes. We note that the houses on either side of the alley look similar. Within this perception image of the lane setting is a smaller action image of the wife and her neighbour, going about their morning chores. Again, resemblances are emphasised.

By selecting a different set of information to frame this image than he used in the images of the preceding bedroom shots, Ozu was able to focus our attention on the outward similarities of the wife's life to her neighbour's. In addition, while we absorb this image, we are also remembering the previous ones with the wife in them – the **perception image** of the bedroom, the **affection images** of the sleeping and then kneeling wife as well as the **action image** of her leaving. These memories merge with the above image, forming an even more comprehensive set of information that includes the perceptions of the alley and bedroom settings as well as movements and feelings associated with both places.

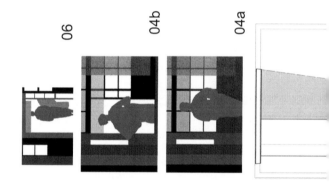

1_13 This is the power of Ozu's cinematic style. He employs simple rules – static camera, 90-degree camera repositions, slowly unfolding space one side at a time. But then he fools the viewer, forcing the audience to always be alert and attentive. Shots 4 and 6 show that our couple's house and life is mirrored by another couple and house across the alley, and the alley joins other houses along its length. In the parallels, we notice differences. The neighbouring husbands and wives are getting up together, while the first husband stays in bed, unwilling to wake up. In less than two minutes of film time, Ozu has already framed a complex set of spatial and social relations.

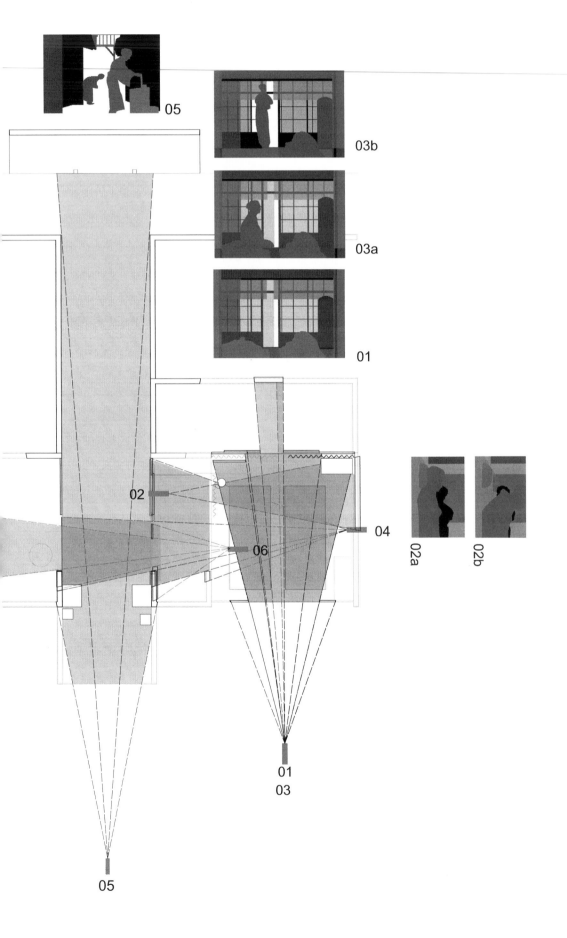

1_14 The wife walks back to the screen doors and opens the curtains and a sliding door to a small courtyard behind the head of the beds.

1_15 In shot 7, the wife has returned to the frame of the first shot, but now she has changed clothes – within the interval of time we were watching the neighbour. In fact, time has been compressed – the real time of her changing clothes has been cut and because of the cut we have jumped ahead in time.

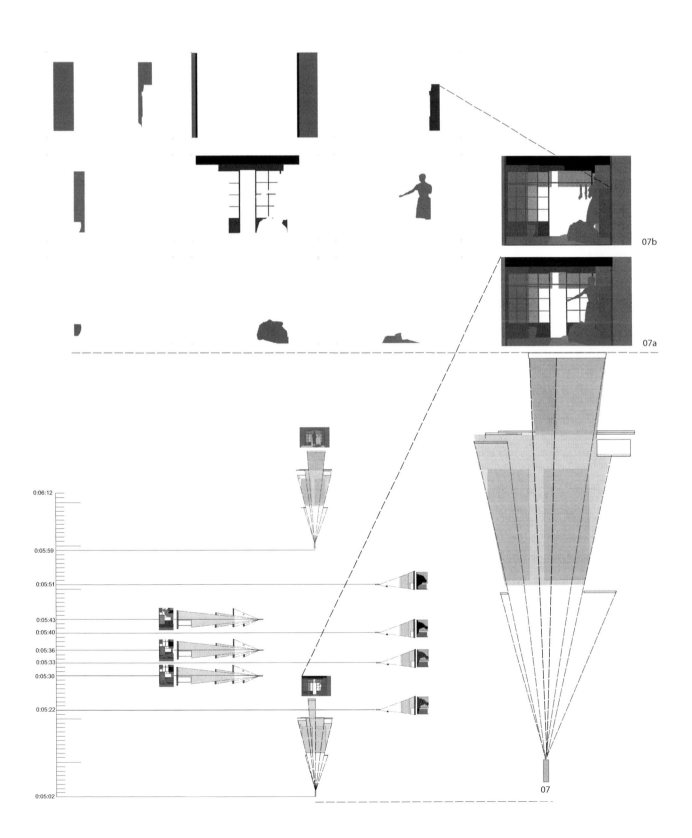

07b

07a

07

0:06:12

0:05:59

0:05:51

0:05:43
0:05:40

0:05:36
0:05:33
0:05:30

0:05:22

0:05:02

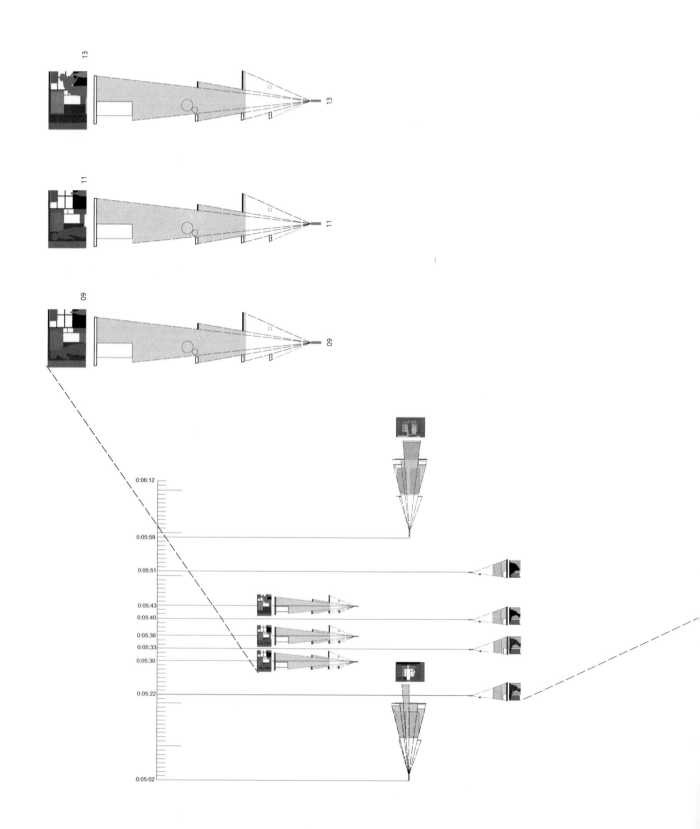

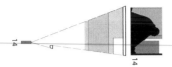

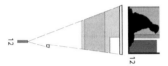

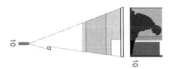

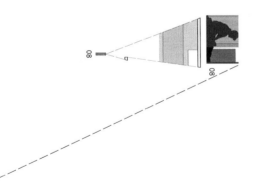

1_16 Shots 8 -14 continue to cut back and forth between the couple in conversation. The seventh shot, like the first and third, is outside the bedroom set and represents an objective point of view, matching the point of view of the audience looking at the screen. The intercutting later shots 8 -14 represent the husband and wife's respective subjective points of view, as if the camera were the wife looking at the husband and the husband looking at looking at her. **Objective** — for our purposes here — means a point of view from outside the set of information, **subjective** means a point of view from inside the set.

1_17 Shot 15, the closing shot, returns to the same frontal point of view as the first, opening shot. Now the husband has finally woken up.

1_18 The conversation in the last part of the opening bedroom scene is bracketed by shots 7 and 15. Shot 7 (ill 14) showed the wife walking to the back screen doors, and shot 15 matches this shot, but with the husband now walking to the same space occupied previously by the wife. They occupy the same space in the room and in the cinema frame but at different times.

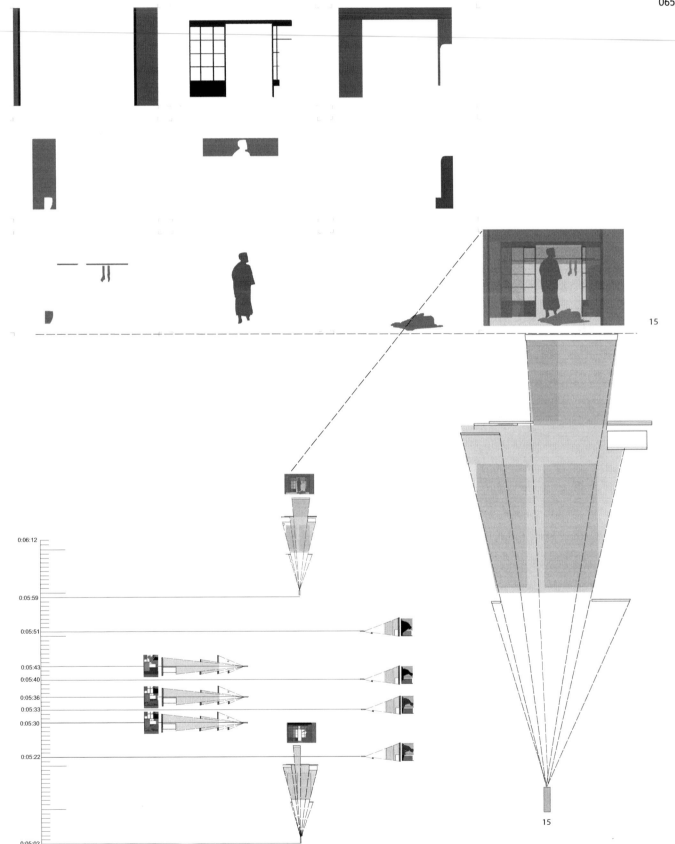

15

15

0:06:12
0:05:59
0:05:51
0:05:43
0:05:40
0:05:36
0:05:33
0:05:30
0:05:22
0:05:02

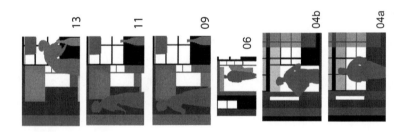

13

11

09

06

04b

04a

1_19 This entire three-minute sequence of fifteen shots first described three sides of a bedroom, the first shot was framed from outside the bedroom set, the second in close-up and the third a medium shot from inside. The camera then followed the wife outside the main set of the bedroom and then followed her neighbour in a similar routine. This diversion revealed the parallel lives of the couple living just opposite the lane. The camera returned to the bedroom, again framed by the frontal views of the 7th and 15th shots, however the camera in shots 9, 11 and 13 now has a greater depth of field that frames a layered space through the lane and to the neighbour's house beyond. Thus we see the couple's bedroom in a complex spatial and social network.

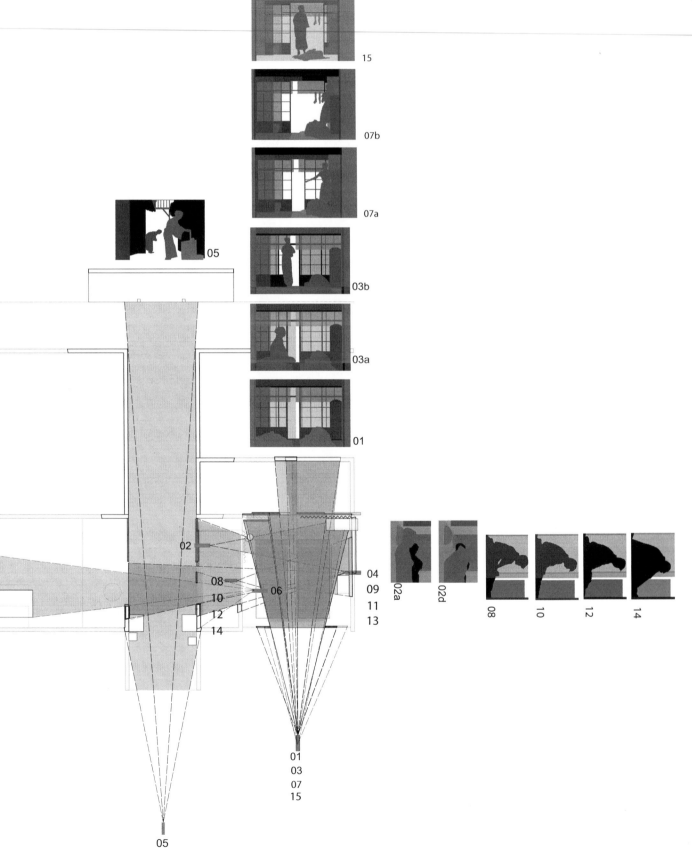

1_20 The repeated return to the initial establishing shot, shown here in the image layered with each return, lets us measure change, not only in movement of the characters in and out of the space of the **relative out-of-field**, but in duration evident by the movement of light from dawn to early morning ever present in the background of the opening scene of Ozu's *Early Spring*.

1_21 Shots 1, 3, 7 and 15 frame the **absolute out-of-field** as an expression of **duration** by returning to almost the same camera position at different points of time. By comparing these shots we can see a slight adjustment of the frame in shots 7 and 15, the gradual opening of the space to the outside, and an increase in lighting.

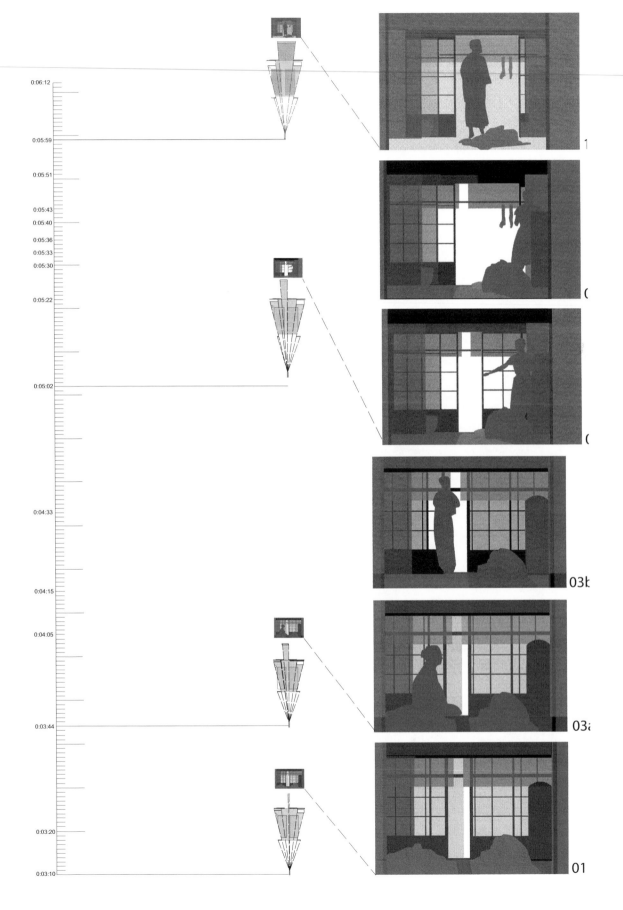

0:06:12
0:05:59
0:05:51
0:05:43
0:05:40
0:05:36
0:05:33
0:05:30
0:05:22
0:05:02
0:04:33
0:04:15
0:04:05
0:03:44
0:03:20
0:03:10

1

0

0

03b

03a

01

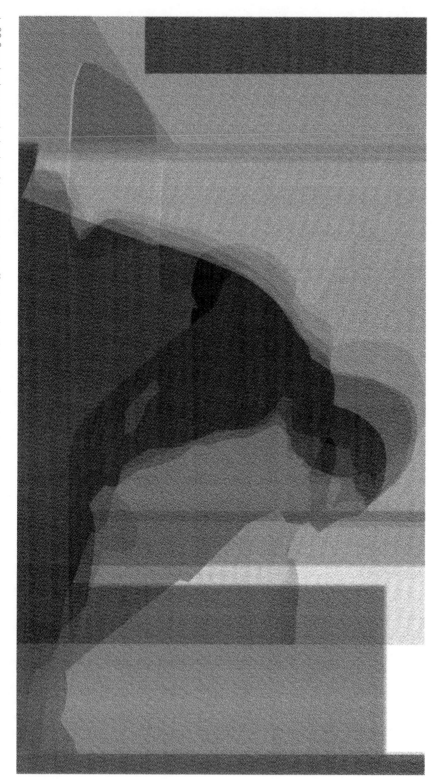

1_22 Seen in close-up, the husband is presented as an affective rather than an active character.

1_23 Shots 8, 10, 12 and 14 frame the husband from a close-up similar to the point of view from which we first saw the wife sleeping in profile in shot 2. We understand the shots of the husband as the point of view of the wife.

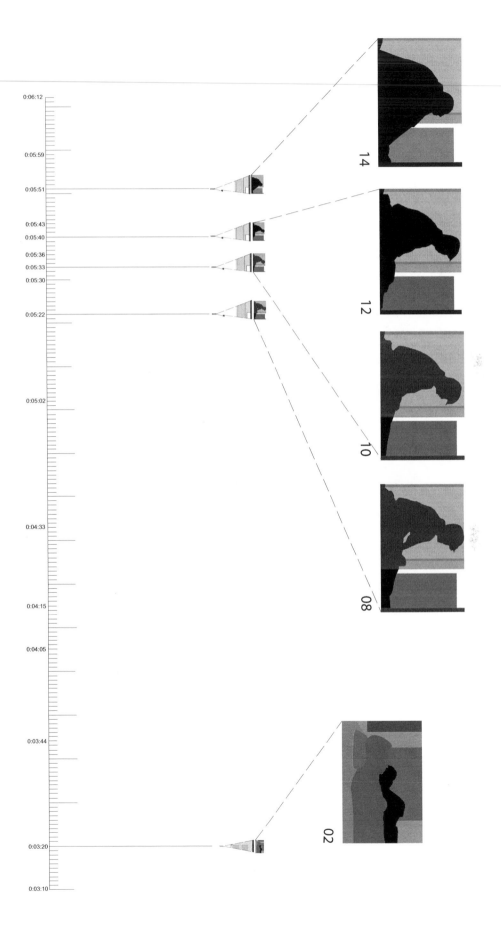

I_24 In a medium depth of field, we see the wife in the kitchen viewed from what we now assume to be the husband's vantage point inside the bedroom. The open doors of her kitchen and the neighbour's reveal a deep background space across the lane. We have returned to the bedroom but the **relative out-of-field** of the neighbourhood is now present as well.

I_25 The wife is presented in shots 4, 9, 11 and 13 as an active figure. We were momentarily fooled by the similar framing of the neighbour in shot 6.

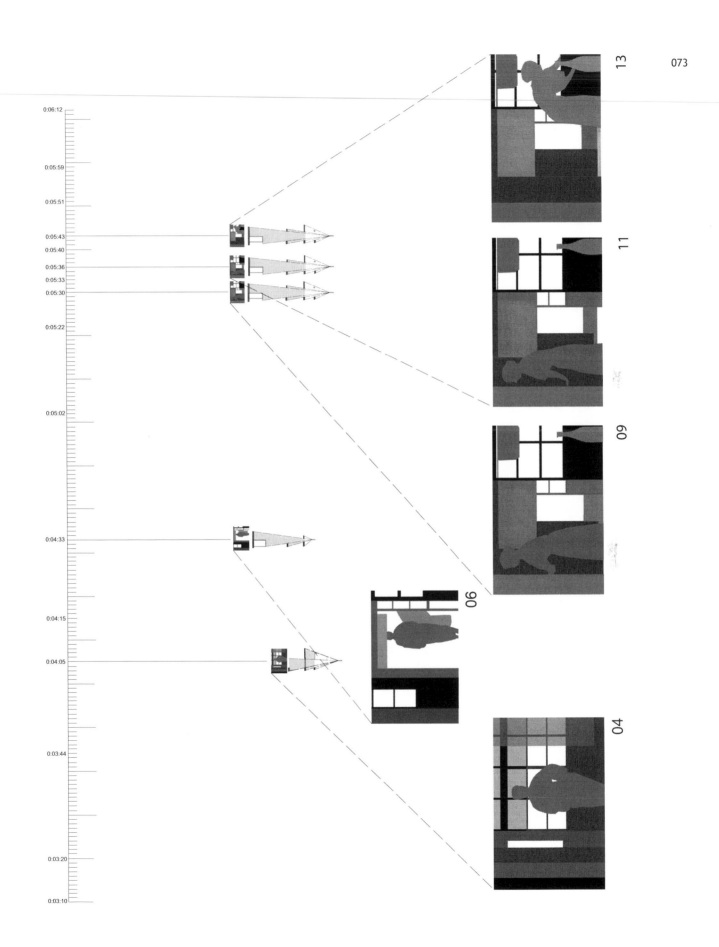

1_26 The rest of the film *Early Spring* follows the daily routine of a young husband and wife structured by 44 scenes which move between home, work and passing through leisure spaces in-between. The first scene is composed of 15 shots in three adjoining sets: the couple's house, a lane and their neighbour's house. Each shot consists of 24 frames per second. Each frame contains an informatic set of relations. Ozu returns to the same room of the opening shot 10 more times over the course of the movie, an attentive and reiterative framing of a critical period of time in a young couple's domestic relationship.

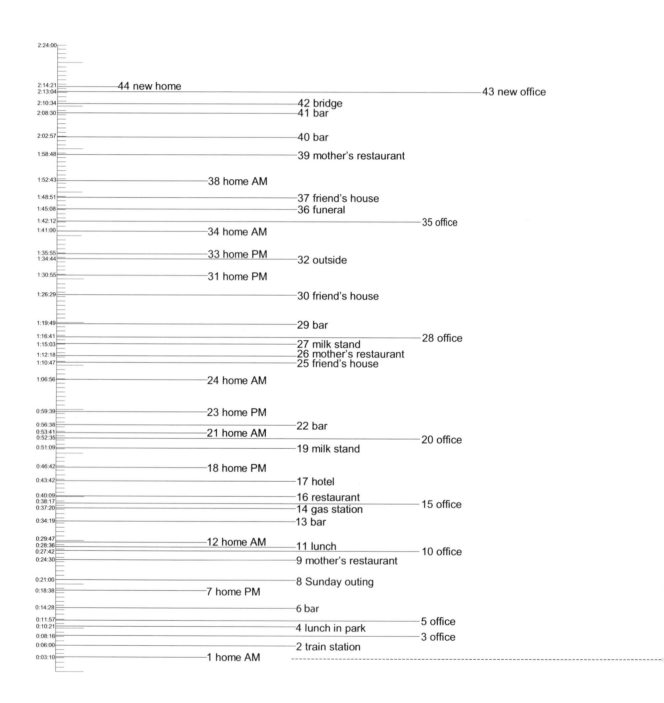

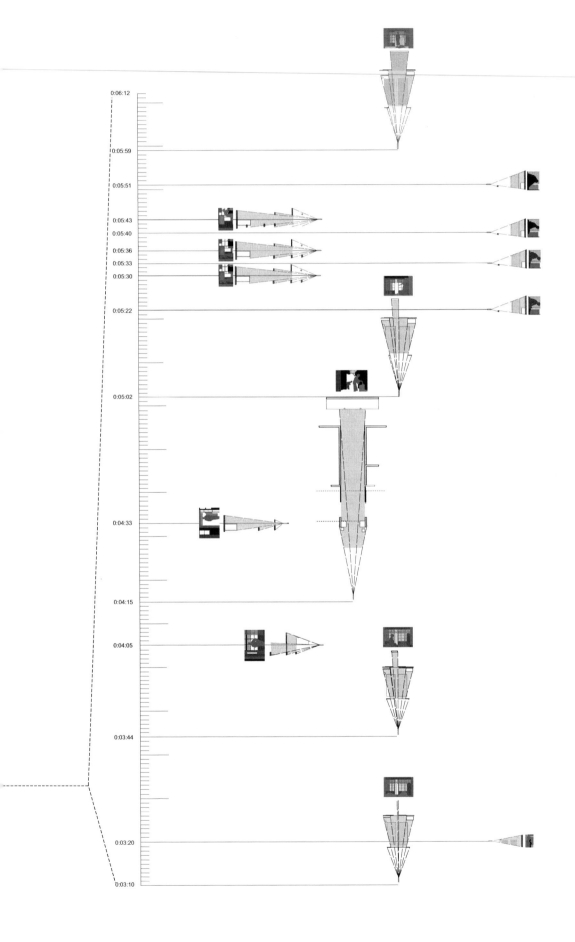

0:06:12
0:05:59
0:05:51
0:05:43
0:05:40
0:05:36
0:05:33
0:05:30
0:05:22
0:05:02
0:04:33
0:04:15
0:04:05
0:03:44
0:03:20
0:03:10

Before we turn to a more detailed look at framing matter-flux in architecture as immobile cuts in the next chapters, lets review what we have just been exploring. We have seen that because we are indeterminate, we allow external influences to which we are indifferent to pass through us, others that we consider important we isolate and keep. The resulting **frames** of space-time become our perceptions. This detaching of sets of information from matter-flux to make **movement images** is what film-makers do when they focus their cameras and what architects do when they draw using the computer camera. The virtual camera becomes a drawing tool for architects working digitally because it can zoom in and out, change points of view, and turn on and off layers by continually framing sets of information as images, thus directing our attention to them. Rendering techniques and pixel manipulation can change the state – solid, liquid or gaseous – of images as well.

We call **perception images** that are indistinguishable from the thing itself **objective** because they attempt to create an image in an unmediated fashion. An image is a **subjective** perception image when it is distinguishable from the thing itself. Objective is a perception image from outside the closed set of information, subjective from inside. We call images that frame feeling **affection images** and those that frame our movements **action images**.

What we have been doing will help you learn to draw an architecture that is in a field of relations within the **open vibrational whole** by examining the '**intervals**' between these images – the pause after exterior movement that creates the opportunity for choices that lead to perception images. We feel subtle sensations in our body in relation to what we perceive. This results in an **affection image**, feelings which are pleasant or unpleasant, depending on our choices. It is from these sensations that we choose to act – to walk away, to move closer, to stay in bed or to get up. This is the sensori-motor mechanism of the body at work: micro-movements in our body that move with such rapidity that we are usually unconscious of them as they have become habitual.

Knowing about the three types of images can also help you direct the *Cinemetric* drawing of your day so you aren't missing important information. This knowledge will help you to understand what happens when movements no longer exist in space or images in our brains. Movement is no longer just the quantifiable measurement of the translation of a body across space, but transformation of the open whole in duration. Images are a selection through framing from flowing matter-flux. Now you are ready to start the process of living the possibilities of a philosophy of '**newness**' and drawing an architecture for it.

1 Gilles Deleuze, *Cinema I: The Movement Image*, trans Hugh Tomlinson and Barbara Habberjam, University of Minnesota Press (Minneapolis, MN), 1986, pp 57–8.

2 Henri Bergson, *Matter and Memory*, Zone Books (New York), 1988, pp 9–10.

3 Deleuze, *Cinema I*, p 69.

4 Floyd Merrell, 'Thought-signs, sign-events', *Semiotica: Journal of the International Association for Semiotic Studies*, 1991, Vols 87–112, p 3.

5 Charles Sanders Peirce, *The Essential Peirce: Selected Philosophical Writings*, Vol 2 (1893–1913), ed by Peirce Edition Project, Indiana University Press (Bloomington, Indiana), 1998. And Floyd Merrell, 'Thought-signs, sign-events', *Semiotica: Journal of the International Association for Semiotic Studies*, 1991, Vols 87–112, pp 1–57.

6 *http://wsu.edu/~dee/GLOSSARY/MONO.HTM*

7 *http://www.sensesofcinema.com/contents/directors/03/ozu.html*

8 Deleuze, *Cinema I*, p 65.

CHAPTER 2

IMMOBILE CUTS

*How can we develop an architectural drawing system
from the intervals in flowing matter-flux?*

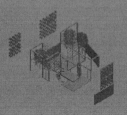

By framing matter-flux, you began the process of becoming a **cybernetic architect** by developing a drawing system based on the perceptions, affections and actions you experience spontaneously while waking. We also used a digital drawing system to analyse Yasujiro Ozu's opening scene in *Early Spring* as an example of how to frame the ordinary, everyday act of waking. We looked as well at how stopping the movement of film through digital technologies can give us insights into the intervals within flowing matter-flux. These framed intervals allow us to perceive the ways our sensori-motor system works. The resulting drawing system combines architectural plans with film stills and time lines as a new hybrid methodology for mapping space, time and movement as **immobile cuts** through matter-flux.

Words in bold are Keywords found on pages 260-265

Immobile Cuts Involve Choosing Sets of Information from Matter-Flux

When you decide what you will do moment by moment in daily life, there is more involved than just selecting sets of information that constitute **perception images, affection images** and **action images.** Now we are going to explore five aspects of framing a system of perception, affection and action images.[1] By making yourself aware of these aspects of framing, you learn to draw architecture as a provisionally closed **set of information** in a field of relations within the **open** vibrational **whole**.

Each of the five aspects of framing listed below is explained in this chapter. We explore the aspects in detail by looking for them in a computer-generated model of Shigeru Ban's Photographer's Shutter House, designed between 2000 and 2002 and constructed between 2002 and 2003. Ban's house is analysed through our understanding of Ozu's orthographic camera system used in *Early Spring*. But when you pay attention in your own living experience as you select sets of information from the open whole, you will notice that you unconsciously move through these same five aspects as a cognitive process of selection. So you already know the five aspects of framing even if you haven't named them yet. They all occur each time you select blocks of space-time. These questions help to bring to consciousness what happens to you on a daily basis, and will help you in more precisely defining where to cut through the flowing matter-flux of architecture in the process of making moving drawings.

Five Aspects of Framing

1 *Informatic: Does the information set you select tend to be saturated with a lot of data or rarefied with little?*

2 *Limit: Does the character of the frame edge tend to be Euclidean coordinates topological invariants or is it dynamic?*

3 *Nature of Parts: Do the parts within the frame tend to have Euclidean coordinates topological invariants or are they dynamic?*

4 *Point of View: Does the angle in space from which the information set is framed tend to be justified pragmatically or can it claim a 'higher justification'?*

5 *Out-of-Field: Does the out-of-field of the framed information set tend to be relative or absolute, or both?[2]*

Knowing about the five ways of framing can also help you to construct a drawing system of your day so you aren't missing important information. This knowledge will help you to understand what happens when movements no longer exist in space and images in our brains: you start to live the possibilities of the '**new**' instead of constantly repeating old patterns of thought and behaviour, and to develop through drawing a new architecture for drawing a new architecture for these possibilities.

Framing as Informatic

Does the information set you select tend to be saturated with a lot of data or rarefied with little?

Exercise 2.1: *To prepare for the exercises in this chapter, create or find a computer model of a modern house comprised of strictly orthogonal Euclidean coordinates. Layer the model as 'sets of information', as shown in illus 2_02. Select different cuts from your computer model with either lots (saturated) or little (rarefied) information.*

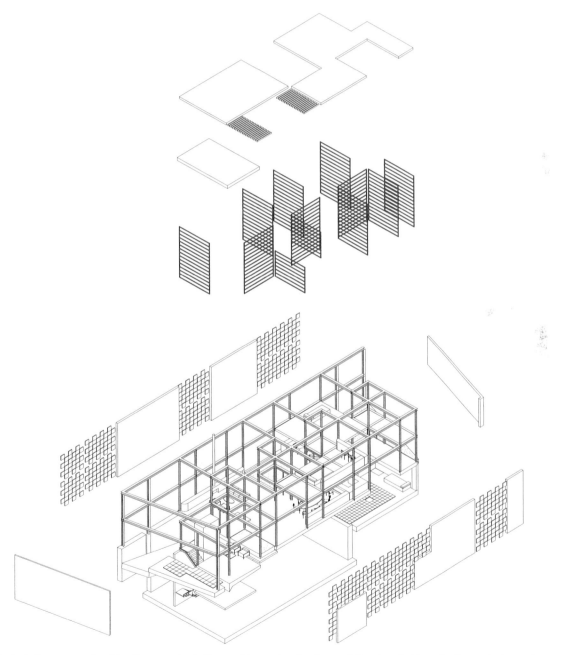

2_01 Exploded axonometric of the Photographer's Shutter House showing the roof, the glass shutters, the four exterior surfaces, and the main structural frame of the house. These architectural elements form the 'set of information' for the house. The number of elelments can be inclusive – saturated – or selective – rarified.

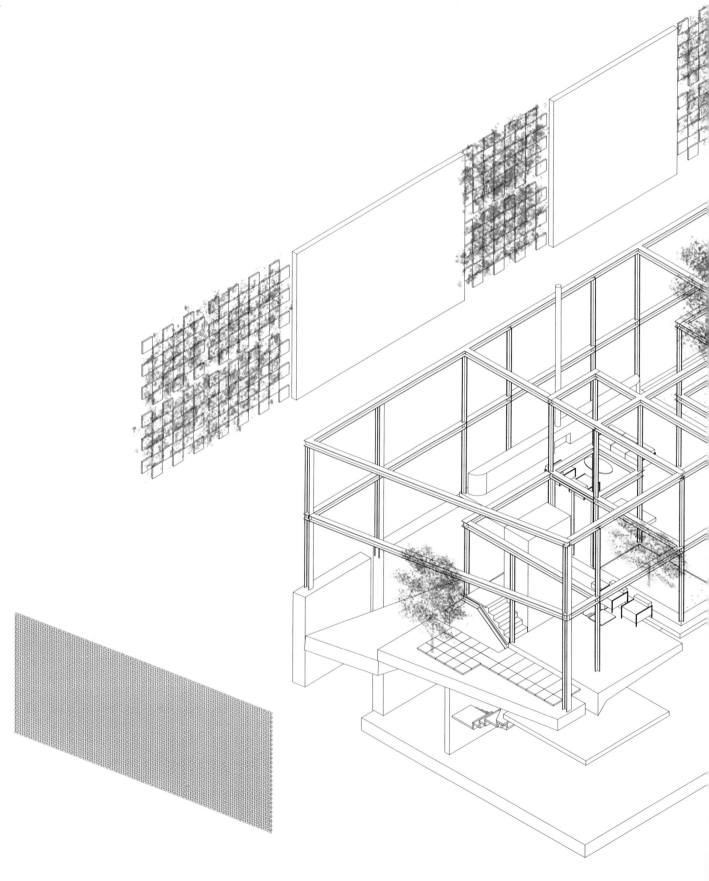

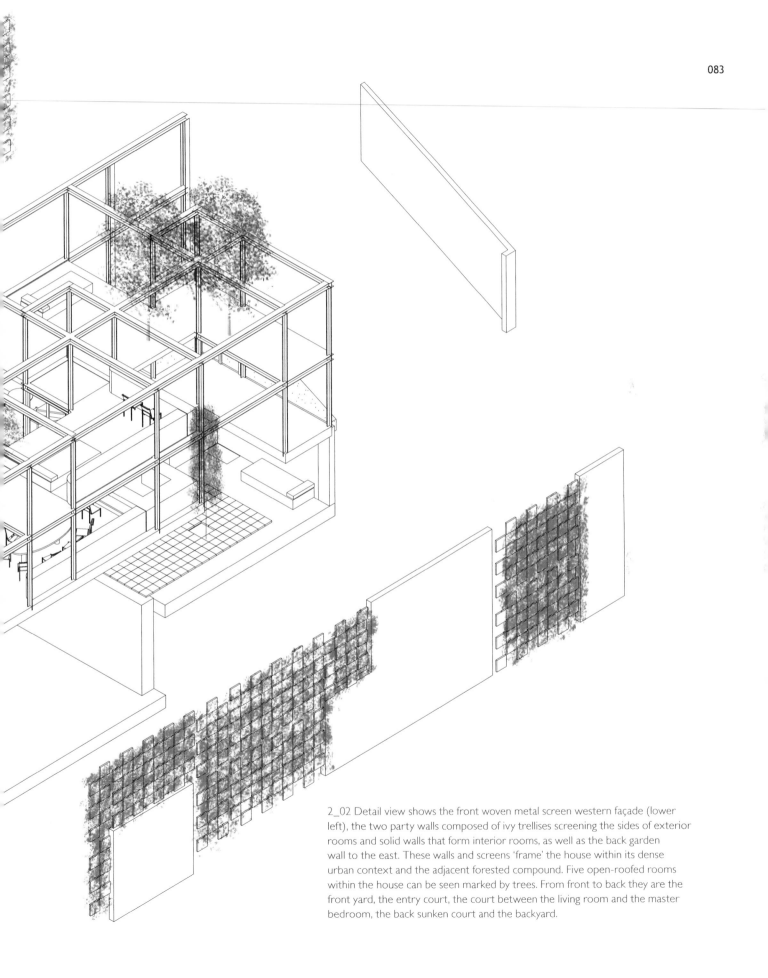

2_02 Detail view shows the front woven metal screen western façade (lower left), the two party walls composed of ivy trellises screening the sides of exterior rooms and solid walls that form interior rooms, as well as the back garden wall to the east. These walls and screens 'frame' the house within its dense urban context and the adjacent forested compound. Five open-roofed rooms within the house can be seen marked by trees. From front to back they are the front yard, the entry court, the court between the living room and the master bedroom, the back sunken court and the backyard.

As we have seen in Chapter 1 *Framing,* Ozu's first four shots of *Early Spring* show us the distinguishing characteristics of the sleeping couple's room (illus 1_02 and 1_11). The four shots create a provisionally closed system of information that helps us to understand the remaining shots from the same scene. The scene is both literally a movie set, shot in a sound stage in Tokyo, but also a set of information selected by the director. The low studio light level limits the amount of information we can perceive, and the shot begins as a rarefied frame with only a limited amount of information available to us. We see light coming through a gridded-screen background, the shadowy profile of a sleeping couple in the middle ground, and a framed opening telling us that we are outside the sleeping area in another space in the foreground.

In the second shot we see a close-up of the wife (illus 1_05 and 1_06). The alarm clock has gone off. We see her husband roll over and cover himself with the blanket. Past him in the upper half of the frame is a plain wall, which we surmise is to the right of the window-screen at the back of the establishing shot. By repeating elements in this frame, such as the sleeping woman and man of the opening frame, Ozu orients us in space, making this room and its events legible, and creates continuity between frames. Because this second image subtracts from the **information set** of the establishing shot and creates feeling, it is a **subjective affection image**. It also begins to contain the first actions in the film – the wife switching off the alarm clock, the husband rolling over, and at the end of the second shot, the wife sitting up – marking a transition to a full action image.

As we have seen, in the third shot (illus 1_07 and 1_08). Ozu positions the wife kneeling in profile but from the angle of the first establishing **perception shot**. The final shot of the sequence showing the wife getting up, presents a third angle, this time 90 degrees to the right. Here we see the wife exiting the bedroom to another room beyond. As we have seen, a close-up is a more rarified set of information which produces an affection image of pure quality or feeling, while a long shot gives a perception image – which can become quite saturated with information because of the greater depth of field.

The master bedroom in the Shigeru Ban's Photographer's Shutter House is situated between the backyard and two courtyards – one at the same level as the master bedroom to the west, and one sunken into the basement to the south. Like the sliding screens in *Early Spring,* the front and back walls of the house are glass shutters, which can fold up to the ceiling, opening the bedroom to outside air, smells, temperatures and sounds. The backyard faces east, so the light comes into the bedroom from this side, but shades can be drawn for privacy from the front, or shielding light from the back.

Ban sets up different types of visual, auditory, olfactory, tactile and physical access to the world outside the bedroom. In addition to the possibility of opening the shades to view the three exterior spaces, and let the morning light in, there is also the possibility of descending a spiral stair adjacent to the sunken courtyard. How does the set of building elements in the Ban house frame the matter-flux of architecture? What can Ozu's way of dynamically framing matter-flux teach us about making limited sets of information in architecture? How can we select **immobile cuts** through buildings in order to analyse the potential of an architecture which, dynamically frames movement and time?

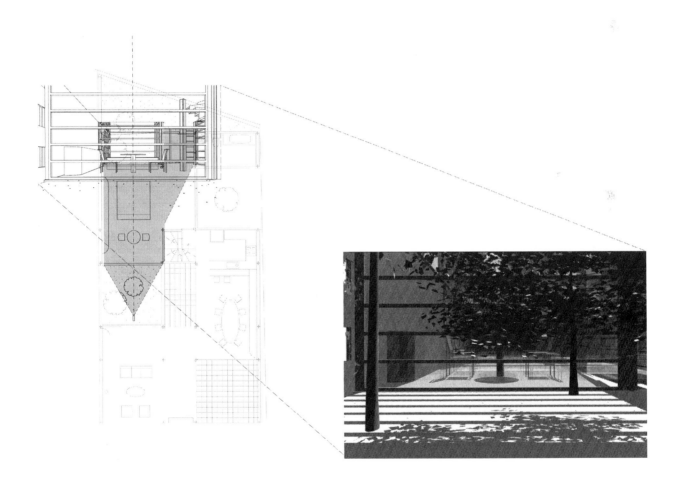

2_03 Immobile cut 1: looking east through the living-room courtyard and the master bedroom towards the early morning light. The elements that frame this set are the trees in the foreground, the glass shutter, and the solid side wall. The information that is framed includes the morning light and shadow, and the reflective qualities of the glass.

086

2_04 Immobile cut 2: looking south towards the sunken court from the master bedroom. Here the structural columns and shutters are again present in the frame, but now the tree and the ivy screen wall are in the background of the set of information. The light is now coming in from the left-hand, east side of the image. A spiral stair is in the foreground to the right, and the light from the backyard casts a shadow on the bedroom floor.

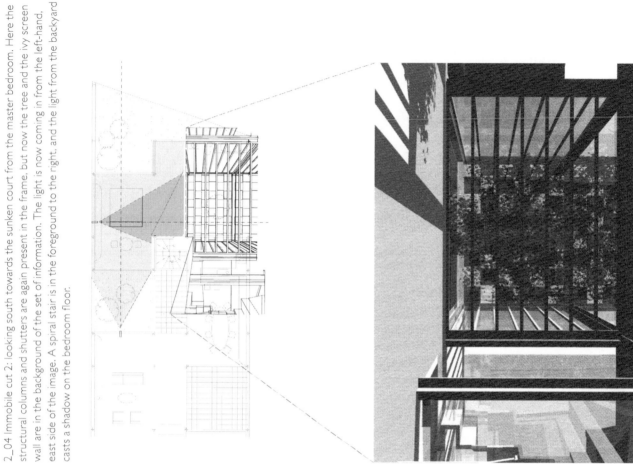

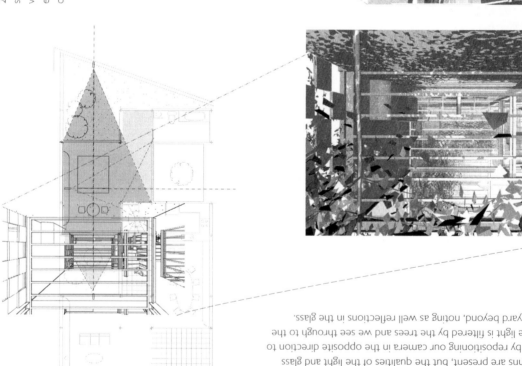

2_05 Immobile cut 3: looking west from the backyard towards the master bedroom with the early morning light coming in from behind. Again the familiar shutters and steel columns are present, but the qualities of the light and glass have been transformed by repositioning our camera in the opposite direction to the first frame. Here the light is filtered by the trees and we see through to the bedroom and the courtyard beyond, noting as well reflections in the glass.

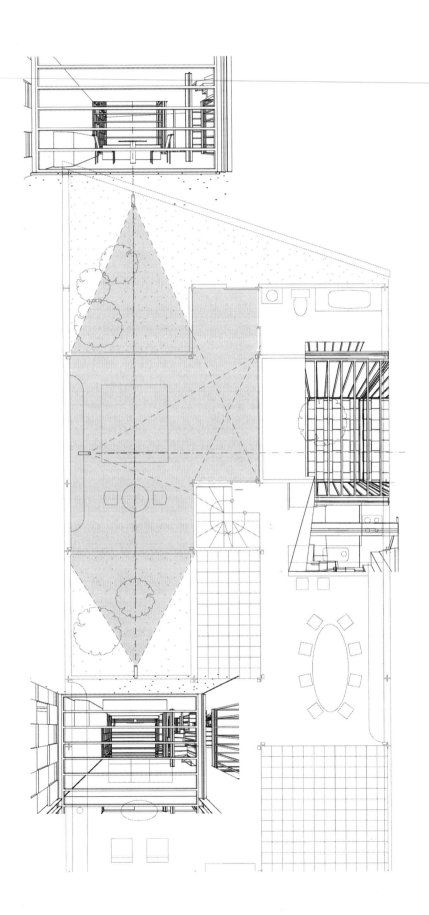

Framing as Limit

Does the character of the frame edge tend to conform to Euclidean coordinates or topological invariants or is it dynamic?

Exercise 2.2: *Experiment with the three different kinds of frame edges in your computer model. What makes a frame edge dynamic or topological? Analyse the variety of spaces framed in the house by taking different cuts through your computer model.*

Artful hand-drawn architectural drawings often create a dynamic relation between the figure of the drawing, the field of the paper, and its edge. When a frame is constituted, not in relation to chosen coordinates as in **Euclidean geometry**, but in relation to selected invariants, it becomes **topological**. For instance, it is often pointed out that the topologist can't tell a coffee cup (with one handle) from a doughnut, since a sufficiently pliable coffee cup (with one handle) can be reshaped into

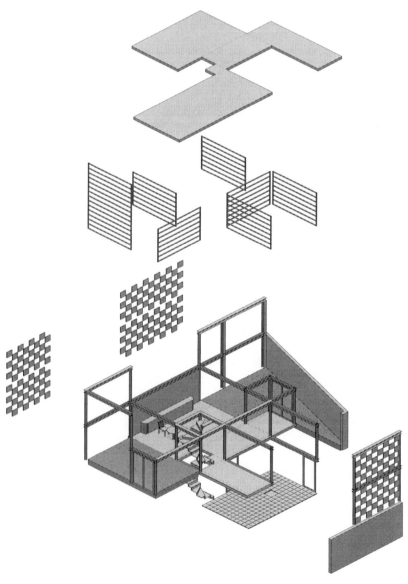

2_06 Exploded axonometric of an immobile cut of master bedroom and three adjacent open-air spaces located at the back, east end of the house. The structural frames are quite regular, formed by a small and large grid, but the space created is complex and uncontained as the space of the bedroom extends out through the courtyards and adjoining rooms. The illustration also shows the three-dimensional variety of the spaces with the living-room courtyard and backyard reaching up to two storeys, while the side courtyard is an excavated space bringing light into the basement.

the form of a doughnut without cutting it apart or gluing pieces of it together. In topology, the coffee cup (with one handle) and the doughnut are the same form: the surfaces of both are considered equivalent because both have a single hole. The invariant here is a continuous surface with a single hole. Often as well a frame can be dynamic without being either Euclidean or topological.

The 'frame of frames' or screen of a computer and of a film, of course, remains constant, but within the computer or film frame the edges of the image can be constructed with Euclidean coordinates or topological invariants. Dynamic framing is possible in digital video editing, where the size, scale or proportion of the frame edge can vary within the animation according to a formula of transformation. However, in both systems, whether Euclidean or topological, the frame acts as a limit to the **set of information**. Such a limit also influences how we perceive the enclosed set of information by using either Euclidean coordinates or topological invariants. Limiting is a creative tool that influences the character of the information set we have chosen and how that information set is perceived.

There are film-makers who limit their frames with topological invariants, rather than with Euclidean coordinates, just as there are architects who limit their forms topologically rather than with Euclidean coordinates. Are the images of the drawing system of your day framed with Euclidean coordinates or topological invariants, or both? And what about the architecture that you draw? How is it limited? The frame of the computer screen is a geometric constant, but projected or

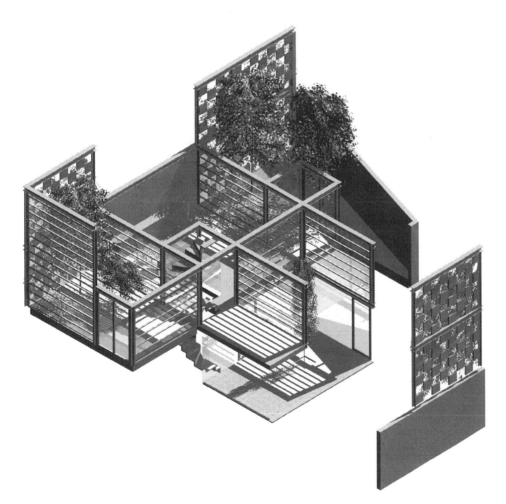

2_07 Rendered axonometric showing the dynamic spatial framing of the space with large and small structural bays and interlocking floor plates. The view shows the direction of the morning light, which projects shadows from the back garden into the bedroom.

090   plotted computer-generated drawings have the potential to frame images in a much more open and dynamic system than film frames. The book you are reading is also limited by the geometric frame of the covers and two page spread, but by flipping pages – and turning the book sideways and upside down, as you are encouraged to do with the illustrations in this book – you introduce a dynamic between images and text. Try looking at the images in the framing section as a cartoon flip book and examine illustrations from different sides of the book.

Ozu's frames are strictly geometric within Euclidean coordinates. However, low light levels blur the edges of the frame in darkness, especially when projected in a dark room or printed on a dark background, making it a dynamic frame. A classic example of dynamic framing is D.W. Griffith's use of a circular oculus, which focuses on a detail in the frame and then zooms out to complete the frame.[4] Ozu brings attention to detail through limited light. Figures are in profile, the edges are not strictly defined. If we examine the frame created light, we see a different geometry or edge to the image, and these fragments of light float in a black space.

2_08 Frontal perspective showing sectional relationship between first floor bedroom flat, behind the two-storey courtyard in the front, and three-storey south facing sunken courtyard on side.

Where are the edges or limits of the master bedroom of the Shutter House? Ban's design begins within the strict limits of a square structural grid. However, there are two sizes of squares in the grid, and already as we have seen in the bedroom, the room itself is not contained within the limits of one grid, but moves between the two. The limits of the master bedroom are the glass walls and doors which, when closed, contain a space of two shifted rectangles, creating a dynamic space with a diagonal orientation across the shift in plan. Also when the shades are open, the visual space of the bedroom includes the trees, sky and shifting light conditions of the exterior. Additionally, when front and back shutters are open, the space of the bedroom is continuous with the outdoors, uncontained in terms of air, moisture, sound and temperature flows, but limited by the back wall of the property and the physical limits of living-room courtyard.

Adjacent to the stair, the bedroom has a door which opens to the kitchen and dining area, which likewise is situated between three courtyards. Additionally, when the shutter is open the courtyard is accessible directly from the bedroom and also has the possibility of opening to the two-storey living room through an even larger, double-height movable shutter. The living room, dining room and kitchen are all shifted rectangles opening into courtyard spaces. This house, seemingly confined by the Euclidean geometries of the structural grid, in fact provides a multitude of dynamic overlapping spaces and different ways of framing the matter-flux both inside and out.

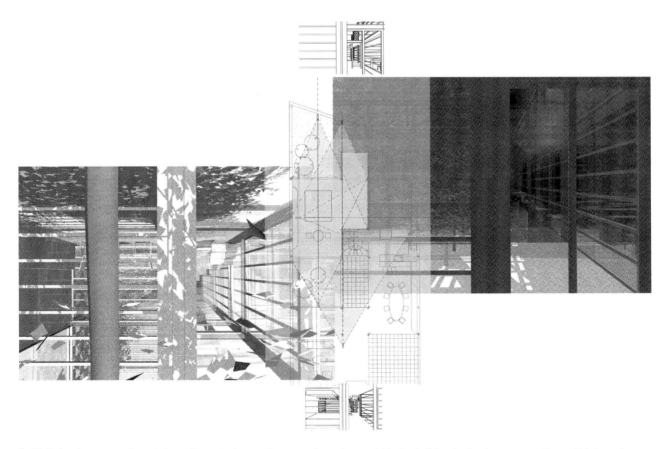

2_09 Reframing east and west views. By centering our frame on the column grid instead of the shutter bay, you see the spatial dynamic between the wide and narrow structural bays. This illustration should be looked at upside down as well as viewed normally.

Framing the nature of parts

Do the parts within the frame tend to have Euclidean coordinates or topological invariants, or are they dynamic?

Exercise 2.3: *Look at the relation between moving figures within the space of your model and the frames of the space itself. Besides framing the edges of an image, you also frame parts with the frame which, either by Euclidean coordinates or topological invariants or by making them dynamic.*

In shot 4 (illus 1_09 and 1_10) of *Early Spring*, Ozu has framed the coordinates of the parts of this image – the interior – and their relationship to each other so the movements of the wife reinforce them. He has vertically aligned her within a field of vertical and horizontal elements, which, like the wife, can move but are nonetheless constrained. For instance, the horizontal blind she raises only moves up or down in order to open or close the rectangular doorway to the alley. The horizontals and verticals of blind and doorframe, in turn, mirror the horizontals and verticals of the screen and most of the other features of the room, making the geometry and relationship of the parts within this image consistently Euclidean. However, the movement of her body within her kimono sets up a complex geometry of fabric and folds in continual movement, which we can track in direct opposition to the strict geometry of the space.

In Ozu's shot 4, the proportions and size of the rectangular door frame send a signal that only one person can pass through it at a time. The movable horizontal blind for the door sends another signal: it clearly indicates that both the interior and the alley beyond it can be either closed to movement and view or used for moving as well as viewing. But because the blind,

which is an element in the circulation route, is made of lightweight, loosely-joined, horizontal elements, noise and light can penetrate, indicating that the space of the room is only partially closed off from that of the lane, which is a space shared with neighbours. Thus, the door frame is a part of a circulation route whose Euclidean details clearly communicate its intended function, even without anyone actually using it.

Just as in a film image, the interior elements in an architectural one can be framed either with **Euclidean coordinates** or **topological invariants** or they can be made dynamic. For instance, when you draw circulation routes into and through architecture and its interiors, you are making **action images**. You don't need people to show the range of supported movements these paths indicate. The architecture itself does this through its own signs. The geometry of the relationship of the parts of circulation routes signals how to use the paths, thus modifying the suggested movements of people on them.

As we have mentioned, the opening of the shutters in Ban's house can be related to the act of waking up in the morning. If we situated the wife in Ozu's film in the Shutter House, we can observe her from the back garden, looking through the glass shutter as she wakes up and opens the back glass wall. (Read image sequence in illus 2_12 from right to left.) She might then proceed to the bathroom first, and later to the kitchen. The bed faces the back wall, and the shifting rectangles of the room direct the movement diagonally across to the bathroom. Coming from the bathroom, with the light on her back, the wife can proceed directly to the kitchen by the stairway without disturbing her still sleeping husband. Likewise we can observe her husband waking up and opening the shutter to the living-room courtyard, creating a continuous space from the back garden to the living room.

2_10 In this fictional scenario where the house is occupied by the characters from Ozu's *Early Spring*, the wife wakes up in the morning and opens the rear glass shutter wall before going to the bathroom (image sequence reads from right to left)

LIVERPOOL JOHN MOORES UNIVERSITY
LEARNING SERVICES

2_11 The fictional scenario continues as the husband wakes up and opens the front shutter to the courtyard facing the living room. Now the dynamic spatial qualities of the movable shutters become evident as the bedroom becomes reframed in the relative out-of-field of the back garden and the living-room court. (Image sequence reads from left to right.)

Framing a point of view

Does the angle in space from which the framed information set is made tend to be justified pragmatically or claim a 'higher justification?'

Exercise 2.4: *Experiment with different framing angles in space. Separate out points of view which can be justified pragmatically – framing the movements of the couple waking up in the morning – as well as claiming a 'higher justification', such as the qualities of the space, light or materials.*

Every film image and view generated from a computer model has an '**angle of framing**', the position in space from which it was drawn. Each of the earlier drawings from *Early Spring* shown in this book has clearly marked on it Ozu's angle of framing. These positions can be explained pragmatically as well as having a 'higher justification' when looked at in digital representation.

In the fifth shot of *Early Spring* (illus 1_12), the angle of framing is pragmatic. A pragmatic angle results from one of two possible positions: 'from the point of view of a more comprehensive set … or from the point of view of an initially unseen … element of the first set'.[5] This image takes the point of view of a more comprehensive **set of information** than the image itself frames. The series of illustrations 2_15 and 2_16 from the computer model of the Photographer's Shutter

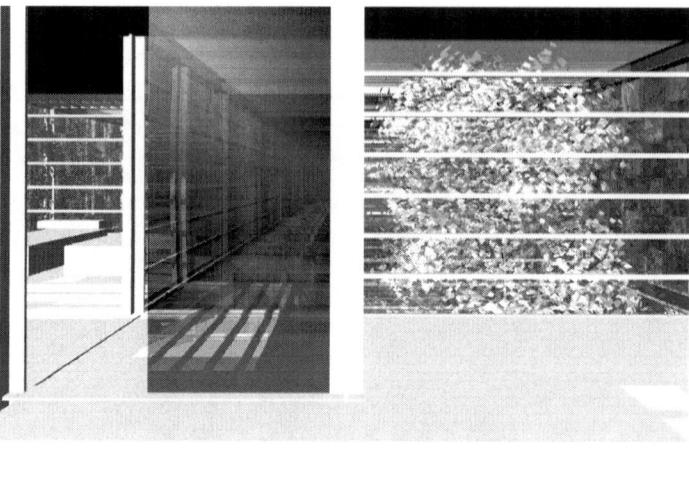

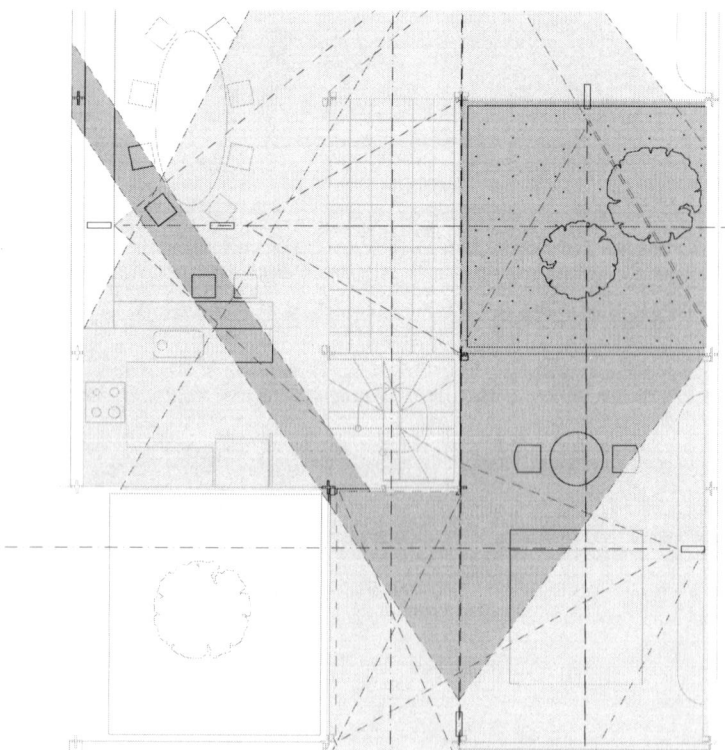

2_12 Two upper level views taken from two different angles show the relation of the children's bedrooms to the courtyard and stairs. The upstairs bedrooms on the upper floor and the maid's room and small studio in the basement are interconnected by this stairway. The qualities of light shift as one moves vertically through the house.

House take views and cuts through the computer model that give images of spatial relations in the house that cannot be viewed by a human observer in the actual house. This use of a camera eye specific to computer modelling lays claim to the 'higher justification' of the deeper architectural concepts of the house.

The angle of framing for all of the Ozu images discussed can be explained pragmatically. Two of them – the close-up of the wife sleeping (illus I_05 and I_06) and the view of her back as she leaves the kitchen (illus I_09 and I_10) – illustrate the second method used for pragmatic framing: 'from the point of view of an initially unseen ... element of the first set'. Ozu framed the image of the profile of the waking wife from the angle of someone within the information set of the initial establishing bedroom shot (illus I_03 and I_04). To do this, Ozu stationed the camera near the floor next to the bed. Likewise, the place from which the wife was filmed going through the door to the alley is within the bedroom space seen in the establishing shot. Both images are pragmatic, having been made 'from the point of view of an initially unseen ... element' in the establishing set.

You can also frame an image from an angle that claims a higher justification. The close-up image of the sleeping wife can help us understand how to do this. Ozu has shown behind her a plain wall that fills most of the upper half of the frame. There is nothing on the wall. It is featureless. Its blankness intensifies the mood emanating from the wife's expressionless face. The justification for an angle of framing that at first seems to frame the dead space of the plain wall is the power of emptiness to carry us beyond the visible to the invisible – a higher justification than a purely pragmatic angle. So the image of the waking wife uses both techniques of framing the point of view: pragmatic and claiming a higher justification.

Seemingly 'dead or disconnected spaces', like the wall in the close-up of the sleeping wife, appear in many films. They are an angle of framing that has no narrative function because they 'refer to another dimension of the image'. They introduce the concept of 'deframing', where there is no visual function. Instead they have a 'legible function'; they make intelligible, not what the eyes see, but what the mind knows.[6] Deframing in moving architectural drawings can serve an additional function. This technique can help free the maker and viewer from the illusion of moving architectural drawings simulating reality. Scanning the top of the computer model of Ban's house with a virtual camera reveals the blank, 'dead' spaces of the roof alternating with the deeper dimension of the courtyards.

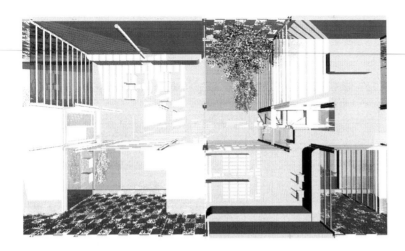

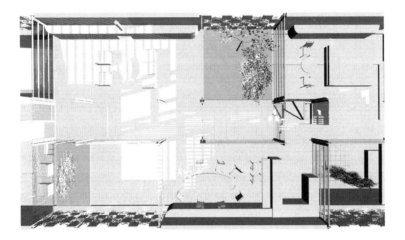

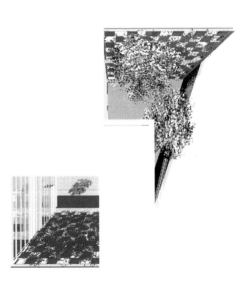

2_13 Immobile horizontal cuts through the Photographer's Shutter House from top down showing roof and courtyards, second floor and ground floor, all looking down. These views are an example of ways to look at the house that are beyond the abilities of the human eye, and as such seek a "higher justification" – in this case they explain the rhythm of enclosed spaces and those open to the sky.

Pragmatics and higher justification intersect continually in the Shutter House. The house is for a young family but, also accommodates an underground photographer's studio and darkroom. The clients of the house, a photographer and a painter, as artists, came with the higher justification of aesthetics. In fact, Ban quotes the photographer as saying: 'I wish I could commission Mies (van der Rohe) if only he were alive … '[7] This demand for the highest aesthetic achievement of modern architecture is coupled with the messy reality of domestic and work life, both of which come together in the house. While we have seen how the geometry and glass shutters frame the experience of waking up and beginning the day at the Shutter House, we can also examine the more public spaces at the front of the house, and how the house in addition to being a family home, is also a photographer's studio that must accommodate creative work, studio assistants, and visitors. It is only in section cuts through the computer model that we can see the two worlds of the light-filled house above and the dark room, garage and photographer's studio below (illus 2_16).

Shigeru Ban describes how he balanced the 'higher justification' of the aesthetic ideals he shared with the clients and the pragmatics of the given programme of providing for both domestic and work life:

> 'The space composition features a set of grid modules with checked patterns of 4m and 2m a side that covers up this inevitably closed site, so that all rooms share a sense of continuity as well as courtyards that are arranged between each room. The dimensions of a room are derived by combining large and small checked modules until they make an appropriate size. Of these modules, the smallest square unit was made into a core supporting the lateral force that circulates from the basement up through the 2nd floor. Lack of planar rigidity on the roof is reinforced by making use of the canopy of thin louvers.
>
> Glass is used along all edges of each room facing the courtyards for visual link between the inside and outside. These glass surfaces are structured as stacking shutters that can be fully open to the courtyards, accounting for the physical continuity of the internal/external spaces. This allows controlling spatial fluidity according to seasons and occasions in both planar and cross-sectional manners, producing a Universal Floor as opposed to Mies' Universal Space.
>
> One side of the courtyard facing the site's border is a checkered plane of greenery, a vertical garden that provides minimum protection of privacy'.[8]

Framing an out-of-field

Does the out-of-field of the framed information set tend to be relative or absolute ... or both?

Exercise 2.5: *Find the two kinds of out-of-field through framing the information set in your computer model.*

In *Early Spring,* a medium shot action image of the neighbour (illus 1_12), whom we first saw in the background of the fifth shot, will help us explore framing an out-of-field. We identify her from the pattern and belt of her kimono, which differs from the kimono of the first woman we observed waking up in her bedroom. The neighbour is entering her home through a door with an adjustable blind, similar to the one we saw in the first couple's home. We see in front of her another person – her husband – wearing his sleeping kimono, brushing his teeth.

In this image (illus 1_12) Ozu constructed a set of framed information with strong mirrored elements to the data describing the first couple. In doing so he focuses our awareness not only on the obvious parallels between the first couple and this one, but more importantly on the subtle differences between them. In this way, he catches our attention because initially we think we are seeing the back of the first woman. As we become conscious that it is a different person, we are jolted into an 'awake awareness'. Our habitual way of seeing is unsettled. It has misled us. Where before we had been 'just looking', now we have become conscious. Something new and unexpected is happening, which relates to the aspect of framing we are exploring here – the out-of-field.

102   We are investigating whether the out-of-field of this information set is relative (part of a larger set), or absolute (a whole into which the set of information is integrated). All framing of **blocks** of space-time refers to one or possibly both of these two aspects of what is beyond the image: the 'relative' out-of-field in which the framed information set is part of a larger set and the 'absolute' out-of-field, an **open whole** into which the information set is integrated.[9]

In the image under discussion (illus 1_12), Ozu composed a frame whose out-of-field is relative because it is part of a larger set, which includes the fourth 'wall' of the space – the passageway from which the neighbour enters her home. This is where the camera and the film-viewers are located. Once we realise that the woman in the image is not the same person we saw earlier, waking up in her bedroom, we become aware that off this lane is a similar door to the first couple's home where, we assume, the husband is probably starting to get up. The first set of **movement images** in the couple's bedroom has now become the relative out-of-field for this action image. There is yet another possible relative out-of-field suggested by the light seen through the window to the left, which we suppose is outside natural light although we see no particulars of the exterior, just luminosity.

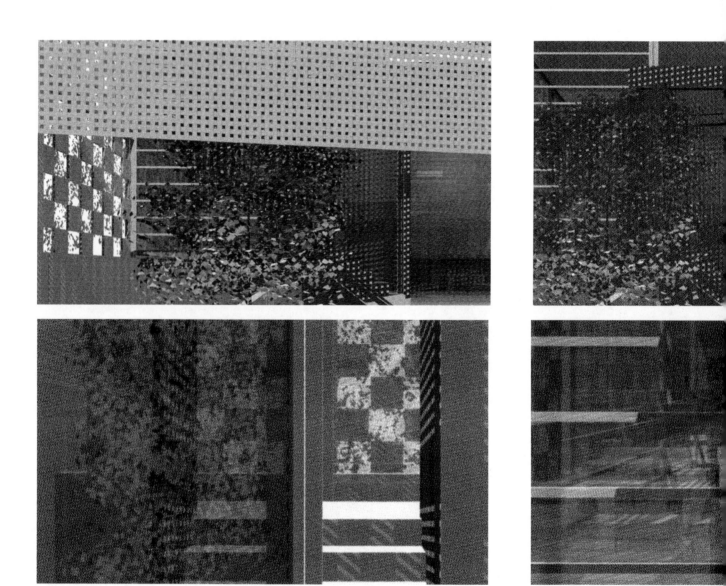

The relation between the relative and absolute out-of-fields is very rich in the architectural experience of Shigeru Ban's Photographer's Shutter House. In illus 2_04 to 2_14 we saw how each part of the house can be adjusted to open up to a larger and larger space through the presence of interlocking structural grids, glass shutters and three dimensional variety. From the entrance of the house, the limiting of information is tied to the dual functions of living and work space. As a photographer's atelier with staff and visitors, the front of the house consists of many screens, glass walls, reflections and refractions which can limit visual and physical access to private areas of the house, but reveal to the visitor essential qualities of the open whole of Ban's architecture – its ability to frame the absolute out-of-field.

2_15 Six views as immobile cuts creating intervals in the movement and duration of entering the house: slipping under the front screen wall, the glass entry vestibule with the shadows of the afternoon light filtering through the screen wall, and the multiple reflections through the series of glass planes at the entry.

To learn more about domestic architecture in its larger context, we will examine the second type of out-of-field – the absolute – by examining closely shots 7 to 15 in *Early Spring*, in which we return to the first couple's bedroom (illus 1_14 to 1_19). The seventh shot is a medium shot, in which the wife has not only returned but changed her clothes. We are surprised to find that her husband is not getting ready for the day, but is still in bed. The wife moves to the back screen to open the courtyard door and the translucent curtains. The eighth shot observes the husband finally getting up while the ninth shows the wife in the kitchen. The next five shots cut back and forth between the couple in conversation. The final 15th shot shows the husband standing in front of the screen where his wife stood earlier (illus 1_17, 1_18).

Where is the absolute out-of-field in shots 7 to 15?

The following question can help us understand where the absolute out-of-field is: Is there an 'aspect [of shots 7 to 15] by which the closed system [of information] opens on to a **duration** which is immanent to the whole universe, which is no longer a set and does not belong to the order of the visible?'[10] In other words, is there an out-of-field in these shots that is absolute – 'a whole into which the information set is integrated'?

Immobile Cuts Through Duration

In *Losing Perspective,* we briefly referred to Henri Bergson's and Gilles Deleuze's reflections on **duration.** For them duration is experienced when you realise that 'there exists somewhere a whole which is changing, and which is open'.[11] This experience of a changing whole contrasts with the popular concept of the universe as closed, with a predetermined clock-like, mechanical course in which past events predict future ones. In the **open whole** of Bergson and Deleuze, the universe endures by changing, through the creation of 'newness'. The processes of the universe cannot be described as linked through cause and effect. When you pause in the **interval** and decide to act in a manner in a manner predicted by habit, you are living within a universe, that endures because it changes.

In the repeated shots from the same vantage in the bedroom in Early Spring, we experience duration when we feel the quality of the diffuse light framed by the squares in the screen. This is not the first time in the opening scene that light subsists. All the frames studied so far (illus I_20, I_21) include this light. All of the frames studied so far (illus I_20, I_21) include this light, which changes its quality and thus its relationship to the other elements in the set as we move through this first scene. The second and 14th shots create duration through 'deframing', the inclusion of the seemingly blank areas of the wall. In the views from the Ban house, we looked at the bedroom spaces in early morning light, while the illustrations of the entry sequence (illus 2_17) depict afternoon light filtering through the west-facing entry screen wall.

Remember the back-light in the first establishing shot of the bedroom with the sleeping couple in *Early Spring* (illus I_03, I_04), as well as in the images facing east in the Shutter House? (illus 2_05). It permeated the far wall bedroom screen in Ozu and the glass master bedroom in Ban's design. Starting with both cinematic and architectural bedroom images, on through the other frames of this sequence, relationships are in movement – between wife and husband, between features of their bedroom, and between the light and the other parts of the images – all are constantly changing and yet enduring. As we experience the movement images in these cinematic and architectural sequences, we come to realise that the relationships of all the elements in this **set of information** are continually transforming. This recurring change alters the state of the **whole**, keeping it open, enabling the unpredictable in the form of '**newness**' to emerge. 'Duration is change … it changes and does not stop changing.'[12]

We grasp these changes because Ozu and Ban, using the art of framing in cinema and in architecture, have awakened our consciousness, which 'only exist[s] in so far as it open[s] itself upon a whole'.[13] For instance, the relation between the light and the waking husband and wife shifts dramatically as the morning light changes. In the second shot of *Early Spring,* the husband rolls over and tries to go back to sleep when the alarm goes off. Now, as we look at him still in bed, knowing that his wife and the neighbouring couple are getting ready for the day, his relationship to the light has the distinct quality of his avoiding getting up. We become conscious that the state of the **whole** has changed since the first establishing shot. The relationships of the parts in this set have shifted. 'Relation is not a property of objects, it is always external to its terms. It is … inseparable from the open, and displays a spiritual or mental existence.' '**Duration** … is the whole of relations.'[14]

In both *Early Spring* and the Photographer's Shutter House, the absolute out-of-field of the light 'testifies to a more disturbing presence, one which cannot even be said to exist, but rather to "insist" or "subsist", a more radical Elsewhere, outside homogeneous space and time'. The more the relative out-of-field is disconnected from spatio-temporal coordinates of commonsense experience, the greater is the disquieting insistence of the absolute out-of-field, 'the more effectively the out-of-field fulfils its other function which is that of introducing the transpatial and the spiritual into the system which is never perfectly closed'. The image becomes 'a mental image', 'open[ing] … on to a play of relations which are purely thought and which weave a whole'.[15]

106   The luminous sections of the screens in Ozu's set, as well as the glass shutters in Ban's design, are the elements bringing the absolute out-of-field into their rooms. These architectural elements integrate set and design with the open whole. Duration is thus present within the frame of set and design because the closed systems of cinematic and architectural information 'open onto a **duration** which is immanent to the whole universe, which is no longer a set and does not belong to the order of the visible'.[16]

Can you experience the absolute out-of-field so you will have a sense of what it is you are integrating into your drawings? The answer is yes. To start, ask yourself a question similar to the one we raised in relation to Ozu and Ban: 'Is there an aspect of your morning routine by which its seemingly closed system of information opens onto a **duration** which is immanent to the whole universe, which is no longer a set and does not belong to the order of the visible'? To find this aspect, recall the **interval** between breathing in and breathing out. Here is where you can experience the absolute out-of-field. Within the interval is access to the **open** vibratory **whole** of **matter-flux** from which not only you emerge as a **centre of indeterminacy** but also the three **movement images** and the **five aspects of framing**. In the interval is the absolute out-of-field, which is also the source of an architecture of 'newness'.

In his Photographer's Shutter House, Shigeru Ban put together the higher justification of the aesthetics of modern architecture and specific cultural relationships with nature within a flexible and dynamic three-dimensional grid. Working with his assistants and the clients over a two-year period, they arrived at a design which mixes aesthetic ideals with the pragmatics of everyday life. We can understand how one experiences the relationship between everyday activities such as work, play, family life and the absolute by looking at various hypothetical scenarios over the course of a day in this house.

2_16 This immobile longitudinal cut from south to north showing the spatial variety in section – the two-storey living room, the sunken court and the lower basement photographer's studio.

1 Deleuze, *Cinema 1*, pp 18, 57–8.

2 Deleuze, *Cinema 1*, p 18.

3 Deleuze, *Cinema 1*, p 18.

4 Deleuze, *Cinema 1*, p 13.

5 Deleuze, *Cinema 1*, p 15.

6 Deleuze, *Cinema 1*, p 15.

7 Shigeru Ban, unpublished notes.

8 Shigeru Ban, unpublished notes.

9 Deleuze, *Cinema 1*, pp 15–16.

10 Deleuze, *Cinema 1*, p 17.

11 Deleuze, *Cinema 1*, p 9.

12 Deleuze, *Cinema 1*, p 8.

13 Deleuze, *Cinema 1*, p 10.

14 Deleuze, *Cinema 1*, p 10.

15 Deleuze, *Cinema 1*, pp 17–18.

16 Deleuze, *Cinema 1*, p 17.

CHAPTER 3

SHOOTING

What happens when movement is related, not to privileged poses, but to any-instant-whatever?

You are now on your way to knowing what it means to be a **cybernetic architect**. The first part of this book calls your attention to the large range of choices you have in framing architectural information as immobile cuts through flowing matter-flux. We introduced you to how your own body experiences can be the references for understanding the process of framing immobile cuts using digital technologies. One consequence of particular importance to *Cinemetrics* is that you are beginning to understand that computers contribute to new relationships between your senses and your motor responses. These relationships are radically different from the sensori-motor schema active when you draw using a drawing board and mechanical tools. You are also experiencing that you can make choices. You are a moving **centre of indeterminacy** in an acentered world, not a pre-programmed robot attached to an electronic gadget. Before reacting to signals given by your computer, you can pause to feel your perceptions by noting the sensations of your body experiences. You can be a sensor of yourself. Then you can take whatever action you choose. You don't have to be propelled by electronic gadgets – to constantly check your email or mobile phone. You don't have to be a **servo-mechanism** to them. They are extensions of you as a living organism. Making conscious the feedback loops between you and your electronic tools enables you to make choices.

Words in bold are Keywords found on pages 260-265

110 You can consciously experience the world as an **open whole** to develop the new **know-how** and **know-about** of *Cinemetrics*. Instead of using digital imaging technologies to simulate the use of hand-drawing tools or to become a moviemaker of films showing architectural walk-throughs, you can use electronic tools developed with cybernetic feedback systems to make drawings that *move* in a field of relations. Using these tools, you will learn to experience and draw moving images of our world as an everyday activity rather than as solely a professional skill. There is nothing esoteric about the *Cinemetric* methodology. When you access the vibrational matrix of the open whole as the source of architectural images, they cease to be isolated objects. Instead, they emerge in relationship to specific human concerns, such as culture, and broader realms, such as ecology, which are not in the computer. They are part of the ordinary **autopoietic** world in which your body is embedded. This chapter will help you understand this process in more detail.

Exercise 3.1: *Shoot examples of people and architecture assuming privileged poses.*

To more fully understand what it takes to be a cybernetic architect and to help you with those unfinished drawings waiting on your computer, let's consider the question that opens this chapter: *What happens when movement is related, not to privileged poses, but to any-instant-whatever?* In this chapter we will use Jean-Luc Godard's film *Contempt* (1963) as our second film example help you to understand these concepts in your daily life. Let's start with **privileged poses**. You are probably familiar with privileged poses from Western art. Remember all those statues of ancient Greek youths in various stances described as ideal? Their body positions are privileged poses. The *Discus Thrower* by Myron, 450 BC, is one example. Classical sculptures actualise forms or ideas considered eternal and transcendent.[1] They 'characterize a period of which they express the quintessence, all the rest of this period being filled by the transition, of no interest in itself, from one form to another form.'[2]

Godard's film is a fictional account of the making of a hypothetical Hollywood adaptation of the epic poem, *The Odyssey*, written by the early Greek storyteller Homer. At the beginning of *Contempt*, Godard shows us from this film within a film clips of the classical Greek gods assuming privileged poses. They are frozen figures that only move when an unseen assistant turns them within the camera frame, not unlike our experience when we walk around a sculpture keeping it as our centre of vision. Later we see the film character of a Hollywood movie producer assume the pose of the Discus Thrower as he heaves a film canister across a screening room. The juxtaposition of Greek gods and Hollywood actors jolts us. Witnessing the melodramatic gestures of the actors, we suddenly see that Hollywood has co-opted the privileged poses of Greek gods, and to Godard, corrupted them in the process.

In architecture, the privileged pose is the facade – the face – of the building, seen in physical fact from a particular designed vantage point, or in photographs and drawings. The revolutionary Russian film-maker Sergei Eisenstein wrote about the affinities between the privileged poses of architecture and cinema after carefully studying architectural historian Auguste Choisy's 19th-century drawings of the approach up the Athenian Acropolis. Choisy draws a sequence of privileged poses through the monumental gateway of the Propylaea, looking towards the 36 foot tall gold and ivory statue of Athena. The architect of the Parthenon – Phideas – has positioned her so we dramatically see her standing pose as a warrior wearing full armour, carrying a spear and a shield, with a helmet on her head – a classical privileged pose.

3_01 In Ozu's film, the camera remained stable, and the movement in the shot passed through the frame. In the following sequence from the movie *Contempt*, Jean-Luc Godard pans the camera back and forth through a five-room apartment in Rome. Here the two characters – again a married couple in a domestic space – pass in and out of the frame as the camera pans back and forth. We have left the world of the **privileged poses** of Ozu's stationary camera, and have entered a realm of **any-instant-whatever**. Illustration continues through to page 117.

Next Choisy sketches a 'shot' looking towards the Erechtheum, a small shrine honouring both Athena and Poseidon, and then another one approaching the Parthenon, the most important temple on the Acropolis. Eisenstein interprets these Beaux-Arts drawings like a film sequence, where the human observer stops at certain places on this sacred route to get privileged views of the architectural ensemble. In the movie *Contempt*, Godard appropriates the modern Casa Malaparte (1938–41) on the Island of Capri as the scene for the shooting of the film within his film in order to caricature Hollywood historical dramas, often set in ancient sites. Godard's presentation of the house in its dramatic setting shows us how, when architecture is viewed as a movement image, the privileged pose becomes just one of the many **any-instant-whatever** that make the illusion of movement possible. We will look more closely at the Casa Malaparte in the next section, where it serves as our second architectural example.

The tendency in Western architecture to make the facade a privileged pose is evident as well in Western perspectival pictures of architecture, such as those described by Robin Evans as the *arrested image*. As Evans points out in *The Projective Cast*, the tendency to make Western architecture into a privileged pose is one of the reasons it often appears static and picture-like, instead of the dynamic continuous environment experienced over time that it frequently is. This is another reason, besides the use of the non-linear digital tools, that it is important for us to lose linear perspective when we draw architecture using the cybernetic computer. What would happen if we put the stages of making and observing a building that Evans charts in diagrams into Paul Ryan's intransitive cybernetic Relational Circuit (in *Losing Perspective*, illus m). In particular, what happens to the pictures associated with hand-held tools in *The Projective Cast*? Evans pictures ten relationships in the transitive interaction between orthographic and perspective drawing, the built object and the human observer. He goes to the limit of what you can do relationally with perspective or projective geometry. In effect, he shows us that we need to abandon pictorial projection if cybernetic relationships between sets of information are to be, not pictured, but indexed and diagrammed. So if a privileged pose is what perspective drawing focuses our attention on, then what is an **any-instant-whatever** and how does it relate to architecture, cybernetics, and computers? 'Any-instant-whatever is the instant which is equidistant from another.'[3] Projected 35 millimetre film stock consists of 24 any-instant-whatever per second to create the illusion of the continuity of movement. Every film you have seen creates movement using any-instant-whatever, but let's use animated cartoons to illustrate them. You have probably seen many animated cartoons and perhaps even made your own. The drawings in an animated cartoon describe figures that are '… always in the process of being formed or dissolving through movement of lines and points taken at any-instant-whatevers of their course'. Animated cartoons are not composed from completed figures or poses. 'Cartoon film … does not give us a figure described in a unique moment, but the continuity of the movement which describes the figure.'[4] We are learning a drawing system with continuity of movement, so the architecture you create will not become an autonomous object that actualises an ideal form but a field of any-instant-whatever within a larger sphere of both human and non-human relations.

You may be wondering when you no longer actualise ideal forms in your drawings and buildings what happens to the symmetrical facade as privileged pose, which to many is such an integral part of architecture. When we relate movement to any-instant-whatever, a building's symmetrical facade, like those on so many Western neo-classical buildings, becomes not a singular and remarkable any-instant-whatever, but an ordinary and regular any-instant-whatever. Why? Because, rather than being 'new', the facade actualises a transcendent form – symmetry – that has been used for centuries. 'Any-instant-

whatevers can be regular *or* singular, ordinary *or* remarkable.' But, and this is the important point, remarkable instants are not 'transcendental forms which are actualized in a movement'. They are 'the singular points which are immanent to movement.' 'The singular is taken from the any-whatever, and is itself an any-whatever which is simply non-ordinary and non-regular.' It is 'new'. Developing a drawing system out of any-instant-whatever, not privileged poses, is integral to addressing the unprecedented cultural and ecological processes that confront the issues that confront you today as an architect, which necessitate continually creating the 'new'.[5]

Exercise 3.2: *Photograph examples of people and architecture as a series of an-instants-whatever rather than as single privileged pose.*

Architects today are increasingly recognising that movement, rather than ideal form, is essential to architecture. They realise that our experiences of architecture are not merely transitions through minor instants to the moment when movement stops and we stand in front of a building as if it were a perspectival drawing by Brunelleschi. They design without creating a privileged facade for their buildings. They create their buildings from the movement of any-instant-whatever that are 'regular *or* singular, ordinary *or* remarkable'.[6] They select instants or **frames** of space-time that are immanent to the movement of the **open whole**.

Shigeru Ban's Photographer's Shutter House, which we just analysed, is an example. Ban designed it as a moving architecture of any-instant-whatever. Throughout the house, Ban produced complex ever-changing qualities of domestic spaces around glass courtyards. We saw how the exposed steel structural columns and beams frame the space, but the glass walls – transparent, translucent, refractive, and reflective – cannot be experienced by isolating one part of the house from the rest of the building. On a rainy day in early August you have the feeling of wandering through a terrarium of moss-covered gardens with condensation building up on the glass. The possibility of opening walls of glass to outdoor courtyards blurs the distinction between inside and out as well.

The house can be appreciated in the low, meditative still frames that we learned through the example of the film-maker Ozu. However, the experience of moving around, through, in and out of the interior spaces and courtyards produces a series of any-instant-whatever, which create the continuity of our movement and embed us, along with the house itself, within a field of relations that extend beyond the building itself. With respect to the glass, the field of relations includes the movement of the sun, the gravitational pull of the earth, the fluctuating cycles of day, month, and season, the process of making the glass, delivering it to the site, putting it in place as well as contemporary discussions about glass and its place historically and its relation to changing patterns of domesticity.

By giving the owners the opportunity to open the walls of glass to exterior courtyards, Ban created the possibility of not just visual vibrancy and difference, but atmospheric changes in temperature, smell and sound within the house in a very different way than opening up windows to the outside. Here the shutters open glass walls to an open-roofed room, inside the house. In the last section, you looked at the changing qualities of the space of architecture through immobile cuts. The computer, in its ability to generate multiple, iterative drawings rather than single images, is a robust tool in helping us draw architecture as moving any-instant-whatever rather than the static privileged poses that characterise the way architecture has been understood in print culture through perspectives and still photographs. The computer is a tool that can be used to engage the field of relations within which architecture emerges. The subject of this chapter, the **Shot** is a way of using the tool to reveal any-instant-whatever.

Exercise 3.3: Take your immobile cuts from Chapter 2 and use them as key frames to create moving sections, panning from one frame to another by rotating from one 90-degree angle to another. You are now creating mobile shots.

The Shot is The Movement Image

This section's question – *what happens when movement is related, not to privileged poses, but to any-instant-whatever?* – builds on our exploration in *Framing* of the question, *What happens when movements are not in space and images not in our brains?* In chapter 1 *Framing* you learned that you cause movement images to emerge out of the **matter-flux** of the open **whole** by selecting **blocks of space-time**. Did you realise that movement images are shots composed of any-instant-whatever? What follows will help you understand how.

With this chapter's question in mind, we now examine the movement of any-instant-whatever more closely through what film-makers call **shooting** and the **shot.** The shot is still another way of describing the movement image. Because you are making drawings that move, we will continue to use terms from cinema because 'Cinema is the system which reproduces movement as a function of any-instant-whatever, … as a function of equidistant instants, selected so as to create the impression of continuity'.[7] Bergson and Deleuze argue that when '… one relates movement to any-moment-whatevers- – that they are shots. One must be capable of thinking the production of the new, that is, the remarkable and the singular'.[8] This is what you are aiming for as well – the production of newness.

We are going to use a selection of shots from Godard's film *Contempt* to examine not only the three types of movement images discussed in *Framing,* but three additional ones: **impulse, reflection, and relation**. Deleuze argued that he deduced these six types of movement images by analysing the non-verbal process of human perception as well as by reading about Charles Sanders Peirce's work on the same subject.[9] If this is so, then you should be able to deduce these images from your own body experiences, just as, in *Framing,* you found through your own observations the **interval** that Deleuze and Bergson describe.

The methodology of *Cinemetrics* encourages you to make conscious your process of perception, not just because Deleuze thinks it important, but because how and what your perceive – the experiences of your body – configures your own particular **sensori-motor** reflexes. These reflexes, in turn, structure your drawing habits that result in your **know-how,** which can either actualise transcendent ideals or create, out of the here and now of the immanent, the new **know-about**.

Exercise 3.4: *Let's see if you can experience the six movement images. After reading this sentence, instead of finishing the chapter, put aside the book and go about your habitual daily routine and try to notice yourself experiencing perception, affection, impulse, action, reflection and relation – especially when interacting with other people you meet at home, school or work. Come back later to read the rest of the chapter.*

Now think back over what you have done since putting down the book. Note, in particular, when you had social encounters in your daily life. Do you have a partner, a room-mate, or a neighbour whom you interacted with? Was there a friend you encountered in the classroom, studio or workplace? While shopping or in a restaurant? What happens when you

encounter another person? Think back over these moments and become aware of the physical space you were occupying at the same time you were aware of the presence of another person. Can you remember an all-embracing sense of your experience? Can you see yourself as if you were a many-eyed witness to your interaction with another person in this space? What were the qualities of the space, its facts, and patterns? Note these.

Next try to remember how your body absorbed stimuli from your interaction. Did feeling these stimuli in your body stir impulses, drives, and desires? Notice which of these responses you didn't act on. For instance, in the midst of your daily encounters with friends or strangers, perhaps you became aware of an urge to look off into the distance through an open window rather than directly engage your friend.

During the course of your daily social interactions, were there moments of disagreement? How did that affect the quality of your sense of yourself, of space, or of the other? Maybe you wanted to ignore an unpleasant feeling from the other person and focus on a nearby gadget or object that someone left around. When someone is talking to you, have you ever felt a desire to pick the gadget up and play with it even though the other person would be annoyed with you because you would seem to be ignoring him/her? Or maybe you felt the impulse to get up and walk around the room while your friend was making a point, or even answer your mobile phone while he/she was talking. We all have many impulses during the day that we don't act on. Try to find the ones you had and note them.

What happened when you delayed your spontaneous drives? Let yourself experience now the possibility of fulfilling some of the actions that impulsively occurred to you. Perhaps something dramatic, like stomping around and shutting a door in the face of your friend. How would that have changed the situation? Lastly, create a thought image that frames all the images of this experience in 'a fabric of relations'.[10]

Exercise 3.5: *Now try to record your experience emerging from your socio-spatial encounters. Use a digital video camera for following the six kinds of movement images. Notice how Godard uses a mechanical dolly rather than a hand-held camera. Restrict your camera/survey movements to ones similar to Godard's – tracks forward and back, pans clockwise and counter-clockwise, and tilting up and down.*

Segments of the experience, described above, of possible interactions at home, school, or work relate 'to the interval of movement which separates, within *one* [person] … a received and an executed movement'.[11] Research into the body itself and how it experiences received movement within within the organism has added another sense to the five familiar human senses of sight, taste, smell, touch, and hearing. **Proprioception**, unlike the five exteroceptive senses that receive movement from the outside world, tells us about the position of the parts of the body, relative to other neighbouring parts

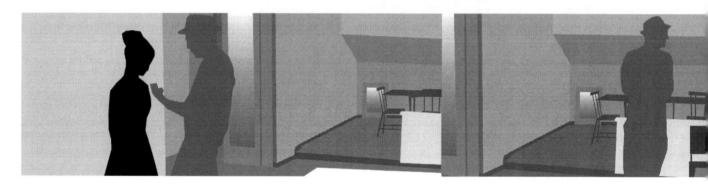

of the body as a result of the received movement. 'Proprioception: from "*proprius*-ception, 'one's own' ception" … provides feedback solely on the status of the body internally'. It gives us what the poet Charles Olsen described as the 'data of depth sensibility'.[12] The 'data of depth sensibility' that you are constantly gathering through your body experiences forms the plastic mass of **matter-flux** from which your drawings of moving architecture emerge.

Deleuze deduced his movement images from the **intervals** of movement and the thoughts emerging from that movement. Remember that it is the interval that Deleuze associates with your transformation from a '**center of indeterminacy**' into a '**living image**'. The stages of your process in the interval, which involve proprioception as well as thought, are what Deleuze names movement images: perception, affection, impulse, action, reflection, relation. These movement images are what you experience in your discussion with your friend when you pay attention to what is happening.[13]

We will now examine an early scene from *Contempt,* filmed in a more ordinary location than the Casa Malaparte. Our purpose is to study how Godard shoots any-instant-whatever to form movement images. In the next chapter we will examine how space is formed as we select these images from matter-flux. For now, we will focus on how these shots frame different kinds of movement images. Our objective is to help you understand how your daily life is a sequence of movement images made up of any-instant-whatever, so your own experience can inform your moving architectural drawing system. To do this, you are now going to use concepts and techniques of *Cinemetrics* to continue and expand a moving drawing system of life's daily routines. But now you will explore images, not through Ozu's static camera, but through Godard's moving camera.

Contempt takes place in three sequences: the first is split between the movie studios of Cinecittà, and the American movie producer's ancient villa in Rome. The second sequence is staged in the apartment of a married couple, and the last scene is filmed at Casa Malaparte where the movie of *The Odyssey* within Godard's film *Contempt* is being shot. In the apartment scene, the film camera follows the exchanges between a writer, hired to rewrite *The Odyssey* script to the tastes of the Hollywood producer, and his wife – here famously played by the French actress Brigitte Bardot. While Ozu's film was shot in

a studio, here location scouts have found a generic modern apartment in Rome filmed as a backdrop and prop for this scene. The opening scene of *Contempt* begins with a long shot at the Cinecittà movie studio with a large camera on tracks in the background (see illus_o in Losing Perspective). The camera is filming a woman walking towards us. We see the act of shooting: Godard films a movie camera on tracks moving forward in pace with the woman being filmed, and shooting her in profile. When the actress and camera come nearer, our point of view moves to a close-up of the cinematographer. Now we see him turn some mechanisms to tilt his camera up and down, and then he rotates the camera in a pan towards us. Now we are looking straight into the lens of the camera, which dramatically reveals the relation of the cameraman to the camera as a moving image is being made. In contrast to our making marks with a pencil when we draw, when we use the camera as a drawing tool, we receive light through the camera lens. Each type of camera lens changes what is actually in front of it. We can slow down the images recorded or speed them up in playback and editing. Meanwhile, the eye actively enters into making what it sees through the camera lens in an autopoietic manner. All of which means that using a camera as a drawing tool is entirely different to making marks on paper with a pencil.

The film is shot in cinemascope, so in addition to seeing the limited movements of the camera, we see the exaggerated horizontal aspect ratio of the frame: 2.35:1. Godard begins his film shooting the act of filming, much like Ryan videoed himself watching a video, as we saw in *Losing Perspective*. In the flat space of the apartment sequence, the slow horizontal pan back and forth dominates the shots, with only a few subtle tilts of the camera, and a couple of moments of dramatic tracks forward. Mostly the camera eye is a passive unseen presence dispassionately rotating back and forth. The apartment is presented in slow panning shots looking at the various rooms of the apartment and the couple. The camera continually turns to keep the couple in its frame. They move in and out of the frame and they fall in and out of an argument as they come home, undress, bath and dress again to go out. Here we observe two people in movement through the various rooms of an apartment, seen through the restricted movements of the mechanical apparatus of a camera: a heavy cinemascope camera on a track, which can slowly move forward or back, tilt up and down and pan left or right.

Now that you have observed and modelled your movements in relationship to another person within an ordinary discussion or argument with the same limitations on the range and types of camera movements, you can compare it to what Godard has done. You are beginning to understand how *Cinemetrics* involves socio-spatial fields of relationships.

Perception Image

Exercise 3.6: *Shoot long distance shots of a variety of places you encounter in a daily routine, first holding the shot, and then mechanically panning, tilting or tracking to form a perception image. Do not follow any action or impulse.*

In the previous exercises, you noted an all-embracing sense of socio-spatial relations even while talking and interacting with other people. By mentally stepping away from conversations and interactions even while continuing them, you create an interval within the matter-flux. Social life as a centre of indeterminacy is like being a billiard ball that acts and reacts to other balls without selecting.[14] As you made choices, an interval formed and you came into being as a **living image** that can frame. Within the context of *Cinemetrics*, the result is a **perception image**.

The Godard apartment scene opens with a perception image. The camera is present in the apartment vestibule, framing the entry door to the left and a view of the kitchen to the right, even before the couple enters. The wife and then the husband walk into the apartment. The camera is still and indecisive for a few moments. The camera first pans to follow the wife into the kitchen and dining area, and then pans all the way around to the left to follow the husband down a hallway and through an unfinished door. The wife carries a book into the living room and the camera next moves forward slightly and then pans to follow her movement. The husband has found his way to the sofa off-screen. The camera does not enter the living room but pans right to follow the couple as they disappear behind a wall to approach the bedroom and bathroom. By continuing to pan right, the camera captures them as they pass from the living room to the opposite end of the hallway that they first entered.

This entire sequence takes nearly half an hour. By its end, the camera has taken us through the entire apartment. Because of the limited positions of the camera, its limits in movement, and the complexity of activities and changes of moods of the couple, we have to continually encounter and re-encounter perception images – the apartment and the couple are never fully present and known. Deleuze says that the moving camera is the eye that is in all things, creating an image that is 'a pure perception as it is in things'. A perception of a perception that can be defined as a 'camera consciousness' emerges from the entire apartment sequence.[15]

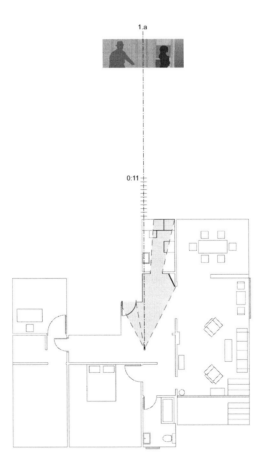

3_02 Shot 1 begins with a stationary camera's horizontal frame split between entry door on the left and kitchen on the right. The couple walks in and the shot holds here for 11 seconds. This drawing is the first in a series of drawings marking the movement of the camera. When the camera holds, the line of direction of the shot is marked as seconds along the center line of the camera. When the camera pans, the duration of the movement is marked along the arc of the curve, and when the camera pans, the duration of the movement is marked along the arc of the curve.

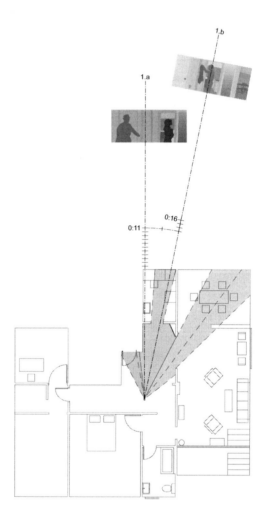

3_03 The camera begins to pan right for two seconds before briefly holding for three seconds as the wife walks into the kitchen and the husband hangs up his coat. The exaggerated horizontal aspect ration of 2.35:1 allows us to scan the frame and watch two spaces and sometimes two characters simultaneously.

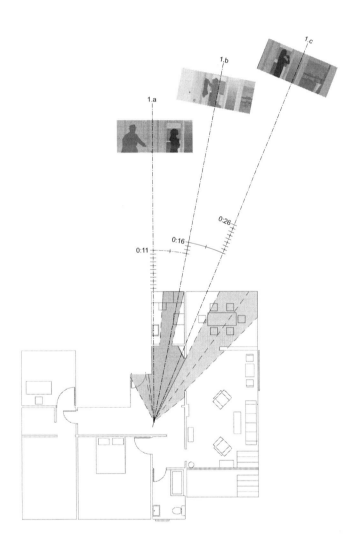

3_04 The camera continues to pan right for two more seconds and stops with the frame split between the kitchen on the left and the living/dining room on the right. The husband walks into the living room while the wife drinks from a bottle of coke, assuming a pose we know from cola commercials, but it is just one **any-instant-whatever**.

122

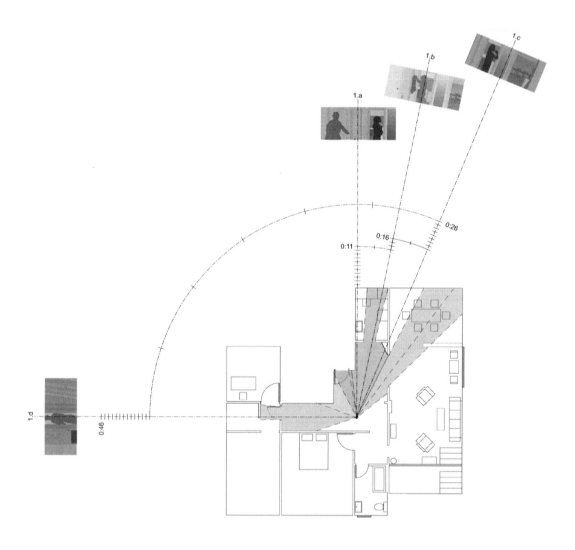

1.a

1.b

1.c

1.d

0:11

0:16

0:26

0:46

3_05 The camera pans more than 90 degrees to the left following the husband as he goes down the hallway and walks through an unfinished door opening at the end of the hall.

Affection Image

Exercise 3.7: *Stop at close-ups of people and architectural surfaces to create an affection image during a panning, tilting of tracking shot.*

When you let yourself feel deeply the effects of the sounds, textures, temperatures, smells, shapes, colours, movements, even tastes of your apartment, studio, or office while talking with a friend or acquaintance, you framed an **affection image**. The human face is often the locus of the affection image in film. In the midst of their discussion and in the process of undressing and bathing, the husband and wife cross paths in the living room in shot 5. They are both wrapped in towels, draped like Roman togas. Suddenly, the writer slaps his wife violently. She turns her face to the wall. The camera cuts to a close-up of the back of her head. The affection image is the shot of the back of her head. Even though we don't see her face, we feel her shock.

If the affection image is the close-up and the close-up is the face, the close-up can also *facialise* objects. When we frame something up close, we no longer see an object within spatial-temporal coordinates, but take in its material qualities outside linear, narrative time. Additionally, an empty and disconnected space called an **any-space-whatever** can create affection images. In these opening shots the any-space-whatever is the way the apartment itself is shot. As we watch the couple move about their apartment, it is almost impossible to orient ourselves by understanding the spatial coordinates of the rooms or features of the site visible through the windows. The camera englobes the space around it, distorting a simple orthogonal relationship of rooms into an immense and unending panorama or comic strip.

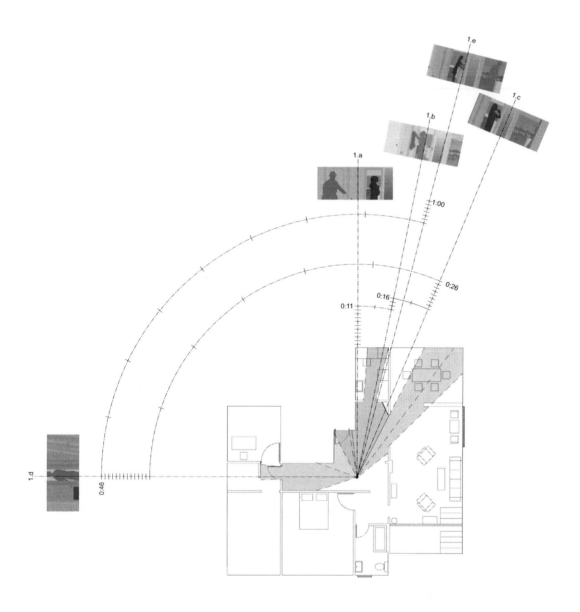

3_06 The camera pans back right to again frame the kitchen/dining area. The couple's paths cross as he goes into the living room and she returns to the kitchen.

3_07 The camera tracks forward slightly towards the wife in the kitchen and then pans right to follow her into the living room. She walks out with a coffee-table book. The camera follows her into the living room panning another 90 degrees as she walks towards her husband as he reads a piece of paper. There is a bronze sculpture of a woman in the centre of the frame as a reminder of the privileged pose of classical art and the classical world, which is the subtext of the film.

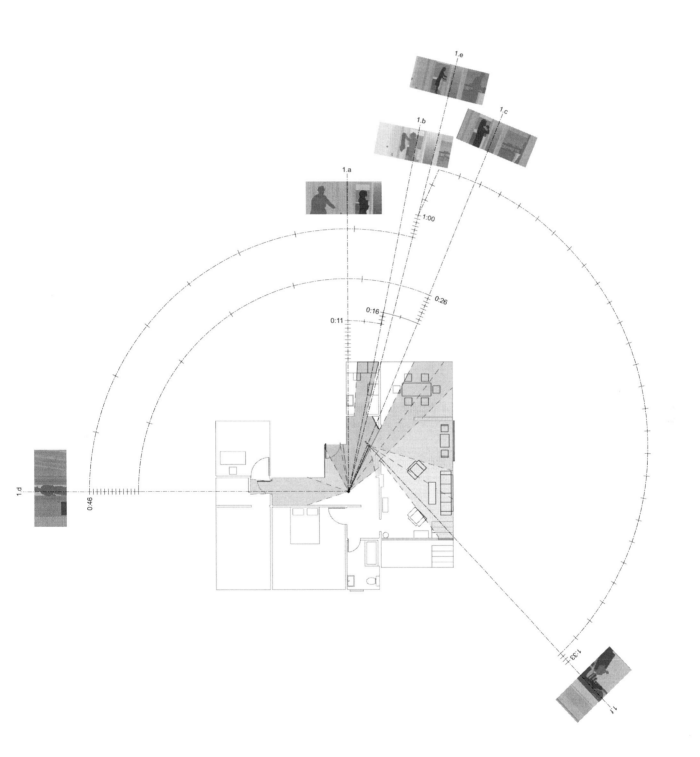

3_08 The camera continues to pan right slightly, now splitting the frame between the living room on the left and the end of the entry hall leading to the bathroom on the right. The wife disappears behind the wall to the right as the husband takes off his shoes while reading his piece of paper. The camera holds the split frame: he is in the living room to the left, she enters the hallway to the bathroom to the right. He gets up and disappears behind the wall as she turns to talk to him. She leaves the frame to the right. Here we see Godard taking full advantage of the elongated proportions of his frame.

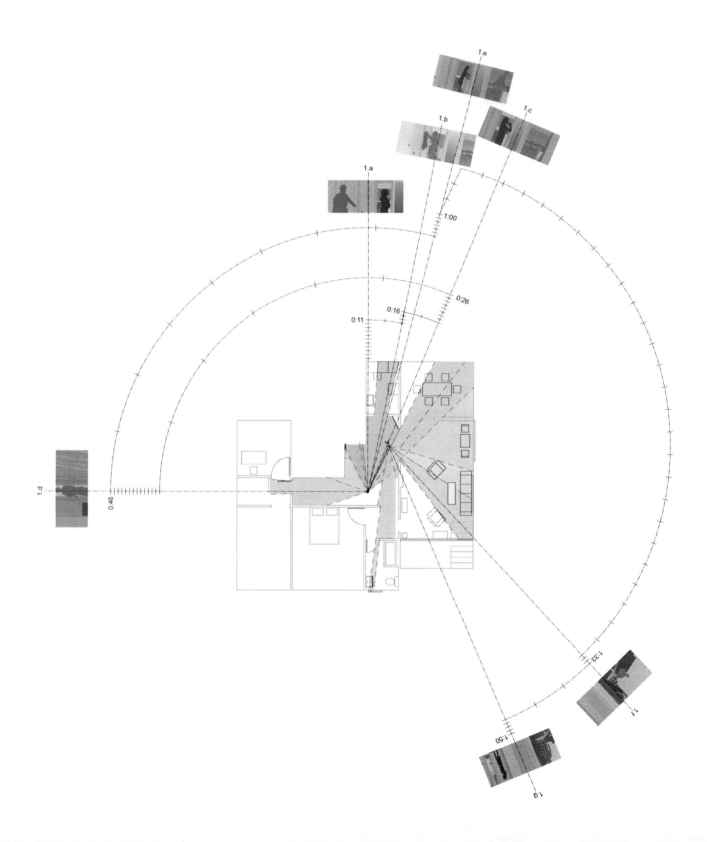

3_09 Within the duration of this first shot — which has lasted nearly two minutes — the camera has rotated nearly 270 degrees showing us the basic layout of the public rooms of the house: the front and back hall, the kitchen and the living/dining area. We also get a narrow glimpse into the bathroom beyond. However, the restless camera and characters never give us a comprehensive **perception image** of the apartment, we just continually see spatial adjacencies, fragments of actions and momentary affective close-ups of colours, surfaces, objects and bodies. The grey tone shows the parts of the apartment that have appeared in this shot, the white wedges reveal the relative out-of-field of the obscured areas where the characters sometimes disappear off frame.

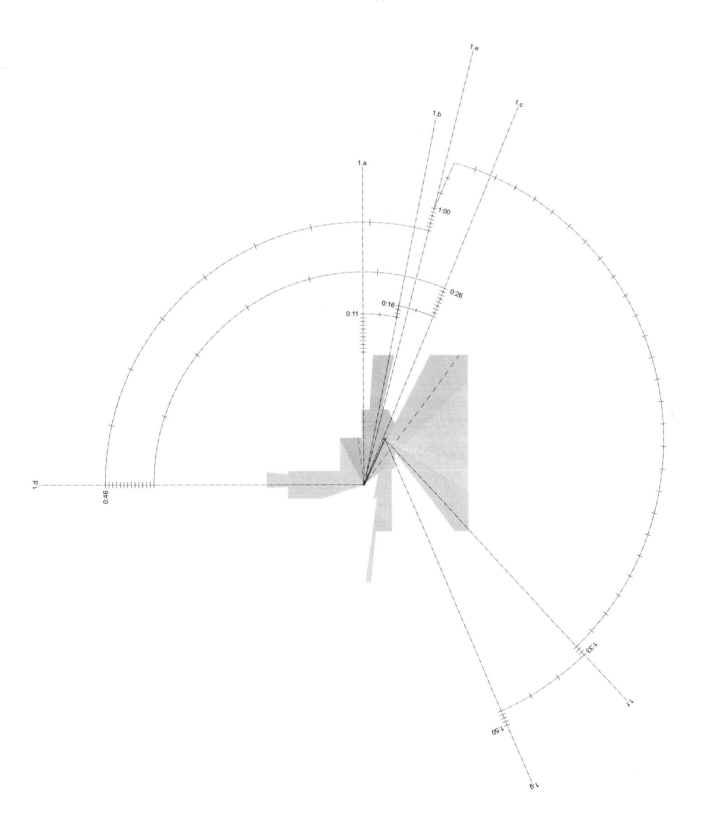

Impulse Image

Exercise 3.8: *During a panning, tracking or tilting shot, allow the mechanical movement of the camera to be interrupted by something that catches your attention: another movement, a colour, light, texture. Start letting impulses interrupt and redirect your mechanical camera movements.*

As the stimuli from your home, studio or office and the effects of agreeable or disagreeable social encounters stirred impulses, drives, and desires within you, you perceived an **impulse image.** An impulse image allows you '… to see impulses and energies permeating and possessing settings and characters'.[16] This is the stage of perception following affection/feeling but before action. The husband slapped his wife in shot 5 by acting immediately on an impulse of anger that preceded the slap.

Later in the apartment sequence, we see the screenwriter leafing through the book the wife carried into the living room in the first shot. The camera provides a close-up of the book as he turns pages depicting erotic art from ancient Rome. Impulse images are 'fragments wrested from actual milieus by impulses', but corresponding to an originary world. They suggest 'a primordial world of drives and forces [as] immanent within and inseparable from the real world of concrete particularities'.[17] The filmed images of the pages in the book take us to another world for a moment, but then the camera returns to recording within the apartment the actions of the couple – in this instance the husband looking at the book of photos we have just seen. In the midst of this scene where a marriage slowly unravels, the erotic images tease the audience whose expectations of a Hollywood movie starring Brigitte Bardot include arousing love-making.

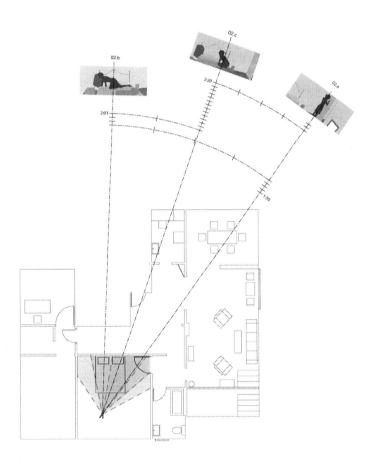

3_10 Shot 2 jumps to the bedroom. The camera is situated at the foot of the bed and we see the wife put on a wig that covers her long blonde hair with a short black bob. The camera pans left to follow her as she reaches for a dress. It then pans up and to the right as she hides behind the door and tells her husband not to come in. He tosses his trousers on the bed and leaves.

130 3_11 Shot 3 the camera returns to its first position in the vestibule looking towards the living room and the hallway to the bathroom. A threshold splits the middle of the pan between these two spaces. The wife walks from the bedroom to the living room, adjusts her wig in the mirror in the hallway, and approaches the bathroom door to show her husband. Godard's preferred composition seems to be a diptych, splitting his camera frame into two separate spaces instead of centering on one space. The camera tracks slightly between the two pans.

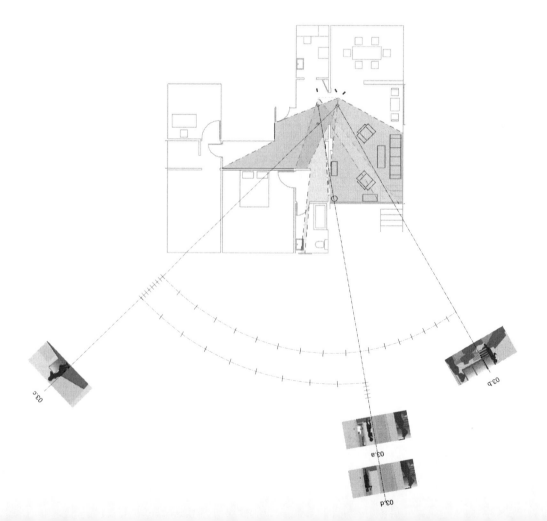

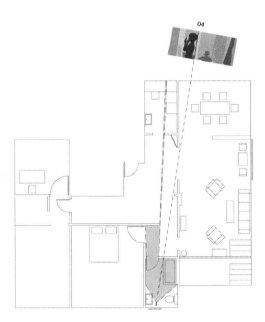

3_12 Shot 4 the camera is situated in the back of the bathroom and in a stable shot frames the husband in the bath and the wife in the doorway. He is wearing a top hat and smoking a cigar. A robe is in the foreground on the right and a mirror reflects the wife on the left of the frame.

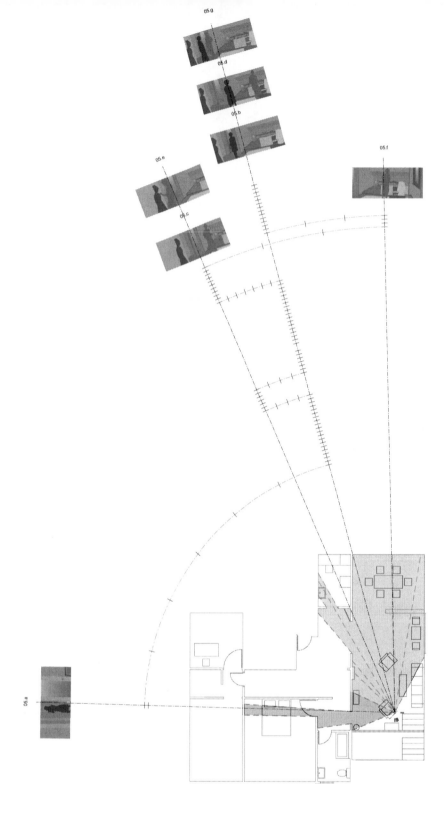

3_13 The camera is now in the far corner of the living room where it is situated to frame the wife leaving the bedroom and walking into the vestibule connecting to the bathroom. It follows her panning right as she walks into the living room and back to the front hall and kitchen. The husband leaves his bath wrapped in a towel. The camera pans back and forth to frame the sculpture as the husband raps it with his knuckles. The camera pans all the way to the right framing the dining area in the background and the husband, and then pans back left as the couple finally meet within the frame. The shot quickly cuts to a close-up of her face after he slaps her.

Action Image

Exercise 3.9: *Follow actions in two ways: from situation to big form action to changed situation, and from small form action to situation to changed action.*

There are two types of action movement images: the big form where an action changes a given situation to a new situation, and the small form that moves from action to a situation to a changed action. The big action image concerns a determinate milieu that '… constitutes a surrounding configuration of forces that impinge on the living image and instigate the living image's actions and reactions'. The milieu designates the ambiance or what Deleuze calls the 'breath-encompasser', which surrounds the body and acts on it. The small form action image moves from action to situation to action. It involves actual behaviours – 'affects and impulses become incarnate in discrete actions [behaviours]'. It is like the difference between a classic Hollywood Western with expansive landscapes and a slapstick comedy where location does not play a major role in the action.[18]

Contempt contains a film within the film: the classic story of *The Odyssey,* the wanderings and battles of Ulysses comprise a classic big action image – the situation of Penelope's fidelity creates the excuse for the big action of war. It is a tragedy because the resulting situation is changed – their previous life together cannot be recovered. But in *Contempt* we don't see any of this large form action. The writer, like Ulysses, is confronted with signs of what he thinks is his wife's infidelity, but unlike Ulysses, he just moves from small act to situation to action to situation again without any ability to change the course of his life.

3_14 After the slap, the wife retreats to the bathroom. The camera pans left to follow her.

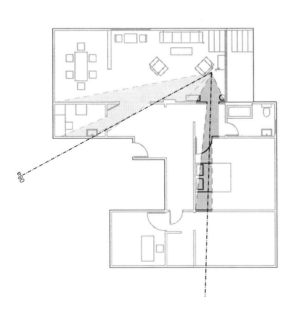

Reflection Image

Exercise 3.10*: Shoot something or someone in transformation as a reflection image.*

A **reflection image** image 'allows a passage from the Large Form to the Small Form [action image]'. It shows 'a deformation, transformation, or transmutation of the action-image'. Hence, the reflection image is 'intermediary between action and relation'. It reveals a 'situation [that] refers back to an image other than that of the situation it indicates,' so 'there is no longer a direct relation between a situation and an action, an action and a situation'.[19]

A reflection image as a transformation of an action image seems to interrupt the flow of the action; it 'pushes the action-image to its limit and transforms Small and Large Forms'. The reflection image arises when 'action and situation enter into indirect relations'. It can be a 'dishonorable situation' that can cause a breakdown of **sensori-motor schema** and the 'dissolution of the **movement-image**'. It is an image 'that pushes action image toward relation image', 'a general process of transformation whereby action-images are pushed to their limits'.[20]

Contempt as a whole is a modern reflection on Homer's *Odyssey*. The small form action of the writer and his wife reflect the mythical situation of the fates of Ulysses and Penelope**.** In the midst of this half-hour long apartment sequence of panning shots which last up to two minutes, is a rapid **assemblage** sequence. The wife has just told her husband she will now sleep in the living room. He asks if that means she doesn't want to make love any more. She tells him of course not – and offers her body to him there and now. In a flash the film cuts between flashback shots of the wife posing naked, running in the forest, getting into the Hollywood producer's car, and then flashes forward to the upcoming scene in Casa Malaparte (illus 3_15). The sequence then continues from the moment we flashed back.

3_15 In the ensuing scenes, the wife has bathed, the couple argues more. Finally, she takes the bed linen and tells her husband she will now sleep on the living-room sofa alone. In a quick montage of images the husband seems to be searching for lost memories of their life together and trying to pinpoint the reason for her change in attitude towards him. There is also a shot which leaps into a subsequent scene in the film where the couple interact on the roof terrace of Casa Malaparte in Capri. We will look at this scene in the next chapter.

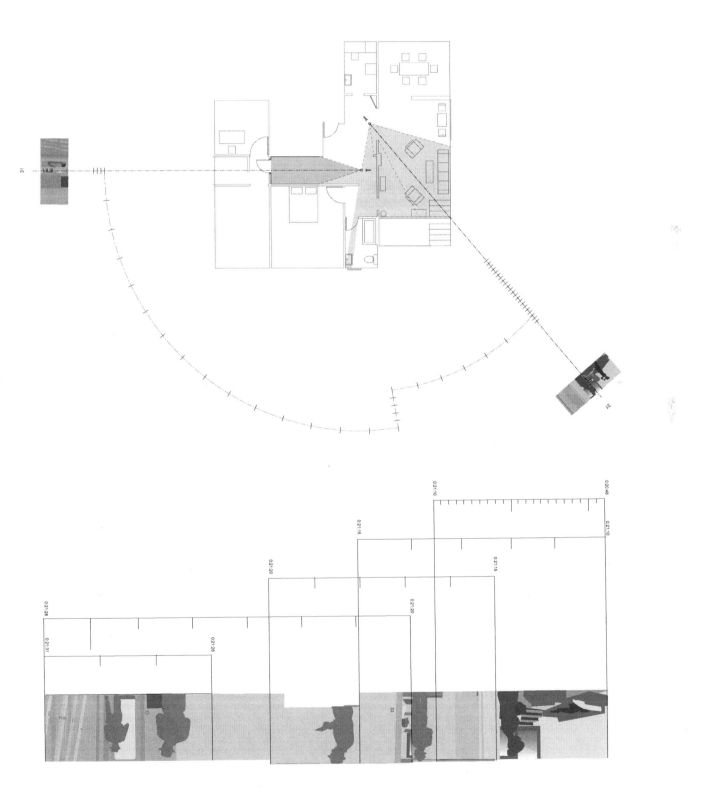

3_16 The shot immediately following the recollection montage picks up where we left off just before the 'cut'. Time has frozen for almost two minutes of film time. We have not moved forward in 'real time'. The husband grabs her robe and covers her up and ties his shoes. The wife gets up and walks to the hall drinking her coke, the camera pans left to follow her, he follows reading his piece of paper. The camera tracks forward following the husband down the back hallway that we saw in the opening shot. He opens the door and steps through it at the same time.

Relation Image

Exercise 3.11*: Draw an architectural plan showing how you created all six different kinds of movement images.*

The final movement image is a **relation image**, which is 'a mental image'. 'It is an image which takes as objects *of* thought, objects which have their own existence outside thought, just as the objects of perception have their own existence outside perception. *It is an image that takes as its object, relations,* symbolic acts, intellectual feelings.' 'The essential point … is that action, and also perception and affection, are framed in a fabric of relations. It is this chain of relations which, constitutes the mental image, in opposition to the thread of actions, perceptions and affections.' The relation image frames and transforms perceptions, affections, and actions.[21]

The images in the apartment **assemblage** are examples of reflection images. The montage itself constitutes a relation image. As we have noted earlier, *Contempt* is not only a film about the problems of a married couple, but is about the problems of shooting a film. By showing us the apparatus of shooting, Godard not only allows us to enter into the spectacle of filming – its settings and its start – but also pulls us away so we are aware of how as a film-maker he is always making choices, selections about what to put into his film. This is why Godard is always creating relation images in his films. We are put into a scene, but also into a set of relations, where we can see people unable to make choices – in this case, the husband in *Contempt* – from the point of view of a director who makes very precise selections of image relationships. Six types of space are generated with the six types of movement images we have just discussed, which we will introduce in the next chapter: *Mobile Sections.*

1. Gaseous space generates with a perception image

2. Any-space-whatever generates with an affection image

3. Space of originary worlds generates with an impulse image

4. Respiration space and line of the universe space generate with the two forms of action image

5. Transformation space generates with a reflection image

6. Symbol space generates with a relation image

3_17 The camera frames the writer typing at a desk in his office. It pans up and to the left to follow the wife as she enters the office and then walks towards the empty bedroom across the hall. The camera returns to the office to frame them together, then him and finally a close-up of a print of a theatre interior above the writer's desk.

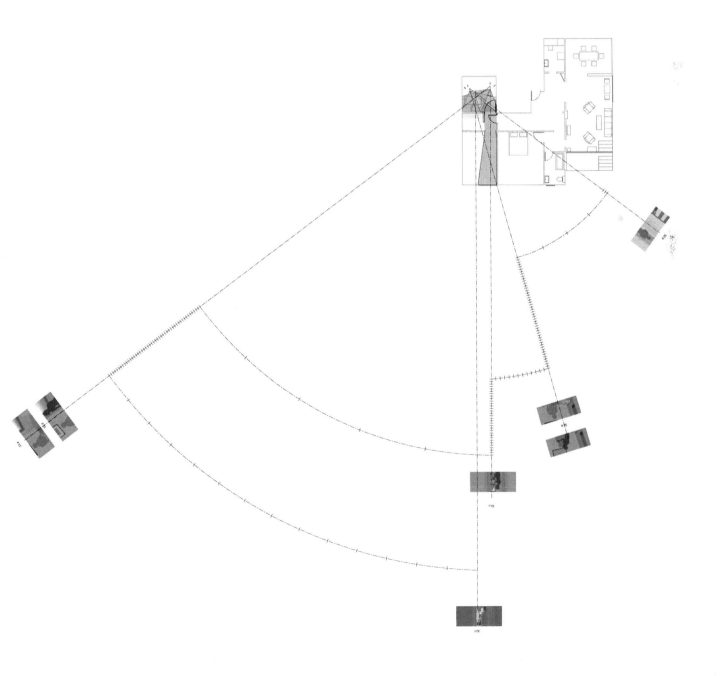

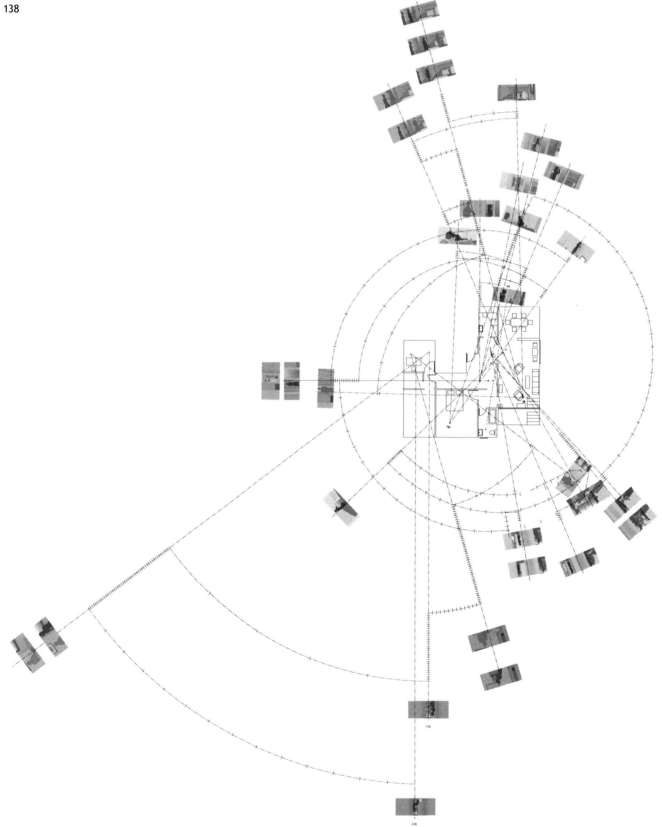

3_18 The camera has not shot every room in the apartment but has circled back and forth in a 360-degree panorama several times. During this sequence, all six types of movement images appear along with the spaces that are generated with them.

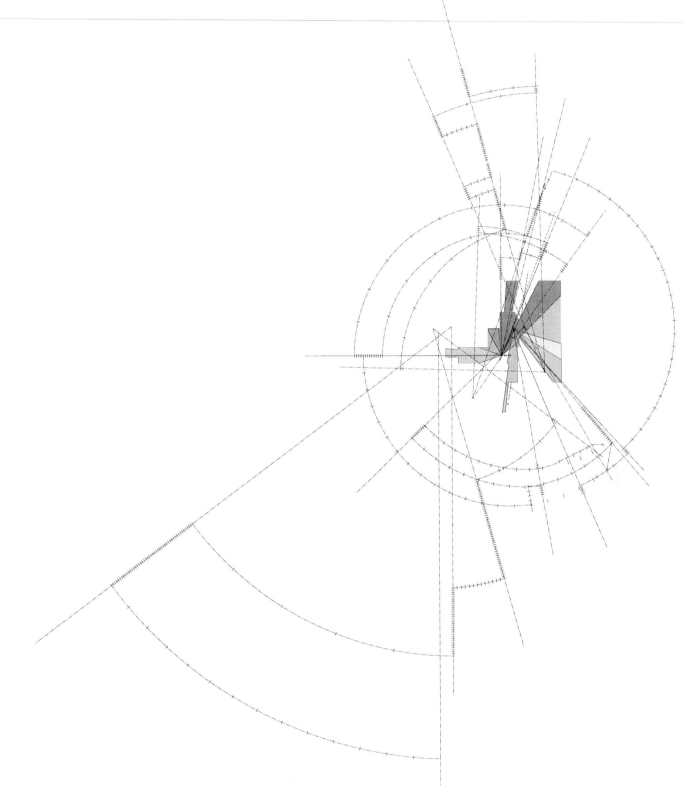

3_19 In spite of the comprehensiveness of the camera and the length of the scene — nearly half an hour — the apartment is 'unknowable' as a plan. The constantly moving camera never clearly shows a perception image of the spatial relationships, instead we feel we are in an unending labyrinth of adjacent rooms.

140   So now you know *what happens when movement is related, not to privileged poses, but to any-instant-whatever*. You lose perspective and begin to find **duration** – movement over time. Once you begin relating movement to any-instant-whatever, you may discover additional responses to this question. Remember that creating a moving drawing system is your goal. When you design a building, it will not be actualised ideal forms, but any-instant-whatever, which can be '… regular *or* singular, ordinary *or* remarkable'.[22] Knowing this, you position yourself to create an architecture of newness within a field of relations within the open **whole**.

29b

3_20 This image can be read as a sequence by reading it from left to right and back right again ending at 29e. The couple are now ready to go out. In this last panning shot, the camera tracks and pans for a complete 360-degree view from back hall to the vestibule and all the connecting rooms as they both walk around. She walks from hall to living room, picks up dishes in the dining room, goes to the kitchen and drops the dishes. She comes down the vestibule hallway and turns down the back hall to the office. She steps through the unfinished door opening. The camera holds as she comes back out reading the paper he has written. This image can be read as a sequence by reading it from right to left and back to the right again.

29c

29e

3_21 The camera pans right following her into the front hallway and dining room as he enters the frame from the living room. She tosses the paper at him. Camera tracks forward as he grabs her arm and tracks right as she walks away into the living room. It stops again with a split frame with her in the hallway. She disappears down the back hall. He stops in the hallway, hands in his pockets. She reappears with sweater, pushes him and walks into the living room. The camera pans left to follow her. The camera continues to pan left as she puts on her shoes and heads out. He follows her and asks her to sit down on the blue chairs. They sit down with the lamp in-between them.

29a

29d

3_22 The last two shots of the scene frame the couple individually. First the camera pursues the wife outside the apartment but holds at the top of the stairs as it tilts down as she walks away down the stairs.

3_23 Finally the camera tracks backwards filming the husband as he walks towards the camera in pursuit of his wife.

1 Deleuze, *Cinema 1*, p 6.

2 Deleuze, *Cinema 1*, p 4.

3 Deleuze, *Cinema 1*, p 6.

4 Deleuze, *Cinema 1*, p 5.

5 Deleuze, *Cinema 1*, p 6.

6 Deleuze, *Cinema 1*, p 6.

7 Deleuze, *Cinema 1*, pp 6, 5.

8 Deleuze, *Cinema 1*, p 7.

9 Deleuze, *Cinema 2*, p 31. Bogue, *Deleuze on Cinema*, p 68.

10 Deleuze, *Cinema 1*, p 200.

11 Deleuze, *Cinema 2*, p 31.

12 http://www.artbrain.org/journal/wolfe.html

13 Deleuze, *Cinema 2*, p 32.

14 Bogue, *Deleuze on Cinema*, p 68.

15 Deleuze, *Cinema 1*, p 84. Bogue, *Deleuze on Cinema*, pp 74, 72.

16 Bogue, *Deleuze on Cinema*, p 105.

17 Bogue, *Deleuze on Cinema*, p 82–4.

18 Bogue, *Deleuze on Cinema*, p 85. Deleuze, *Cinema 1*, pp 186–96.

19 Bogue, *Deleuze on Cinema*, pp 92, 93. Deleuze, *Cinema 1*, p 182.

20 Bogue, *Deleuze on Cinema*, p 96. Deleuze, *Cinema 1*, p 179. Bogue, pp 99, 94, 97.

21 Bogue, *Deleuze on Cinema*, p 100. Deleuze, *Cinema 1*, pp 198, 200.

22 Deleuze, *Cinema 1*, p 6.

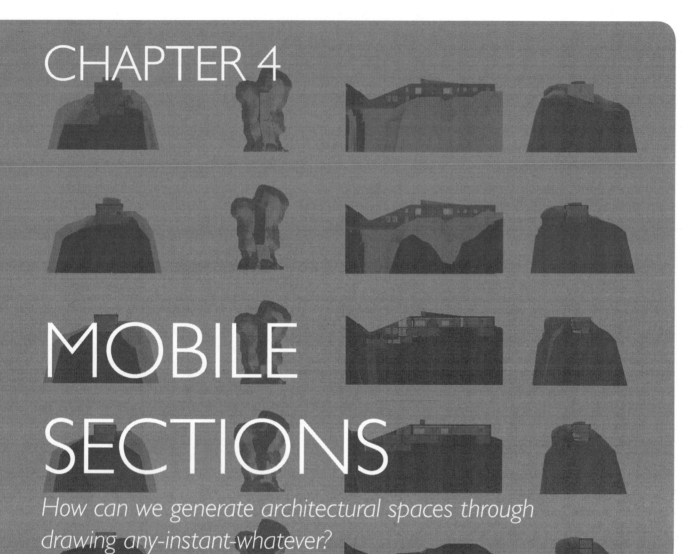

CHAPTER 4

MOBILE SECTIONS

How can we generate architectural spaces through drawing any-instant-whatever?

We are now at the midpoint in developing the *Cinemetric* drawing system. We previously discussed how to frame architectural space as immobile cuts in flowing matter-flux. Additionally, we started to practise connecting the new sensori-motor relationships experienced when using the computer with intervals in matter-flux. We explored how even the simple act of waking up involves these intervals. In *Shooting* we began to learn the power of mobilising the camera as a drawing tool through shooting any-instant-whatever rather than thinking and drawing privileged poses. We also connected this new **know-how** to drawing the multiple feelings and sensations experienced in socio-spatial relations. Mastering both of these techniques – the camera as a moving drawing tool to shoot any-instant-whatever in socio-spatial relations – will help us develop digital drawing skills as a process of creating buildings responsive to the new **know-about** of architecture in an expanded field of relations.

Words in bold are Keywords found on pages 260-265

Cinemetrics emphasises the creation of the 'new', not to encourage novelty for its own sake, but to support drawing an architecture cognisant of the dynamic cultural and ecological relations evident in today's globalised world. The next three chapters introduce additional tools for drawing architecture within these complex relations. Some of these tools may already be familiar to you, others you may be encountering for the first time. Some you may want to explore in the form of thought-exercises.

One of the objectives of this chapter is to introduce you to a generative process for making space that engages the multiple cultural and ecological relations of the building you are drawing. Key to the *Cinemetric* moving drawing system are the cybernetic relationships between our body's involvement in the dynamic physical world of everyday life and our experiences while we are drawing in the virtual digital world. This cybernetic web is a critical part of the field of relations that enables us to consciously make moving drawings embodying cultural and ecological connections. This process is what will facilitate an architecture, not of privileged poses, but of any-instant-whatever.

But how do we begin to observe these cybernetic relations as any-instant-whatever? We will adapt for use in *Cinemetrics* the **semiosis** of Charles Sanders Peirce, whose phenomenology we introduced in *Framing*. Semiosis is a system for classifying our non-verbal body awareness of our **autopoietic** world. Peirce invented the word semiosis, by which he meant any form of activity, conduct, or process that involves non-linguistic signs – all those feelings, gestures, actions, and thoughts associated with becoming aware of the 'direct appearances' that he developed in his phenomenology. Examples are our facial expressions and body positions, the clothes we wear, the places we go, the food we eat – that warmed-up favourite muffin with hot coffee. These are all signs that, when we notice them, give us a greater understanding of how we relate to ourselves as well as participate in making the world around us. They give us a sense of how we ourselves are 'a sign among signs'.[1]

Peirce's phenomenology and semiosis inspired Deleuze's six movement images. What if we began to understand, not just ourselves, but architecture, as Deleuze did cinema, as **signaletic matter**, ' … which includes all kinds of modulation features, sensory (visual and sound), kinetic, intensive, affective, rhythmic, tonal, and even verbal (oral and written)?'[2] With this understanding, we can note not only the sensori-motor process of drawing, but also its relational implications for architectural spaces and the places where we build. Through semiosis, we can develop an architectural drawing system that enables us to generate space from any-instant-whatever rather than privileged poses. We can begin to design architecture as signaletic matter in a relational context.

Peirce developed his semiosis from his phenomenology of **firstness**, **secondness** and **thirdness** by making each sign a composite of these three basic categories. He also constructed signs as triadic combinations of objects, representations and interpretations rather than dyadic linguistic relationships between sign and signified. Peirce's semiosis can help us understand our relationships to the world as signaletic matter when we do something as ordinary as going for a walk. It can help us to understand how we create both movement images and multiple spaces as we walk. Then we can connect what we observe about ourselves walking to the new processes of drawing digitally that we are developing. Semiosis is thus a deepening of our experience of ourselves that helps us to understand how we become aware of the relations between our own personal interior world, the outside realm and our drawings. This awareness can prevent our drawings and thus architecture from becoming frozen abstractions when we consciously incorporate this knowledge into our moving images.

In the box on the next page are the most basic signposts, with brief definitions from Peirce's taxonomy, of our changing selves as we move through our everyday field of relationships. We have given a name to each signpost to make it easier to identify with its meaning because Peirce kept the signs abstract. He also argued that all of them are necessary to be fully aware of how we continually remake ourselves. The exercise below will help us connect his words to our own **autopoietic** experience of creating images and spaces from signaletic matter while out walking. The signs are introduced in the sequence that Peirce classified them. When we experience them, we put them together in constantly changing assemblages of signaletic matter. As you become aware of how you scrutinise '… direct appearances', you may want to note down the specifics of your own order.

Each sign has a descriptive name that we added to the quotes from Peirce. The names denote different states we are in during ordinary activities. According to Peirce we are 'inseparable from the sign: [we are] a sign among signs'.[3]

1 **Sign of a pre-sentient being**, someone who becomes aware of the 'mere possibility of feeling'.[4]

2 **Sign of a sensor**, someone who experiences but with no 'definite linkage to a … object'.[5]

3 **Sign of a person with impulses,** someone who vividly and spontaneously experiences 'some possible quality that might be embodied in a future object'.[6]

4 **Sign of an actor on details,** someone who has 'direct experience of and information concerning the … object [of attention]'.[7]

5 **Sign of a large-scale actor,** someone who sees 'the nature of a general, a universal, *or* type'.[8]

6 **Sign of a change-reflector,** someone who 'sets something apart from something else as *this instead of that*'.[9]

7 **Sign of a reflector on an expanded field of relations,** someone who understands how 'any general type of law, however established, … requires each instance of it to be really affected by its Object in such a manner as to furnish definite information concerning that Object'.[10]

8 **Sign of an artist,** someone who relates iconically by 'call[ing] up an image in the mind which image … tends to produce a general concept'.[11]

9 **Sign of a critic,** someone who judges analytically; 'its intended interpretant signifies it as being actually affected by its "semiotic object"'.[12]

10 **Sign of a thinker,** someone who is 'a sign of a law that results from thinking'. The 'immanence of the [thinker] is fundamental'.[13]

On the following page is an exercise, using Peirce's semiotics as interpreted and charted by scholar Floyd Merrell, to help us to understand the signs of ourselves and their relation to the images we make and the spaces we generate.[14] You will find similarities to the first exercise in the previous chapter. We have done this intentionally not only to reiterate what we learned previously but to add more complex environmental relations of site and landscape. This may be an exercise that you decide to do as a thought experiment, especially if you practise a sport regularly, train for extended bike rides, or participate in other activities that teach you greater body awareness.

Exercise 4.1: *Go for a walk outside. As in earlier exercises, focus on framing flowing matter-flux and shooting any-instant-whatever. After half an hour or so, stop and read through the following paragraphs as a way to review your walk semiotically as well as in relation to the six movement images and their associated spaces, which will be discussed in more detail at the end of this chapter. We describe two assemblages of signs. Try them both. As you repeat your walk, consciously look for different ways of moving between the signs of yourself, the movement images and their spaces.*

As you walk outside, perhaps you vaguely feel something. You are really not sure. At that moment, you are a pre-sentient being (sign 1). Did you spontaneously pause to pay attention to the feeling? We now know when we pause we move from

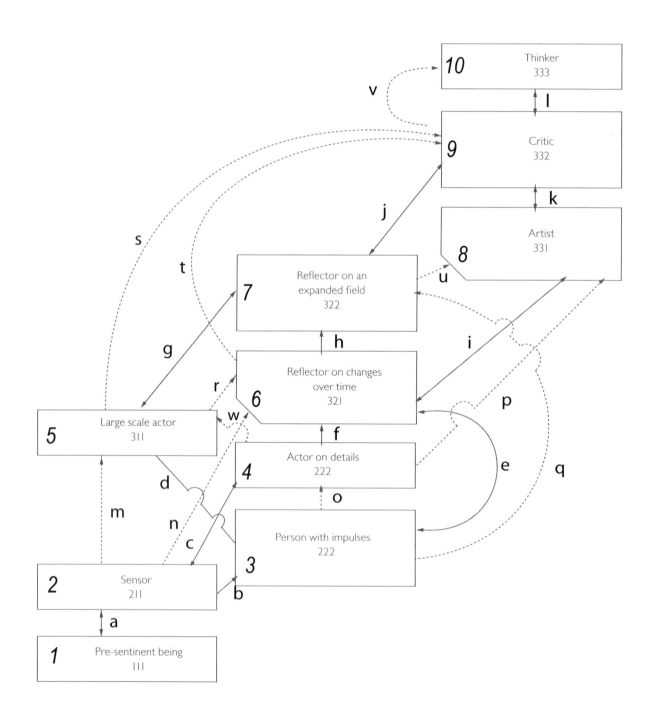

being a centre of indeterminacy to being a living image. At the same time, space started to curve around you, beginning to form its nature in relation to the set of information you chose, in this case, the place to pause. You, in effect, made yourself and your world by selecting both yourself and your world out of matter-flux – a self-creating, **autopoietic** act. In this gaseous space it can feel like we see everywhere at once.[15] Within the context of making moving drawings, the result is a **perception image** generated with a gaseous space.

Now soak up the place. Take in stimuli from the surroundings. Feel through all your senses. Heighten them: what does your body manifest **proprioceptively** as you feel, hear, see and taste? You have become a sensor and formed an **affection image** with an any-space-whatever, a space without any definite link yet to a specific place, such as the blur we experience in most airports. What we are experiencing is a space of 'qualities and powers … abstracted from specific coordinates yet still enmeshed in a material, sensual medium'.[16] From here you can move through the signs in either of two assemblages. Does either of them describe the process you are accustomed to?

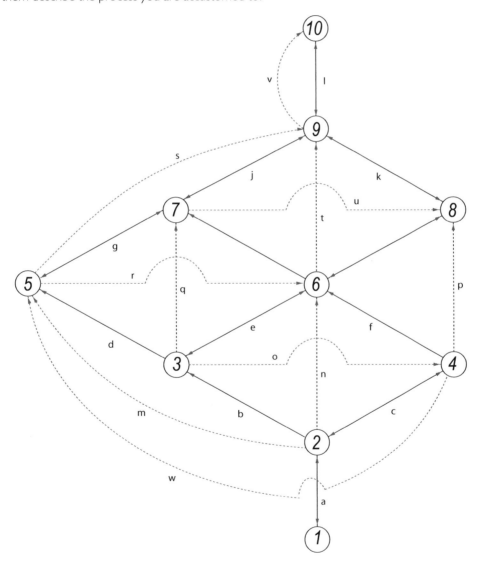

4_01 and 4_02 From Floyd Merrell a: Can you imagine the ten signs of yourself as **any-instant-whatever** in a changing **semiosis** rather than as **privileged poses**? Here we add ten signs of ourselves to Merrell's diagram of Peirce's semiosis. The lettered arrows are called 'operators' which show the transformative links between signs; b: Merrell constructed this diagram to show the network or possible lines of generation and de-generation between the signs of ourselves. Redrawn from Merrell, Floyd. "Thought-sign, sign-events," *Semiotica: Journal of the International Association for Semiotic Studies*, 1991, Volume 87-112, pp. 1 – 57.

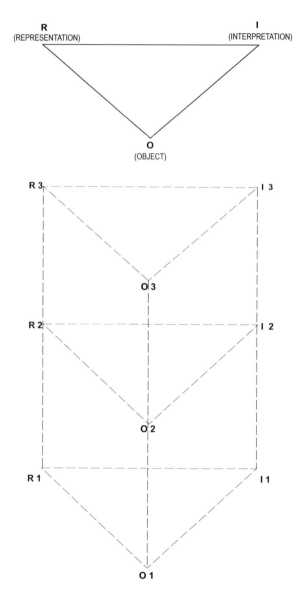

Indexical Assemblage

Feeling the body stimuli as a sensor (sign 2) stirs impulses, drives, and desires; notice these sudden urges but don't act on them. You are now witnessing yourself as a person with impulses (sign 3), a person who forms an **impulse image**, framing space as an originary world, which allows us 'to see impulses and energies permeating and possessing settings and character'.

Perhaps you feel an overwhelming desire to be far from work, on a beach, say, on a long extended vacation – no more deadlines! A larger vision transforms your initial impulse to pause. If you act on this impulse, you experience yourself as a large-scale actor (sign 5), forming a large-form **action image** with a respiration space. This space emerges via 'a global composition of an encompassing ambient whole within which individual elements are already situated and structured'. To draw this space, we become like a painter who 'reflect[s] the vital breath, that is, create movement'.[17]

Study the overall urban skyline or panorama. But rather than fulfilling your initial urges by immediately acting, hesitate and note what happens if you delay your spontaneous drives. Let yourself think about experiencing the possibility of fulfilling some of the actions that impulsively occur. You are now a reflector on an expanded field (sign 7) about what to do next and have made a **reflection image** in a transformation space.

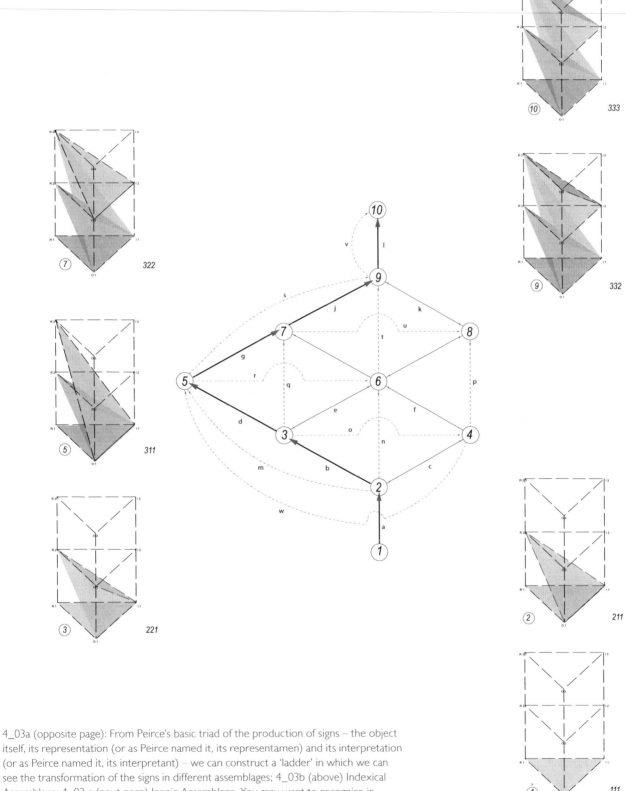

4_03a (opposite page): From Peirce's basic triad of the production of signs – the object itself, its representation (or as Peirce named it, its representamen) and its interpretation (or as Peirce named it, its interpretant) – we can construct a 'ladder' in which we can see the transformation of the signs in different assemblages; 4_03b (above) Indexical Assemblage; 4_03 c (next page) Iconic Assemblage. You may want to recognise in Peirce's semiotic triad: firstness or representamen , secondness or the object, and thirdness or the interpretant.

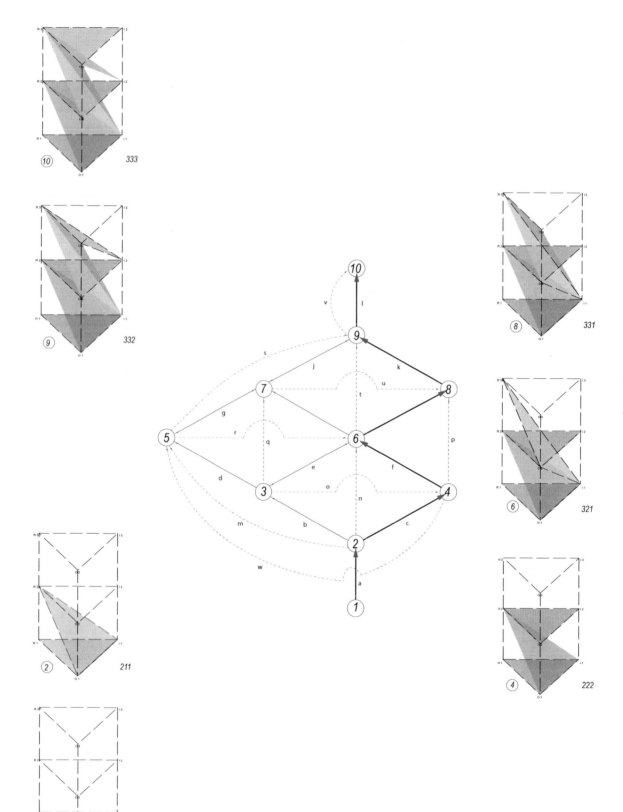

Iconic Assemblage (an alternative to the first assemblage)

When you are on your walk outside, after sensing the surrounding stimuli, perhaps you feel a desire to focus on a crack in the pavement or the branching of a tree limb, then, in fact, you do just that. You have become an actor on details (sign 4), making a small **action image** and forming a skeleton space, a contracted space in which we see vectors for the lines of the universe. The movement of the small action image is from action to situation to changed action. No longer does it image the breath of the respiration space, but 'the skeleton, the little fragment of space which must be connected to the next fragment'. A useful way to conceive of this space is as a 'wrinkled' or a 'broken' movement – 'step by step, zig-by-zag, from intensity to intensity',[18] for instance, the space you form when climbing or driving up a hill on a route with switchbacks.

If you are on an unfamiliar street, you may hanker to look more closely at changing details, becoming a change-reflector, (sign 6), making a **reflection image** with its transformation space. A reflection image as a transformation of an action image seems to interrupt the flow of the action. It generates with a transformation space that '… pushes the action-image to its limit and transforms Small and Large forms'.[19]

By moving through this second assemblage of signs you next act as an artist (sign 8), forming a relation image with a symbol space that associates the previous signs iconically.

Both assemblages of signs described above converge in the final two signs of yourself as a critic (sign 9) and lastly a thinker (sign 10). Now you create a critical **relation image** with a **symbol** space of either or both of the above assemblages. How? … by framing digitally in 'a fabric of relations' all the images in either or both combinations.[20] For instance, to deepen the first **indexical** assemblage of signs, start where you left off when you were reflecting on an expanded field. Now you relate critically the images of the first sign assemblage. From there you move to the final relation image, which emerges from thinking about your experience.

Or you can intensify the second process in which you were assembling the images in an iconic pattern. Now think about these images critically. The final step for the second, as the first, combination is thinking about your experience of yourself within an expanded field of signaletic matter. Note that the resulting image is one of at least two types of possible thought-relation images, each with their own symbol space. The particular type of thought-relation image depends on whether or not you combine the signs in the first indexical or in the second iconic assemblage. We will see in the next chapter that is exactly what both a film director and a cybernetic architect do.

Taken as a whole, these signs of ourselves in an expanded field help us to understand the images and spaces we make both on and off the computer in relation to the ecological, cultural, and social upheavals of our time. We have already experienced many of them in earlier exercises. Now semiosis helps us to systemise our experiences so we can deepen our awareness of the relationships between body involvement in complex spatial relations off and on the computer. Semiosis is fundamental in helping us to understand how we autopoietically generate space from the signaletic matter of any-instant-whatever as we draw moving images. Semiosis also helps us to lay the groundwork for the multidimensions of drawing as a cybernetic architect in an expanded field.

To reinforce understanding the interrelations between the signs of yourself, movement images and their spaces, we will analyse Casa Malaparte as an architectural space generated in part through the responsiveness of a specific person, the writer Curzio Malaparte, to a particular land formation – a rugged peninsula on the island of Capri. Casa Malaparte is additionally the site of the final segment in Godard's *Contempt*.

154   Casa Malaparte is particularly interesting to analyse. In addition to providing the setting for one of the last scenes in *Contempt*, historical scholarship demonstrates that the house represents a break with the linear production from drawing to building characteristic of modern architecture. Scholar Marida Talamona has shown that the house as built differs substantially from the drawings Italian Rationalist architect Adalberto Libera made for Curzio Malaparte. Looking at letters and photographs of the site during the years of construction, Talamona concludes that Malaparte consulted many people, but it was he, together with the local mason Alfonso Almitraro, who eventually changed the design of the house during the process of construction. For our purposes, the photographs of the site that Talamona discovered that contain images of the house scratched on top of its rocky site suggest feed-back relations between building, site, 'shooting', drawing and Malaparte's experiences that help us to understand the cybernetics of designing.[21] These images show an architecture in a field of relations between Malaparte's signs of himself as writer, prisoner, man and the cultural and environmental conditions of the site.

The following analysis of the movement images of the Casa Malaparte reiterates how we form images in the different signs of ourselves that we have just reviewed, and also how we generate six different kinds of space in that process. Architectural space has been traditionally defined by describing the six sides of a cube: top, bottom, front, back, left and right. This restricts its description to the limits of the building. The relative out-of-field of cinematic space has been described as the space beyond the top, bottom, left and right of the frame, as well as behind the scene and behind the camera. The absolute out-of-field space subsists within anomalous areas within the frame – "empty", gaseous, and liquid spaces that are the matrix for the more conventional relative-out-field spaces. From our exploration of the six kinds of movement images we can see that *Cinemetric* drawing encompasses a range of scales from the detail of the close up to the larger out-of-field of the long shot. The six different kinds of spaces generated from the movement image are situated within the expanded field of cinematic space.

Exercise 4.2: *To fully engage yourself in the analysis of the Casa Malaparte, first find or create a computer model of a free-standing house of radial geometries formed by site or land conditions, such as the Blades Residence by Morphosis. Shoot mobile sections through the house, but restrict your camera movements to mechanical pans (rotating the camera from a fixed point), tracks (moving forward or backward while looking towards the front, back or either side) and tilts (moving the camera up and down along a vertical axis). Incorporate pauses into your 'shots' of this house in all the following exercises in a manner similar to Godard's in* Contempt.

We see a **perception image** in the opening shot of the Casa Malaparte scene, which lasts for about 24 seconds (illus 4_04). Godard's camera tilts up to frame a set of information showing a craggy coast, and the vaporous ocean and sky. At the left edge of the frame is the screenwriter. We recognise him from his suit and hat. He and his wife have been invited to the film producer's rented house on the island of Capri – the final scene for his film of *The Odyssey*. The befuddled screenwriter has arrived late and without his wife, after arguing with her. She wanted to go with her husband, but instead rides in the film producer's boat – an action she feels her husband has pushed her into. She suspects that her husband is offering her to the film producer as a bonus for his rewriting an existing script to the tune of $10,000, much more than he could earn writing a play in Paris. She experiences contempt for him.

In this opening shot we are also aware of a 'camera consciousness' because the camera holds the shot longer than we anticipate, making us aware of the camera's presence.[22] It is the camera eye that reveals, near the left edge of the image, the just-arrived screenwriter, standing motionless on a rocky outcrop. He looks out over the hazy expanse, which forms a gaseous space. As noted, Godard has framed a perception image. It, as all **movement images**, is differentiated in three ways, each of which describes a basic feature of the image in question: one differentiation involves the spatial genesis of the image as a signal of possibility. The other two ways indicate the methods of composing the image in relation to the out-of-field. The signal of the relative out-of-field is our everyday world as a function of the living image where variation of all images is in reference to a living image. The signal of the absolute out-of-field is the open whole as a function of the whole where variation in movement is in relation to all.[23] The perception image generates after you are in sign 1 – pre-sentient being – where you experienced the mere possibility of feeling.

These three differentiations of every space are critical to your efforts to draw the spaces you intend to build within a larger field of cultural and site relations. Hold the differences in your imagination as you draw: space is not an emptiness but instead matter-flux from which generates the many variants of space. Remember that each of the different types of space we describe generate with a movement image as a specific signal of possibility that is composed with reference both to our everyday world and to the open whole.

The opening three shots of the approach to Casa Malaparte are examples for exercise 4.3 below. The signal of possibility within the perception image is its generative gaseous space. In this space we see as if we 'were a scattered cloud of eyes',[24] as we did on our walk when we first witnessed ourselves in an expanded field. The signal of our everyday world is the space's relative out-of-field. The frame selects the limitless sky, the vastness of the Mediterranean Sea, the craggy rocks of Capri's geology, the scrubby vegetation with little soil in the arid and windswept island climate, and the lone figure of a man. In the foreground, screenwriter and rocks form part of a space of solid objects that extend beyond the camera frame as we, rather than a camera, would see the space. The frame does not contain the space. This is the signal of the relative out-of-field. The signal of the open whole is the absolute out of-field of the image. In the distant sea and sky, water and air have dissolved in a gaseous matter-flow that moves through everything, expressing the **open whole**.

Exercise 4.3: *From the computer model you found or created in Exercise 4.2, generate six kinds of spaces in the next six exercises. In the first exercise: can you as a living image generate the space that curves around you? It cannot be represented in a single picture, but in a series of moving any-instant-whatever. First generate a gaseous space by taking long-distance panning shots of the house you have modelled. Do not show details, but atmospheric relations of the building in its landscape by experimenting with different filters, low contrasts and granulated pixellisation. Think of dissolving the building into the landscape from solid to liquid to gaseous.*

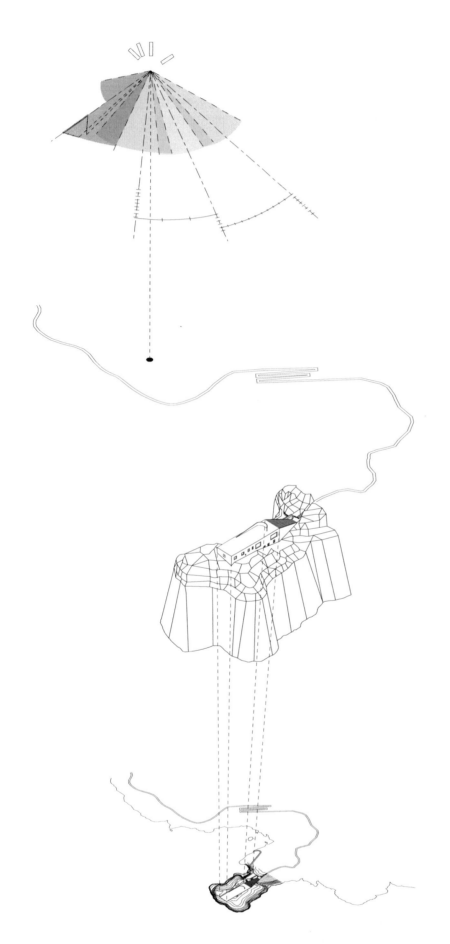

1:10   pan left

1:18   hold

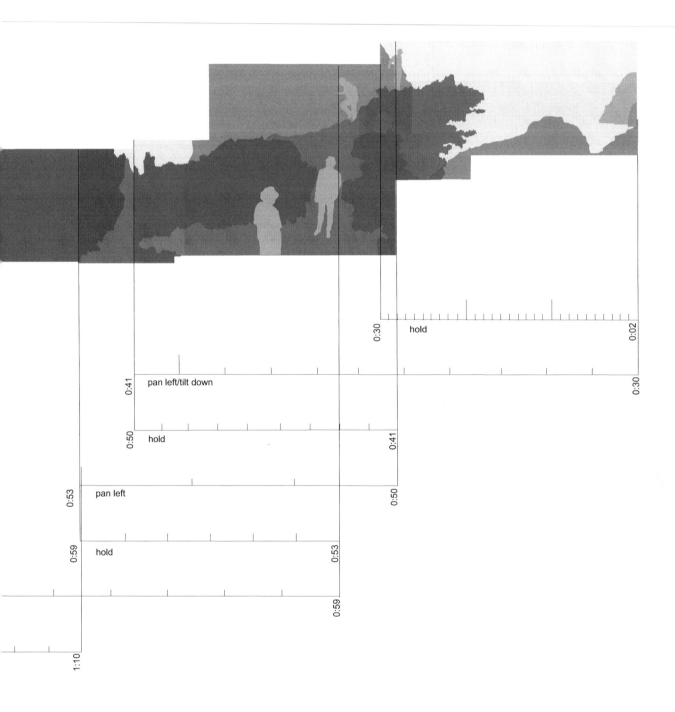

0:30
hold
0:02
0:30

0:41 pan left/tilt down
0:50 hold
0:41
0:50

0:53 pan left
0:59 hold
0:53
0:59

1:10

4_04 Shot 1. The camera tilts up to reveal a dramatic landscape dominated by the long horizon of the sea indistinctly meeting the sky. The writer is a tiny figure at the far top left of the frame clinging to a cliff side with a few scrubby pines. The camera pans left and tilts down as he climbs down the hill. The camera holds as he meets the fictional film director of the film shot within *Contempt* – played by the famous German director Fritz Lang. The camera pans left as the writer and film director begin a conversation as they walk down a path. The shot holds still for eight seconds after they disappear into the vegetation.

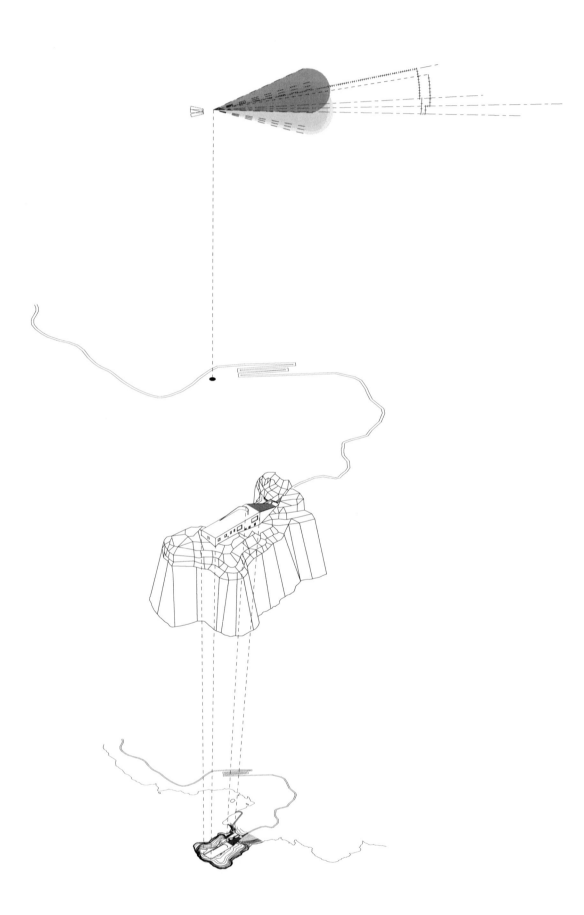

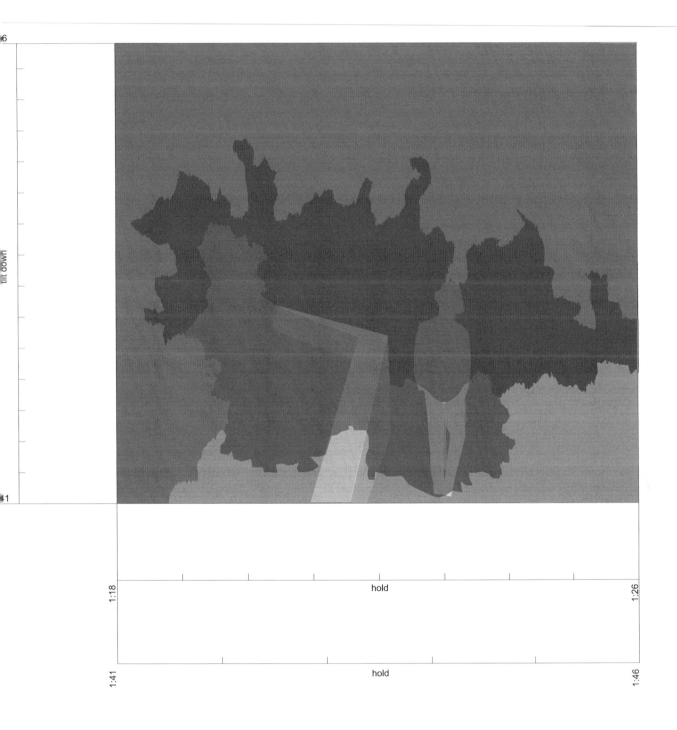

tilt down

1:18   hold   1:26

1:41   hold   1:46

4_05 Shot 2. A still camera is positioned at the landing of a switchback ramp. It first holds and then tilts down to follow the writer and director still in conversation as they approach the landing and camera. The camera remains still while they turn around the bend and continue down the path, now with their backs to the camera. The tilt continues, and then the camera holds as they again disappear into the vegetation.

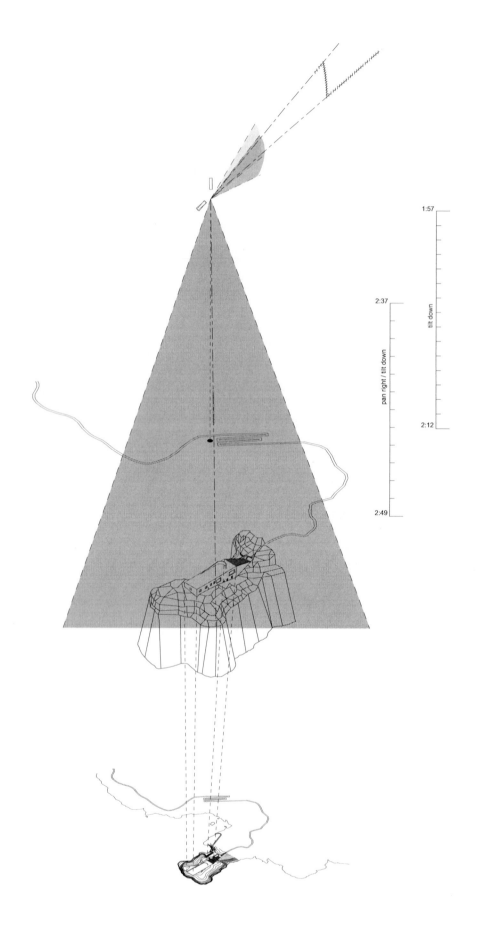

1:57

tilt down

2:37

pan right / tilt down

2:12

2:49

1:53

hold

2:12

hold

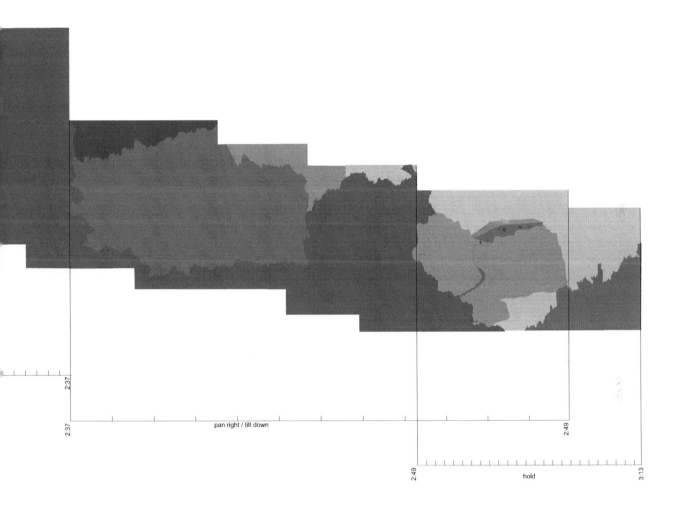

2:37

2:37   pan right / tilt down

2:49

2:49   hold   3:13

4_06 Shot 3. The camera is resituated well below the ramp which we see in profile. The two men continue to walk down the ramp and the camera tilts down to follow their movement until it stops, then inexplicably pans right and tilts down. Finally the camera stops panning, framing a dramatic overview of Casa Malaparte sited on a promontory jutting into the Mediterranean. A monumental wedge-shaped stairway and roof terrace with a curved sail-like wall command our first impression of the house. Two tiny figures can be seen on the roof. One of the figures descends the stairway as the shot holds. This is an example of a 'higher justification' framing mentioned in the first chapter. The camera was pragmatically following the two men in conversation before it reached a point where it could dramatically reveal the architectural setting for the concluding scene of the Casa Malaparte sequence.

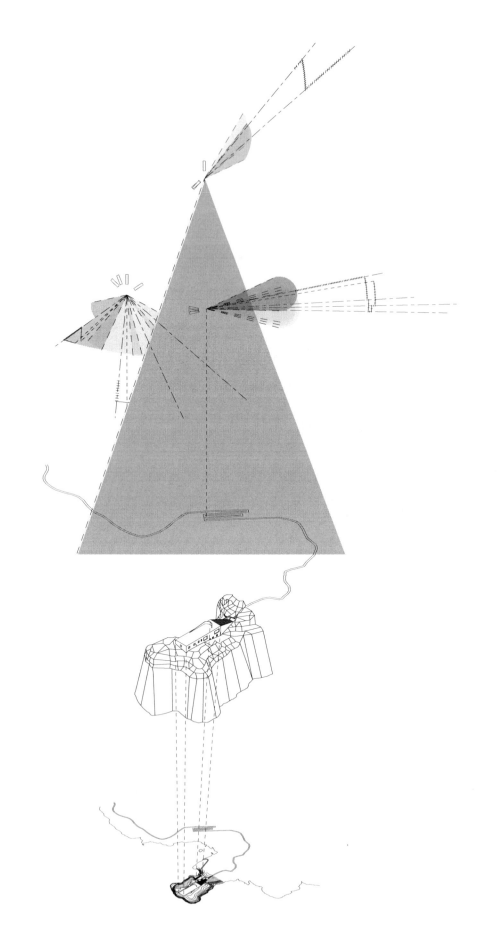

4_07 The first three shots situate Casa Malaparte as intimately linked to its site – a dramatic peninsula jutting into the sea. A tiny house amid a rugged terrain, yet a monumental setting for human drama. The elements of this set, as opposed to the two interior sequences we have previously studied, include the vastness of the sky, the sea, the mineral quality of the rocks, and the specific character of the vegetation.

Any-Space-Whatever Generates with an Affection Image

We can imagine from the restless movements of the screenwriter as he runs up the grand stairs to the roof of Casa Malaparte, looks over the edge of the roof terrace, and runs down the stairs towards the entrance to the house that he is feeling deeply his immediate troubles and is unaware of the specifics of the place. He is preoccupied with his own pressing thoughts and concerns. These shots constitute an **affection image** resulting from his anxiety and the lack of orientation to

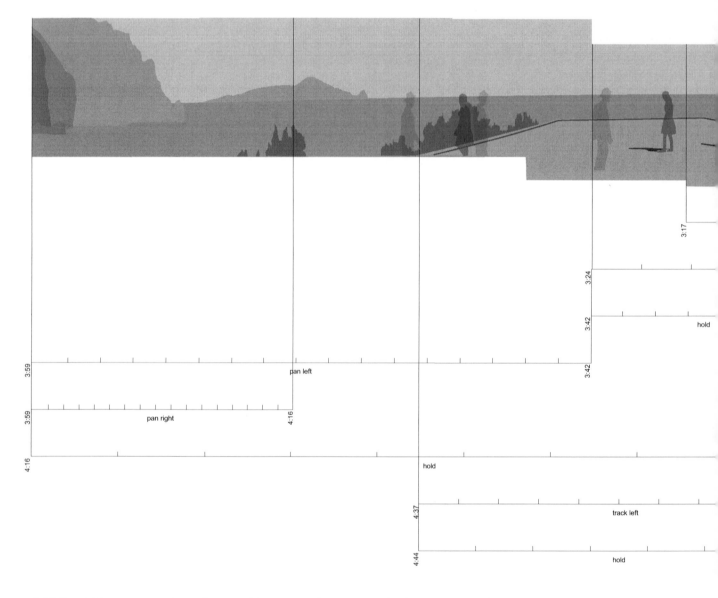

4_08 Shot 4. Now we are on the roof terrace of the house, and we see the wife of the writer, one of the miniature figures from the previous shot. The still camera is at her eye level and pans left as she gets up from reclining against the sail-like wall and walks to the left of the frame. The camera holds as she waves to someone off screen. The pan continues left and up slightly. The pan stops looking left at the east coast of Capri's dramatic view of the cliffs meeting the sea, with the mountains of mainland Italy in the distance. The wife leaves the frame and the camera holds at the view for a moment. The writer then enters the same held frame. The time that has lapsed is too short for the couple to not have met on the staircase, but he seems to have not seen her. Is Godard testing our sense of space and time? We know the two actors would have had to pass each other off screen. The camera pans back to the right following the husband looking for his wife. It stops, looking directly out to sea. The camera tracks left as the husband stops again, this time near the left edge of the terrace, and looks down at something below.

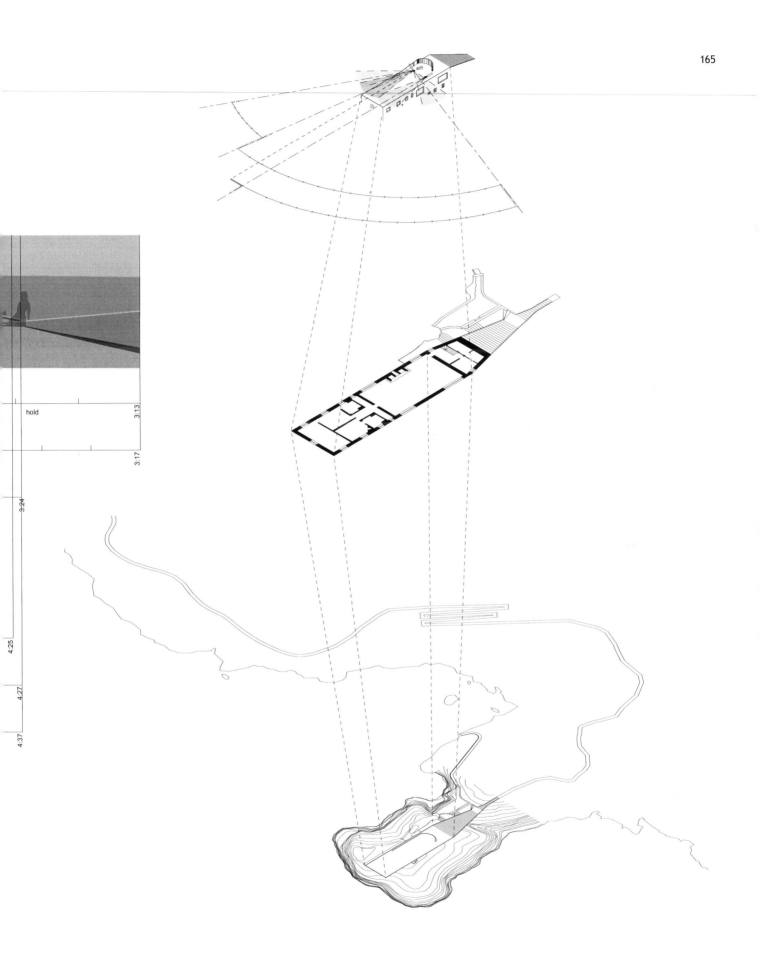

hold

3:13

3:17

3:24

4:25

4:27

4:37

spatial coordinates (illus 4_08 to 4_12). Affection images involving faces are easy to find in films, such as shots 12 and 13 on the Malaparte roof when Godard has the camera frame the faces of the screenwriter and his wife in close-up (illus 4_16). Our objective here is to understand the affect image at the scale of architecture and site, which the shots in Illustrations 4_04 through 4_07 help us to achieve. The affection image generates with any-space-whatever when you are in the sign of a sensor.

At first glance, you may think that the opening shots of this clip show a privileged space. That is, until you remember that a privileged space is just an any-instant-whatever that follows another, instant by instant, as we discussed in *Shooting*. What generates difference in a sequence of any-instant-whatever is a singular space. Godard makes this space singular for the audience by juxtaposing the anxious screenwriter with a sculpture of a powerful Greek warrior, shown, against an indeterminate blue, right before we see the dejected screenwriter standing on the rocky shore. Shot 1 is a sequence of singular any-instant-whatever, which wakes us up. The space becomes a singular any-space-whatever because we have just seen the heroic past of the Mediterranean embodied in the Greek sculpture. It lets us see the modern world with new eyes. The signal of the open whole is the absolute out-of-field of the image. In the distant background, sea and sky, water and air merge into a flow that expresses the open whole moving within everything, an open whole that endures because it changes, in this case from ancient Greek to modern times. The field of relations in architecture includes history and culture as well as space.

So much to pay attention to. It may seem like a lot to take in, let alone use. It may also seem at first reading that the ideas are unfamiliar ones, but if you keep relating them back to your own everyday experiences and to the film sequences, you will find you already know them. That is one of the benefits of attentive recognition.

Exercise 4.4: *Encircle the house in your model with panning, tilting and tracking close-up cameras that frame only parts of the house at one time, creating an affect image with an any-space-whatever. Don't forget to incorporate pauses in changes in direction in your 'shots', as Godard does.*

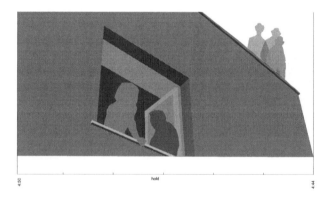

4_09 Shot 5 is taken from below looking up at the back window of the house with the writer looking down from the terrace in the top right corner of the frame. The wife impossibly appears at the window. Examining the floor plan and the later film sequence, she would have had to walk down the grand stairs, into the house, up the interior entry stairs, through the great hall, and finally Malaparte's bedroom to appear at the window in the short time her husband has walked across the roof.

4_10 Shot 6 frames the window from the inside looking out. The wife looks up and seems to notice her husband is watching her, so she kisses the producer. The setting for this scene is the study of the writer Curzio Malaparte, the builder of this house which he called 'a house like me'.

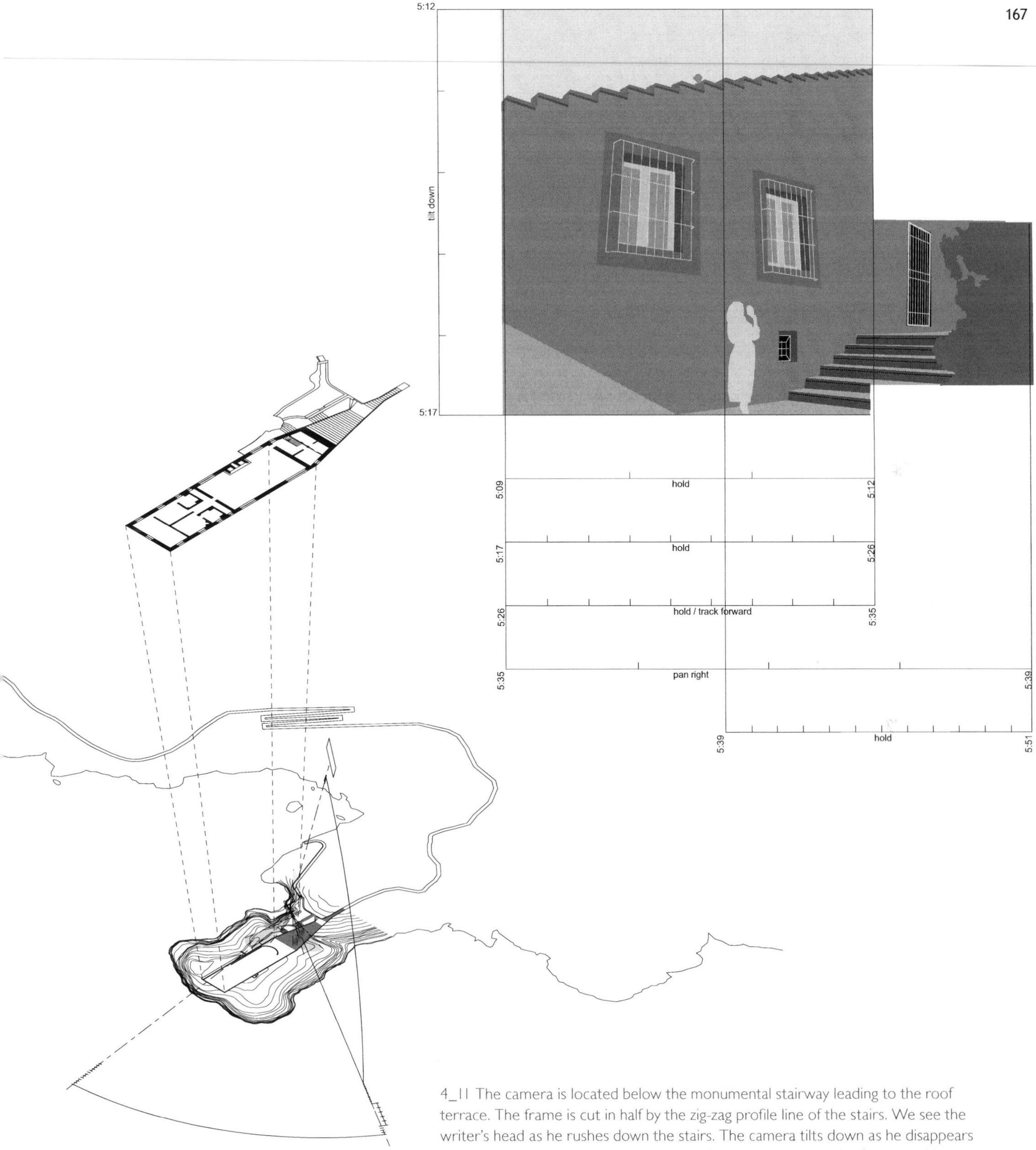

5:12

tilt down

5:17

5:09 hold 5:12

5:17 hold 5:26

5:26 hold / track forward 5:35

5:35 pan right 5:39

5:39 hold 5:51

4_11 The camera is located below the monumental stairway leading to the roof terrace. The frame is cut in half by the zig-zag profile line of the stairs. We see the writer's head as he rushes down the stairs. The camera tilts down as he disappears off frame to the left. As it tilts down, the film director enters the frame, and is met by the translator who has been leaning against the house, brushing her hair. The writer reappears in the frame and they all head to the entry door as the camera follows them, panning right. It holds as they enter the house.

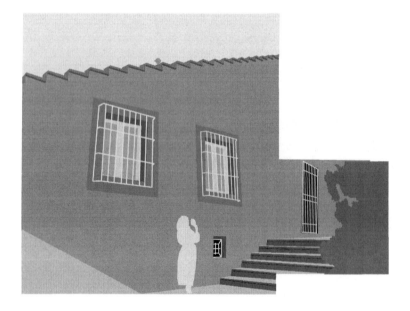

4_12 While the previous apartment sequence was dominated by horizontal pans, with these shots we begin to see sectional relations of the house through the tilting up and down of the camera, and its repositioning at critical junctions in the vertical circulation surrounding the house. Through these four shots we see the panoramic view from the roof terrace, the relation to the prominent window at the far end of the house, and the relation between the monumental stairway to the roof terrace and the minor side entry to the house.

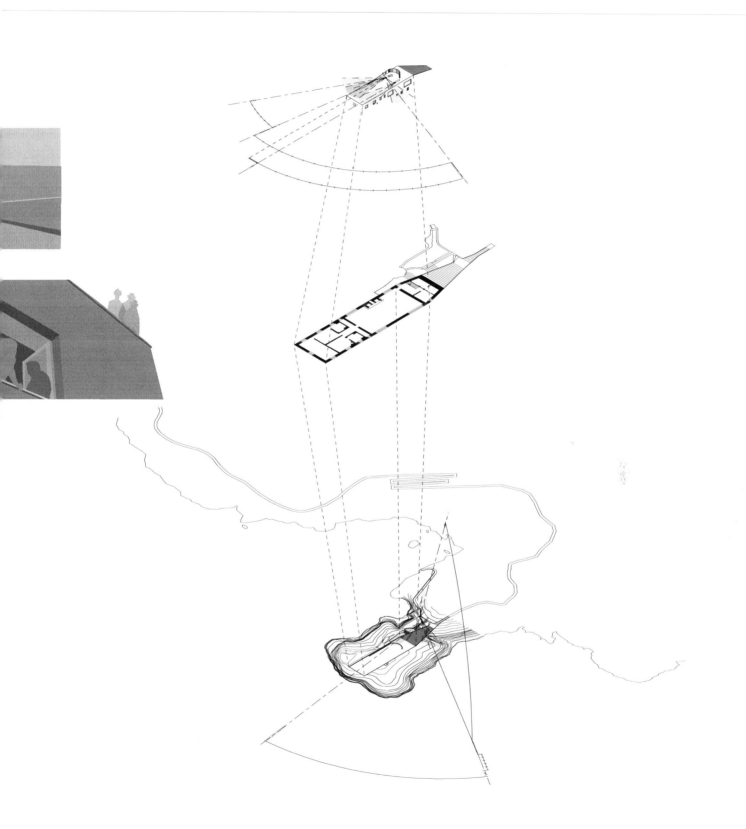

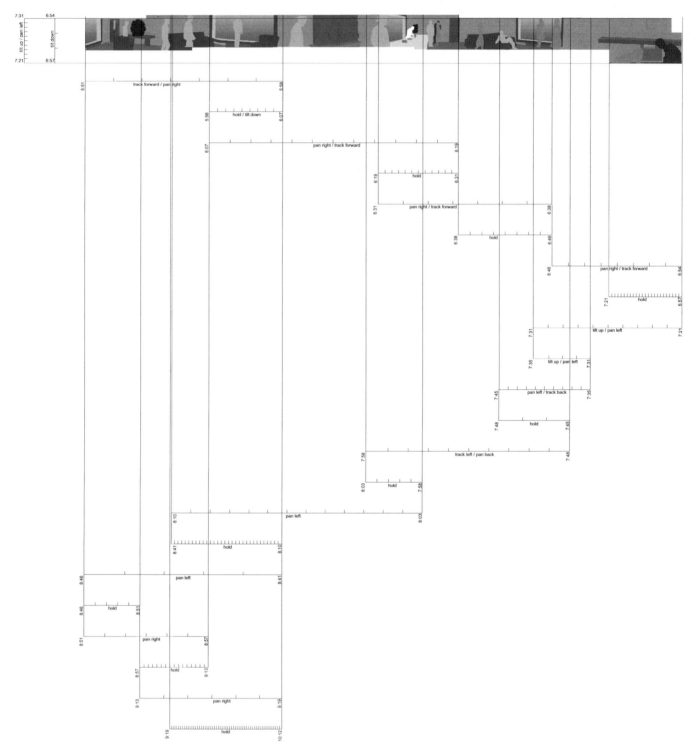

4_13 Shot 8 is a long back and forth panorama giving us a 360-degree view of the main hall of the house. Large picture windows dominate the room with their views towards the sea. Their picture-like quality is reinforced by the architectural detail of their moulded frames. The camera turns back on itself and tilts down at the fireplace – a central focus of the room – the surprising feature of a window in the back of the fireplace is pointed out to the writer's wife by the film producer. This pan is nearly five minutes in duration, and during its rotation we see all the main characters move into the space and a dramatic moment as the writer finally confronts the producer and quits his job rewriting the script of *The Odyssey*.

When the stimuli that you experienced as you paused on your walk stirred impulses, drives, and desires, you experienced yourself as a person with impulses. You made an **impulse image,** framing space as an originary world. This is the stage of perception following being a sensor but before being an actor on details or at large-scale. It is the stage in the Malaparte sequence just before the screenwriter makes his decision not to rewrite the screenplay. The scene takes place in the living room of Casa Malaparte as he paces around the huge central room with large windows facing the dramatic landscape (illus 4_13). Now the genesis of space is originary worlds, which allow us 'to see impulses and energies permeating and possessing settings and characters' – a signal of possibility.[25] One compositional signal is our everyday world – the solid objects we and the film characters experience. The other compositional signal is the open whole as a function of matter-flux – our awareness of what endures.

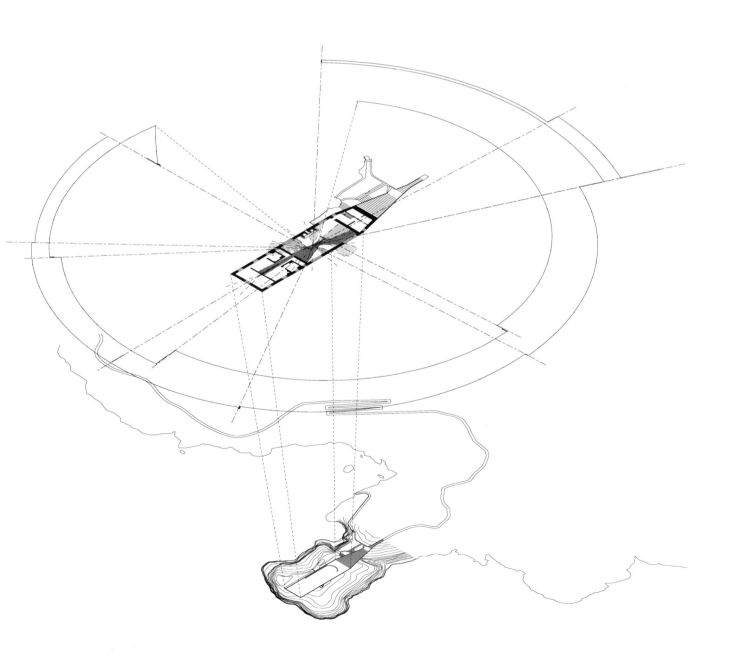

In originary worlds, '… settings, characters, and stories issue from a peculiar kind of vision, one that sees a primordial world of drives and forces [as] immanent within and inseparable from the real world of concrete particularities'. In the interior shot of the Malaparte sequence, Godard shows us an actual space as a symptom corresponding to an originary world that is a 'fragment wrested from [an] actual milieu by impulse'.[26] Curzio Malaparte's surrealist furniture and architectural details – such as the window in the fireplace or the struggling sculptural figures on the wall carved from tree trunks – suggest a fetish that hints at primitive drives and primal desires. The wood sculpture is a signal of our solid object world. The other compositional signal – that of the open whole – continues to subsist in the background expanse seen through the large floor-to-ceiling windows. This landscape is present not only as view of the physical context of the house, but also as the cultural context of the classical world that both Godard and Malaparte refer to.

Exercise 4.5: *Can you identify an originary world in the waking exercise from chapter 1 Framing or the socio-spatial exercise in chapter 3 Shooting? This is the third type of space you might draw. Shoot a rotating panoramic interior of the house model from various positions that create an impulse image with a space of originary worlds.*

Respiration Space and Line of the Universe Space Generate with the Two Forms of Action Image

There are two types of action movement images: the big form that moves from a situation to an action to a changed situation, and the small form that moves from an action to a situation to a changed action. The big form **action image** concerns a determinate milieu that 'constitutes a surrounding configuration of forces that impinge on the living image and instigate the living image's actions and reactions'. The milieu designates the ambiance, which surrounds the body and acts on it. You made this image on your walk as a large-scale actor. The small form action image moves from action to situation to action. It involves 'affects and impulses incarnate in discrete actions [behaviors]'.[27] You made a small action image on your walk as an actor on details.

Connected to each of the two types of action images are two complementary spaces: the skeleton space that generates with the small action image or the respiration space that generates with the large action image. The erratic and distracted zig-zag movements of the writer show him to be a small-scale actor on details, while the resoluteness of his wife's attention to the larger meaning of the course of events marks her as a large-scale actor.

Respiration Space Generates with Big Form Action Image

The genesis of the big form action image in the Casa Malaparte clip is a respiration space, in which 'an englobing vision lets one see contraction and dilation of milieu and action. It is a global synthesis'. The respiration space is a signal of possibility. It is an expanded space, which joins extremes and sets the stage for action.[28] The shot of the rooftop of Casa Malaparte (illus 4_14) with the view of the sea and the cliffs of Capri forms a huge respiration space.

There are two signals of composition for the space of the large action form: the one for the open whole refers to what is organic – the background of Shot 9. The other for the everyday world refers to what is functional – the curving wall which provides a shelter on the roof.[29]

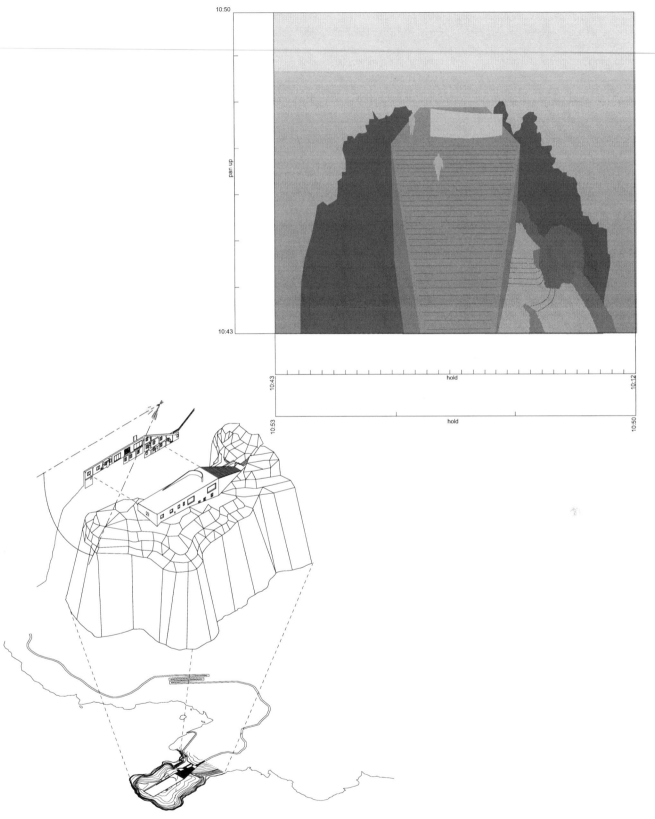

4_14 Shot 9 dramatically looks down at the monumental stairway which symbolises and defines the house. the shot holds still as the writer walks out of the side door, which we see to the right of the frame, zig-zags diagonally up the stairway. The camera tilts up to follow him. The camera stops, framing the roof as a new ground plane with the sea and horizon beyond. He is a small actor on a large stage.

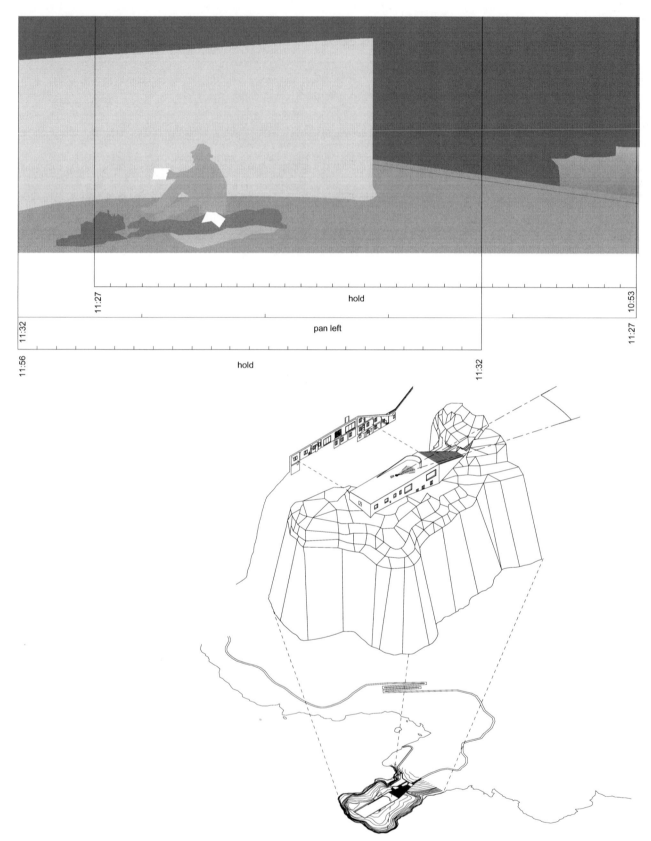

11:27

hold

10:53

11:32

pan left

11:27

11:56

hold

11:32

4_15 Shot 10 is within the shelter of the curved wall we see the wife sunbathing. The camera remains still as her husband watches her and then pans left as he approaches. It stops again as he sits down next to her.

12:14 hold 11:56

12:40 hold 12:14

13:12 hold 12:40

4_16 Shots 11, 12 and 13 are close-up **affection images** of the couple in conversation.

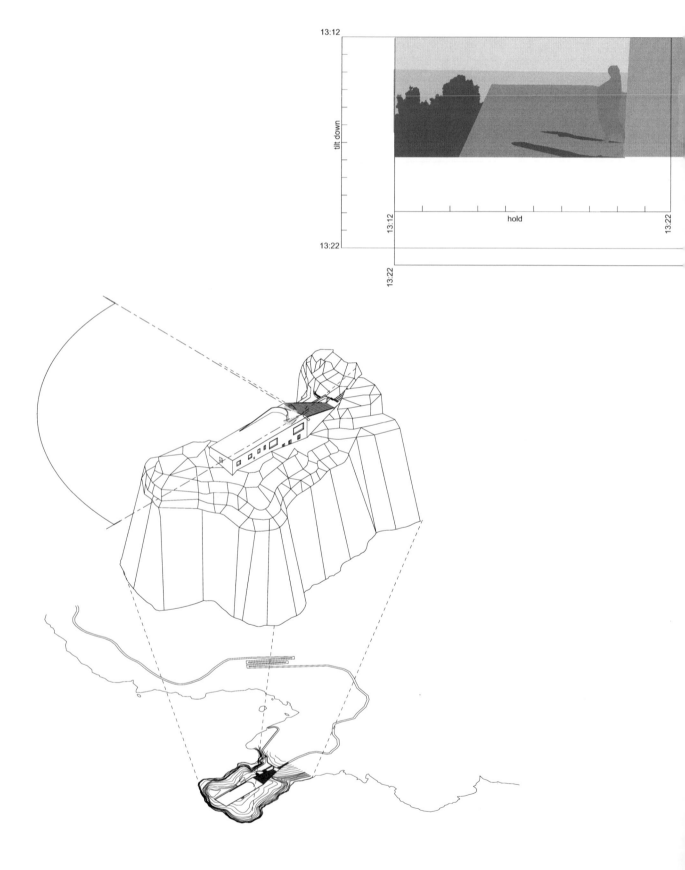

13:12

tilt down

13:12

13:12   hold   13:22

13:22

13:22

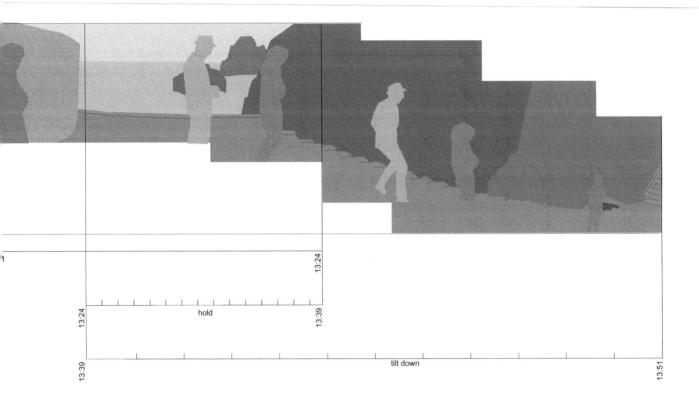

4_17 Shot 14 frames the rooftop with the curved wall to the right of the frame. The wife appears from behind the wall wrapped in a robe. The camera pans right to follow her as she hurriedly goes downstairs with her husband following her.

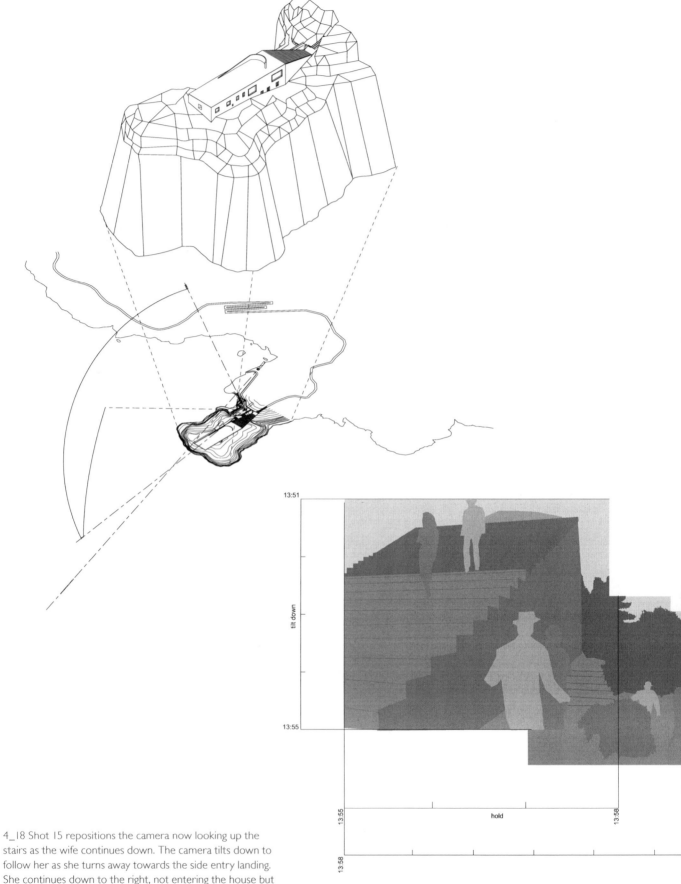

4_18 Shot 15 repositions the camera now looking up the stairs as the wife continues down. The camera tilts down to follow her as she turns away towards the side entry landing. She continues down to the right, not entering the house but descending another stairway to the sea.

13:51

tilt down

13:55

13:55

hold

13:58

13:58

Skeleton Space, Line of the Universe Generates with Small Form Action Image

The small form **action image** concerns actual behaviours: 'affects and impulses incarnate in discrete actions [behaviours]'.[30] Its signal of possibility is its genesis with a skeleton space or line of the universe, 'a contracted space in which we see vectors for the lines of the universe'. Its movement is from action to situation to changed action. You made this image and space on your walk as an actor on details when you looked at the crack in the pavement.

The signals of the composition of the skeleton space are both markers of the commonsense world. There is no signal of wholeness. There is only lack and distance, which are 'illustrated by the possibility and reality of the sudden reversals of the situation'.[31] The last shots of this sequence involve the couple leaving the rooftop and zig-zagging down the many flights of stairs from the house to the sea. The camera is positioned at turning points in their paths, so we watch them approach the camera from below and then the camera pans and tilts down to shoot the couple from above, revealing a skeleton space that zigs and zags.

Exercise 4.6: *Construct mobile sections through both the house and land showing interior and exterior simultaneously. Again these can be constructed through simple tracking section cuts through the building, or rotating from various points within the building. This type of moving drawing can be constructed orthographically or as sectional perspectives. The goal of this drawing is to capture the two forms of action image. Attempt to identify in this moving drawing the generation of both a skeletal space relating to the interior small form, and a respiration space relating to the exterior landscape.*

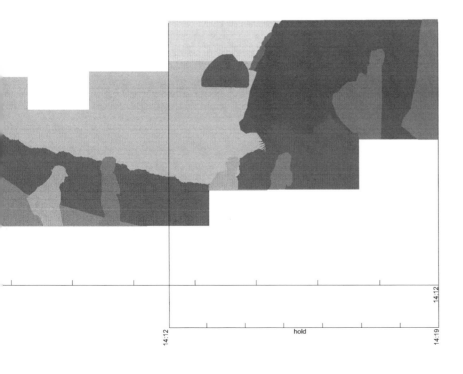

14:12   hold   14:19   14:12

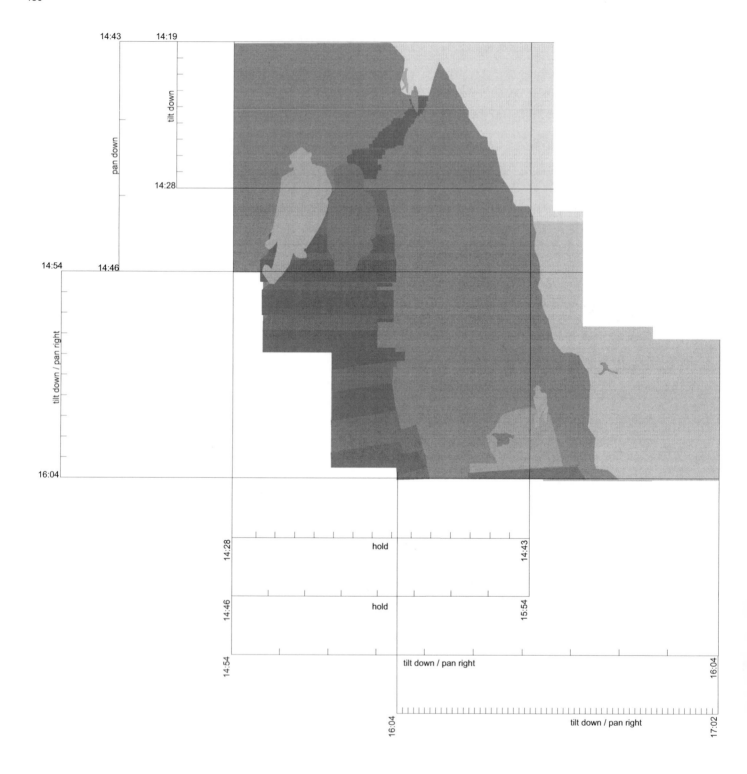

4_19 Shot 16 the camera is again positioned looking downslope and tilts downhill as the couple continues down a stairway carved into the steep cliff side. The camera stops as they sit on the stairs and talk. She gets up, leaves the frame and the camera tilts down and pans right to follow her. The camera stops, framing a ledge overlooking the sea. The husband sits on the ledge and the wife continues off frame. We understand she has jumped into the sea off screen as her robe is thrown into the frame. After a long pause she reappears in the frame in the background swimming out to sea. Finally, at the end of shot she swims out of the edge of frame, never to be seen by her husband again.

Transformation Space Generates a Reflection Image

A reflection image allows for passage from large to small form **action image**. It shows 'a deformation, transformation, or transmutation of the action image … [that] is "the intermediary between action and relation" image'. It reveals circumstances that refer 'back to an image other than that of the situation which it indicates', so 'there is no longer a direct relation between a situation and an action'.[32] You made this image and space at two different scales on your walk as a reflector on change and a reflector on an expanded field.

The last shots of the film clip are literally a reflection. The camera finally halts as the couple reaches a landing carved into the rock. The frame is dramatically split with the writer on the left half of the frame sitting on the landing and lowering his hat over his head. The right half of the frame is a striking fissure showing the surface of the sea below. The wife disappears further down the stairs and tosses her robe up to the landing. We see her reappear as a tiny swimming figure, moving towards the top of the frame. The shot ends after she swims out of the frame. The next shot moves a little closer to the sleeping man. The brilliant blue water in the previous frame has transformed to a steely grey. The sun is setting, the man wakes up. His wife is gone.

The reflection image's signal of possibility is its genesis with a transformation space in which there is a change in the way one normally thinks of something. Its composition signals are a figure of attraction and a figure of inversion. You experienced this on your walk when you considered your actions.

Exercise 4.7: *Overlay stills from your moving images to look at the deformation, transformation, and transmutation of the two kinds of action images in their different spaces, forming a reflection image in a transformation space.*

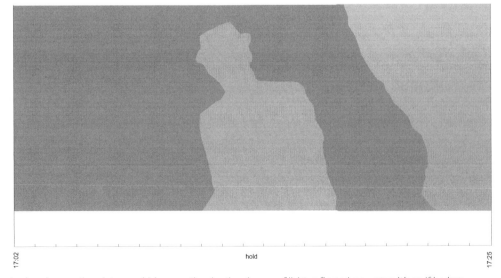

17:02   hold   17:25

4_20 Shot 17 is a close-up of the husband some time later — which we gather by the change of light reflected on water. It's as if he has awoken from a dream.

Symbol Space Generates with Relation Image

You experienced symbol spaces when you worked as an artist, critic, and thinker by creating **relation images** of your walk in each of these signs of yourself. The final movement image, a relation image, which is a thought image, emerges with a symbol space.

The essential point in a relation image is that action, and also perception and affection, are framed in 'a fabric of relations'. It is these relations which constitute the relation image. The relation image, with its accompanying symbol space, frames and connects the perception, affection, and action images in each of the three signs of yourself as artist, critic, or thinker.[33]

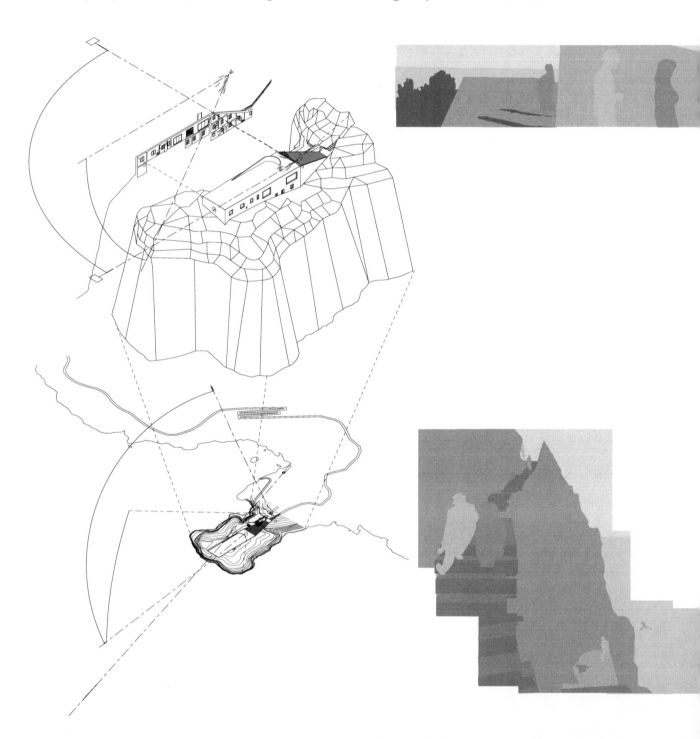

In the Casa Malaparte clips, there is a relation image and **symbol** space when we see the screenwriter asleep, leaning against the rock at the end of the clip (illus 4_21). The shot is a symbol of his inability to comprehend the gravity of the situation with his wife, who has told him she is moving out of their apartment. Instead, he falls asleep and does not awake until after it is too late to stop her from leaving Casa Malaparte. In fact, he doesn't even know that she has already left.

The symbol space is the final space we will discuss. Its composition signals are the mark, a characteristic of the commonsense world, in which its terms refer back in customary series. Its signal of the open whole is the de-mark, in which a term is set outside a series. (Hitchcock famously showed a windmill 'whose sails turn in the opposite direction to the wind' as a clue or de-mark in one of his movies.)[34] Now try to make drawings of symbol spaces as an artist architect, critic architect, and a cybernetic architect. Draw on experiences, similar to those on your walk, when you scrutinised 'what appears' as an artist, a critic, and a thinker.

4_21 The preceding shots continue the **mobile section** of the entire sequence in which Godard starts from the hillside above the house, to the roof terrace, inside the house, and then back up to the roof, and then dramatically down to the sea.

184 ***Exercise 4.8****: Generate a matrix of selected stills from your shooting analysis of your house and landscape looking for relations and movements between different kinds of signs and images. Use the semiosis diagram as a guide (illus 4_03).*

In summary, *'How can we generate architectural space through drawing any-instant-whatever?'* Space forms as we move through the signs of ourselves within a living world, making movement images that have both a relative and absolute out-of-field. The nature of space has changed from what we usually think of when we study architecture. It is no longer an emptiness to be filled with things. It is no longer static, waiting to be organised by perspective. It is a generative moving medium, having its own powers and forces that become manifest and vary in relation to our movements in an expanded field of cultural and environmental relations. Space has its own laws of duration that reveal its relation to the open whole.

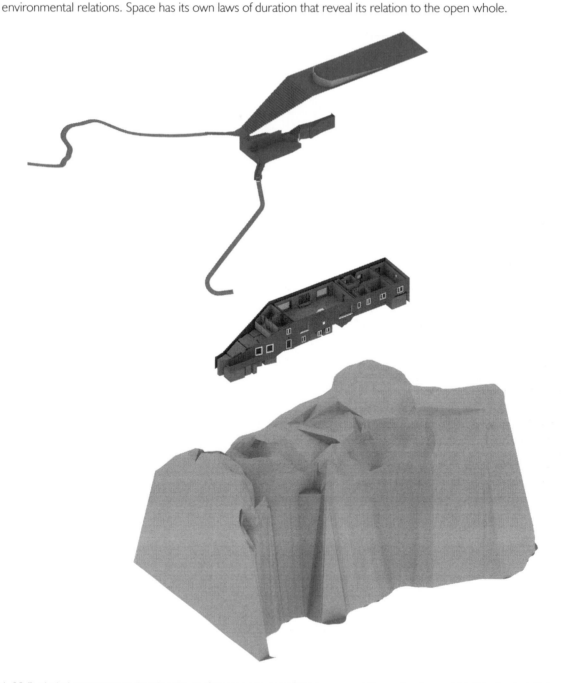

4_22 Exploded axonometric showing the roof terrace, interior of the house, and the peninsula on which it is situated. Malaparte created his house as a **symbol** space for his life.

1 Floyd Merrell, 'Thought-signs, sign-events', *Semiotica: Journal of the International Association for Semiotic Studies,* 1991, Vols 87–112, p 28.

2 Deleuze, *Cinema 2*, p 29.

3 Merrell, 'Thought-signs, sign-events', p 28.

4 Merrell, 'Thought-signs, sign-events', p 20.

5 Merrell, 'Thought-signs, sign-events', p 20.

6 Merrell, 'Thought-signs, sign-events', p 22.

7 Merrell, 'Thought-signs, sign-events', p 22.

8 Merrell, 'Thought-signs, sign-events', p 22.

9 Merrell, 'Thought-signs, sign-events', p 24.

10 Merrell, 'Thought-signs, sign-events', p 24.

11 Merrell, 'Thought-signs, sign-events', p 25.

12 Merrell, 'Thought-signs, sign-events', p 26.

13 Merrell, 'Thought-signs, sign-events', p 28.

14 Merrell, 'Thought-signs, sign-events', pp 17–18.

15 Bogue, *Deleuze on Cinema*, p 105.

16 Bogue, *Deleuze on Cinema*, p 105.

17 Bogue, *Deleuze on Cinema*, p 89.

18 Deleuze, *Cinema 1*, pp 188, 187, 192, 194.

19 Bogue, *Deleuze on Cinema*, p 96.

20 Deleuze, *Cinema 1*, p 203.

21 Talamona, Marida, *Casa Malaparte,* trans Vittoria di Palma, Princeton Architectural Press (Princeton), 1996, p 46.

22 Bogue, *Deleuze on Cinema*, p 72.

23 Bogue, *Deleuze on Cinema*, p 69.

24 Bogue, *Deleuze on Cinema*, p 105.

25 Bogue, *Deleuze on Cinema*, p 105.

26 Bogue, *Deleuze on Cinema*, p 82.

27 Bogue, *Deleuze on Cinema*, pp 85, 33.

28 Bogue, *Deleuze on Cinema*, pp 85–6. Deleuze, *Cinema 1*, p 188.

29 Deleuze, *Cinema 1*, p 142.

30 Bogue, *Deleuze on Cinema*, p 85.

31 Deleuze, *Cinema 1*, pp 168, 201.

32 Bogue, *Deleuze on Cinema*, p 92. Deleuze, *Cinema 1*, p 182.

33 Bogue, *Deleuze on Cinema*, pp 103, 100. Deleuze, *Cinema 1*, pp 198, 200.

34 Deleuze, *Cinema 1*, p 203.

CHAPTER 5

ASSEMBLING

What happens when the sensori-motor schema breaks down and perceptions no longer result in action?

Now that you know how to generate six kinds of images and spaces, using a moving architectural drawing system, you are ready for **assembling** – the putting together of a *Cinemetric* drawing of your day a space you are analysing, or the spaces you are generating. This section also introduces you to additional techniques to develop further the moving images and spaces you have been working on using *Cinemetrics*.

Words in bold are Keywords found on pages 260-265

First, let's remind ourselves why we are creating drawings that move between different kinds of images. Because, as we have shown, movement is no longer understood as only a transposition of objects in space. Instead, it is also a transformation of the **open whole** that happens in time when we consciously frame, deframe and reframe sets of information from the whole. The breaks in our sensori-motor systems explored in this chapter help us to understand in more detail what this means. When our feelings no longer result in actions, we can understand movement for what it is: not merely an activity that covers distance in time, but a qualitative change in **duration** – in the open whole. Creating optic and sonic images in the breaks between affection and action can lead to forming time images. Within these images movement is a qualitative consequence of time rather than time being a result of movement in space. Using a drawing system based on these relationships between time and movement can help us to address the current expanded field of cultural and ecological relations within which architecture is spatially and temporally embedded.

Traditional assembling – editing or montage in film – as in typical architectural animations, entails piecing together shots in a linear, causal succession so the shots describe sensori-motor connections between sequential events. This gives us an indirect image of time as a consequence of movement or transposition in space rather than a transformation of the **open whole**.[1] In Deleuze's philosophy of film, 'More than style of cutting, montage expresses a logic of composition – a concept or a regulating Idea in the philosophical sense – that informs the system of the film globally and in each of its parts. Montage indicates a particular organizing principle or *agencement* of images in the form of Ideas.'[2]

In previous exercises you have recorded activities in your daily life – getting up, interacting with other people, going for a walk outside. You recorded these activities, using very controlled camera movements. In *Framing* you were asked to construct still-frames of the act of waking up in the morning. In *Shooting* you were asked to construct mobile shots of socio-spatial interactions, limiting camera movements to mechanical pans, tilts and tracks. Now in *Assembling*, in addition to editing previous work, you will use a hand-held camera to directly interact with moving bodies in space.

Exercise 5.1: *In this first exercise, arrange the images of your day and routine from all the previous exercises into a chronological, continuous narrative – into a traditional linear assemblage.*

Collecting, differentiating and connecting images isn't something we haven't done before. We do this all the time in life and work. Usually we describe our day as a series of events: leaping out of bed and getting right to work on unfinished drawings, not taking the time to wake up slowly or think of anything else but finishing the work we are so excited about. Such a description portrays the morning as a spatial ordering of **movement images** that presents time as equivalent to the 'normal' course of the day – getting up and going to work. When we describe our day in such a way, in effect, we construct a narrative of continuous spatial moments sequenced in time according to our own personal storytelling style. If we think about it, we probably know a friend's style of narration well enough that we can predict the general manner in which they describes their day even before they start talking. We have listened many times before and know their 'regulating idea' – the style they developed to create a sense of continuity in their life. Conventional architectural animated walk-throughs rely on such normative narratives, constructing apparent continuity out of millions of choices of images and signs that can be digitally generated in computer modelling. This style of storytelling is one that belongs with perspective, the printing press and other tools used frequently when we organise selected blocks of space-time in a linear manner.

Let's compare the overarching organising principle or style of the film directors so far studied: Ozu and Godard. Ozu edited the clip from *Early Spring* we explored in *Framing* and *Immobile Sections* in order to create a sense of continuity. The alarm goes off, the wife wakes up, gets out of bed, and goes about her chores. In the apartment scene from Godard's *Contempt*, analysed in *Shooting*, the screenwriter and his wife arrive at their apartment, get undressed, bathe, fall in and out of an argument, dress and go out again. Such a familiar sequence of shots in an assemblage belongs to the linear organic regime of movement images in which our images reveal the habitual sensori-motor schema of our accustomed everyday reality. In this

commonsense world we distinguish between what is objective and what is subjective, what is real and what is imaginary,
what is physical and what is mental.[3]

But wait a minute. Wasn't there much more to our morning and to the Ozu and Godard film clips than the normative narrative just described? The stillness of Ozu's camera keeps us interested in the careful framing of every detail in his spare scenes and sets, and through the neighbours we see that this couple is just one of thousands whose lives have been altered by the post-war economy in Japan. And in the apartment scene in *Contempt,* the moods of both characters are so volatile we cannot follow any of their behaviour patterns to logical conclusions. There was the montage sequence in illustration 3_15, which flashed back to earlier scenes in the film and previewed a scene in Casa Malaparte that would come later in the film. There was more to our morning and the film clips that we have not considered – memory, which plays a decisive part in assembling cinematic images or the drawing system of our day. Memory complicates the framing, shooting, and assembling of matter-flux because it enters into the process of selecting from the open whole. It problematises narration as an accurate description and can even cause us to question what is true. Memory also affects our process of drawing. Let's see how.

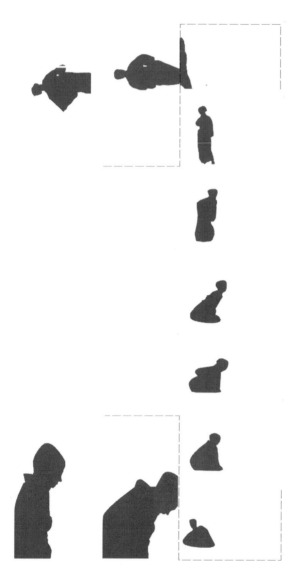

5_01 The **assemblage** of the 2nd to 4th shots in Ozu's *Early Spring* consists of perfectly matched, continuous movements showing the wife getting up from three camera angles. This sequence has to be shot and reshot several times to give the film viewer the sense of temporally, organic continuity. The wife's action of getting up had to be repeated while the film director changed camera positions in order to give the illusion of temporal and spatial continuity. Narrative continuity is a fabrication in cinema and in moving drawing.

Memory Circuits

Memory plays a pivotal part in our lives. Memory guides our habitual sensori-motor routine when it operates automatically. We hear the alarm in the morning and our memory unconsciously recollects that the clock is set to the latest possible moment that we can sleep. We open our eyes, see our computer, and our memory reminds us involuntarily that we have work we would like to finish. When we leap out of bed, our memory instinctively gets our feet onto the floor, and we automatically know the way to the bathroom and so on. Without our being aware, this type of memory converts blocks of space-time into the objects of our everyday reality, in this case, the objects related to waking up. Bergson called this type of memory **automatic recognition.** It is one of the reasons we think objects are in space. We are not usually conscious of the process of selecting from matter-flux the blocks of space-time that become our familiar routine. Our narrative description of waking up, or of what we did during the working day and over the weekend collects and connects most often only the '**shots**' based on automatic recognition.

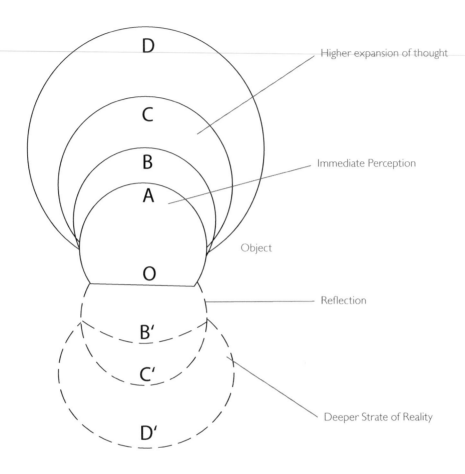

D

C

B

A

Higher expansion of thought

Immediate Perception

Object

O

Reflection

B'

C'

D'

Deeper Strate of Reality

5_02 Bergson's schema of attentive recognition where the line O represents an object and loop A stands for immediate perception. B, C and D represent successive higher expansions of thought, while B', C' and D' stand for deeper strata of reality which result from **attentive recognition.** Redrawn from Bergson, Henri. *Matter and Memory.* Trans. N.M. Paul and W.S. Palmer. New York: Zone Books, 1991 (Originally published in 1896).

But there is a second kind of recognition: **attentive recognition**. It occurs when we consciously pay attention to an object. This kind of recollection occurs at the same time as automatic recognition. We can become aware of it if we pay attention to what we are doing instead of just reacting habitually. Bergson charted the process of attentive recognition in diagram form so we can see how the object and each memory-image are connected. 'As we pay closer attention to the object, we summon up memory-images from broader and more distant past contexts, each widening context encompassing the narrower.'[4] By repeatedly recording our daily life in moving drawings, we are able to use memory and reflection images to understand subtle differences in the flowing of matter-flux in duration.

In the diagram, the object of attention is labelled O and immediate perception is circuit A. There is no attentive recognition, just automatic so there is no 'A'. Circuits B, C, and D represent 'growing efforts at intellectual expansion.'[5] Circuits B',C',D' indicate 'deeper strata of reality',[6] B',C',D' are each an 'external projection of an image, actively created, identical or similar to the object, … which comes to mold itself on the contours of the object.' The process of attentive recognition 'has the effect of creating anew, not simply the perceived object, but the more and more vast systems to which it can be connected.' If we had included in the descriptive narrative drawings of our day, the repeated time element of objects remembered differently, making it possible for us to recognise the alarm, the computer, and so on from one everyday object to another not automatically, but qualitatively different, then we would have integrated attentive recognition into our drawing system.[7]

Imagine, what it would be like if each time we awoke, we felt 'the effect of creating anew, not simply the perceived object, but the more and more vast systems to which it can be connected'. No more dull morning blues! What a different relationship we would have to drawing as well. By focusing on differences rather than the boredom of routine, we don't have that feeling that it has all been done before. No more troublesome questioning: 'How can I possibly contribute?' Instead, attentive recognition supports making the visualisation of what we are drawing 'new' – something fresh emerging from our own ability to be aware of what we are doing in an expanded field of dynamic relations. Nothing remains the same when we really take the time to pay attention so why would we want to repeat what has already been done? Memory fuels the present by adding depth when we frame space-time. Ozu repeatedly returns to the bedroom of the opening scene of *Early Spring,* giving us successive reflective circuits of the room and the couple as they change during the course of the film. The room is used first as a bedroom, and then is a room to do chores in or have tea with a neighbour. Later it is used as a dining room and a reception room for the husband's guests. Let's look at a specific building to see what further meanings **attentive recognition** can have for architecture.

Can you think of any buildings where memory has entered into the design process? The owner and 'architect' of the Casa Malaparte, the surrealist writer Curzio Malaparte aka Kurt Suckert (1898–1957) characterised his house as a 'self-portrait cut in stone' (*ritratto pietra*) or a 'house like me' (*casa come me*). Mixed into his fantastical writings are descriptions of places that recall the house and tell us about his relation to it. For instance, the writer, deported by the Fascists in 1933 to the island of Lipari, north of Sicily, described his experience of imprisonment and Casa Malaparte in his novel *The Skin* (*La Pelle*, 1949):

> 'I now live on an island, in a melancholy, austere house, which I have built myself on a solitary cliff by the sea. The image of my longing.
>
> 'Cell 461 remains in my soul as its secret character. I feel like a bird that has swallowed its cage. The cell is within me like a child inside a pregnant woman.'[8]

As Malaparte so vividly describes, memory is within us physically. Not only does it feed, like an unborn child, on us, but memory also nourishes us and our work in ways both known and unknown. Memory images pop into our mind when a design decision that we are struggling with digs them up. How? Just as Bergson indicates: the object we are focused on drawing – say a particular feature of a building – casts a light into deeper strata of our reality, finding a resonance with an identical or similar object that moulds itself onto the feature we want to draw. Often we don't even recognise the origin of the feature until, possibly, after we have drawn it. Then, becoming aware of its origin, we can either rethink whether or not we want to use the feature or elaborate on it in unexpected ways.

We have used Bergson's diagram of attentive recognition to relate specifics of the Casa Malaparte to possible memories of places that its owner knew. The correlation is a **fabrication**, or what Deleuze calls a **fabulation,** but serves to illustrate potential ways that Malaparte engaged his memory in the design process for '*a melancholy, austere house, which I have built myself on a solitary cliff by the sea. The image of my longing.*'[9]

Malaparte borrowed the stairs that widen upwards as they lead to the stunning roof terrace on the entry stairs to the Church of Annunziata on Lipari, the island of his imprisonment. Stairs and terrace together form a classical open-air Greek theatre – the setting for imagined dramatic action. The main hall of the house with its stone floor and mural-like views through the large windows is like the atrium of a Roman *domus* – recently excavated in nearby Pompeii. Malaparte's favourite mistress' bedroom – with its wood-burning stove – resembles the Alpine interior of his youth. Finally, beyond his own bedroom at the rear of the house is the writer's studio – a solitary space to remind him of his prison cell in exile. For historian Marida Talamona, the view of Casa Malaparte from the water is like a Roman tomb, suggesting that perhaps the writer built this house as a lasting monument to himself.[10]

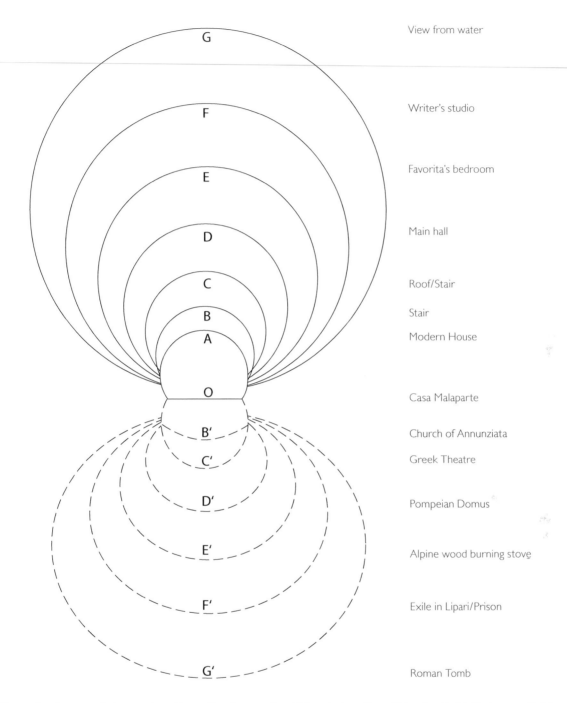

G — View from water

F — Writer's studio

E — Favorita's bedroom

D — Main hall

C — Roof/Stair

B — Stair

A — Modern House

O — Casa Malaparte

B' — Church of Annunziata

C' — Greek Theatre

D' — Pompeian Domus

E' — Alpine wood burning stove

F' — Exile in Lipari/Prison

G' — Roman Tomb

5_03 Bergson's schema applied to an **attentive reflection** on Casa Malaparte by critic and historian Marida Toalamona. Building analysis from Talamona, Merida, *Casa Malaparte*. Trans. Vittoria di Palma. Princeton: Princeton Architectural Press, 1996.

Exercise 5.2: *In order to break with automatic recognition to access the richness of attentive recognition, let's try to break with your current sense of the logic of continuity as seen in the narrative of getting up in the morning, interacting with people, and moving from interior to exterior spaces. Instead, repeat the exercises from* Framing *and* Shooting *and hunt for subtle affinities and differences based on memory connections between the images you have drawn. Then arrange your images based on attentive recognition. Find repetitions of objects in your shots. Connect the repeated images of the same object framed at different times. Generate spaces from drawing the differences in time rather than changing positions in space. Like Ozu, return to the same space at different times of day and under different conditions of use.*

Sheets of the Past and Peaks of the Present

But what about the remembered experience of our senses? We altered our normal morning pattern by paying attention to our body. We noted that our joints were stiff, then smelt coffee brewing and tasted our favourite muffin. Does this experience involve memory? How can we put these sensory stimuli that interrupted our normal sensori-motor routine into the drawing system of our day? And how do these body experiences influence our architectural drawing?

When we focused on our body sensations, our attention was not moving from object to object in space – bed to floor to computer – as happens in automatic recognition, but instead our thoughts were moving in time. The sound of the alarm automatically reminded us it was morning. But, instead of getting right up, we did something different, putting our attention somewhere new. We paid attention to our senses. Then, amazingly, we smelt coffee and tasted a muffin. How did that happen? Come to think of it, a memory of sitting in a café last Saturday morning, with a steaming latte and a warm muffin, the newspaper open at the movie listings, stimulated us several days later to smell and taste the latte and muffin while lying in bed. Before we knew what was happening, we searched our memory for other similar times, not connected in space or in linear time to our weekend memory. We began condensing remembered images of latte and muffin from years ago into the smell and taste we were experiencing, lying in bed.[11]

When we remember something, 'we place ourselves in the past straightaway, and then "transverse a series of different *planes of consciousness*", in search of the given memory'. Bergson visualised this process 'as a cone, with its point representing the past's coincidence with the present and its widening volume representing an ever-growing expanse of coexisting past events. Each plane is a cross section of the cone of the virtual past' – a sheet or layer of the past.[12]

Deleuze gives the classic example of Orson Welles' film *Citizen Kane* as an example of a film organised by peaks of the present and sheets of the past. The movie begins with a peak of the present: Kane's death and his dying words: 'rose bud'. The rest of the film is structured by a reporter's search for people from Kane's life who could provide recollection images of him. With each interview the reporter leaps from the present to a flashback image from Kane's life. Sheets of the past and peaks of the present can be experienced in space and the deep focus shots carefully constructed for this film contain within them sheets of time. Search for memory in layers of time was evident in *Contempt*. Early in the film the wife is offered a ride

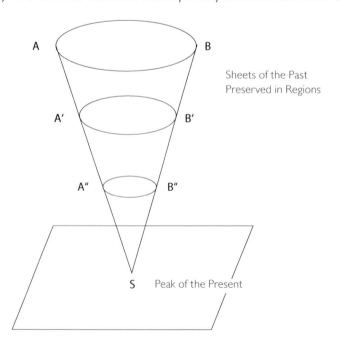

5_04 Bergson's schema of how memory is preserved in **sheets of the past**. The present is point 'S' in the ever expanding cone of the past. One must leap to different regions to retrieve memories. Redrawn from Bergson, Henri. *Matter and Memory.* Trans. N.M. Paul and W.S. Palmer. New York: Zone Books, 1991 (Originally published in 1896).

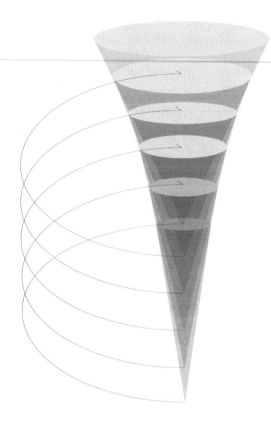

2 Rose bud irretrevable memory

4 Kane's childhood home

6 Kane buys the Inquirer

8 Kane's first marriage

10 Kane's second marriage

1 Xanadu: Kane's dying words: rose bud

3 Thatcher library

5 Berstein's office

7 Nursing home

9 El Rancho nightclub

11 Return to Xanadu

5_05 Bergson's cone applied to the scenario of Orson Welles' *Citizen Kane*. The film begins at the end of Kane's life (1), and then proceeds with a reporter interviewing various people from Kane's life to find the meaning of his dying words: 'rose bud'. The film moves back in time at each successive interview to regions of Kane's past, but the reporter is never able to retrieve the meaning of rose bud which is buried in an early childhood memory of Kane's. Scenario from Carringer, Robert L. *The Making of Citizen Kane*, Berkeley, University of California Press, 1996.

in the film producer's car. When the scene is first presented it passes quickly and we cannot discern much importance to this any-instant-whatever. However, through reflection images, first when the wife remembers the incident as a betrayal by her husband, then when the husband remembers the same scene without seeing its significance, we can see examples of two people reflecting on the same sheet of the past. Can you find layers of time in your moving drawings?

Exercise 5.3: *Arrange your images in reverse chronology as 'sheets of the past', putting the most recent first. Find a structure that retrieves these images from distinct regions of past memories. Try not to use a narrative structure. What other kinds of structures are there?*

'The layers of the past surround a kernel of immediate perception', which are **peaks** or **points of the present** condensing disparate historical moments into a single point in the present.[13] The image of staying in bed instead of getting up is an image freed from our habitual sensori-motor schema that organises our narrative description of our day. We heard the alarm but didn't get up. Instead, we paused to try to feel matter-flux and be aware of our senses. These images are not part of our normal pattern in the morning. They are not movement images. They unlink the linear sequence of perception, affect, and action. How would we describe them acoustically or visually? Can we create sonic or **optical images** of them?

Sonic and optical images emerge out of the affection image of any-space-whatever when we break our habitual sensori-motor schema because we cannot act on what we are feeling. In them, objective and subjective lose relevance. Sonic and optical images open the way, not to movement images and the organic linear regime, but to the **time image** and the multi-faceted **crystalline regime**. They initiate a process of description that engages, not perception, which occurs in space, but memory, which occurs in time and can lead us to a direct crystal image of time. As we learned in *Mobile Sections,* we can act as artist and link colours, forms and spaces from layers of time, or we can reorganise our observations as a critic looking for the significance in details we may overlook at first.

Optical images involve 'pure seeing' that remains 'unassimilated within the ongoing action'.[14] They emerge from doing but are detached from immediate action. They often help us to learn to see more deeply into our lives. For instance, memories of coffee and a muffin, stretching beyond last Saturday in the café, dug up other occasions involving coffee and a muffin – let's say the memory of an incident, years ago, that eventually convinced you to become an architect. Do you remember? It was on a trip with your graduating high school class, let's say to Manhattan. The whole group took the train, arriving in Grand Central Terminal, stopping in the Grand Concourse to grab a coffee and a muffin. The volume of the space and the muffled sound of thousands of commuters' footsteps linger in your mind. The ceiling of the vast space had just been cleaned. Standing there, looking up at its constellations of stars, a trip to an Anasazi village, tucked into the side of a cliff in the Southwest, floats to mind. Amazing, this ancient people had painted the stars above their dwellings on the overhead surface of the cliff shelf. Recalling this trip today, you can still easily imagine the powerful presence of the silent desert sky at night for the people living there a thousand or so years ago. Even now ambient electric lights have not blotted out the intense immediacy of the millions of stars surrounding the desert cliffs. Stunned, you now wonder how you could have forgotten such a moment.

At the time of the high school trip to Grand Central Terminal – seeing its painted zodiac and remembering the Anasazi stars and desert stillness – you began to feel a vague but persistent dissatisfaction with your plans for after-high school. You couldn't put your finger on exactly what was bothering you but those plans didn't interest you any more. The forceful image of the zodiac ceiling in Grand Central had merged with the star-studded overhead surface of an Anasazi cliff dwelling and the millions of stars in the silent desert sky. This multi-faceted image kept popping into your mind at unexpected times. But you didn't know how to act on its dazzling allure. A personal event of geological magnitude had occurred, leaving you unable to respond. Your sensori-motor schema broke down. Unable to act, you formed an optical image based on memory – on layers of the past becoming peaks of the present.

Optical images emerge with the breakdown of our sensori-motor schema. They mark the occurrence of 'something intolerable, unbearable, something "too powerful … that exceeds our habitual patterns of sensori-motor capacities"' and resulting actions. This is why the image of the merged Grand Central ceiling and cliff paintings is not a cliché. If we could draw all the temporal elements contained in this image, we might capture the optical purity of that moment. If so, the image would combine with 'immense forces' and powers so it is legible, so it is something to be read, not just seen. Such an image opens us 'to powerful and direct revelations', connected, not through 'causally related present instants', but through memory.[15]

Now we can begin to answer the opening question: *What happens when the sensori-motor schema breaks down and perceptions no longer result in action?* Duration is no longer measured indirectly by the time it takes to translate movement into action, which we can draw using the six movement images. Instead, a multifaceted **time image** generates from the optical and sonic relations that replace action. Transposition in space is replaced by transformation in time. A crystalline regime, rather than a linear narrative, emerges in which we intuit the whole as universal becoming, as change and creative evolution, in which we think, rather than act.[16] Now the spaces we have generated through the exercises can be fed back to the expanded field that our domestic and workspaces operate in – the specific time and place of our existence.

You may be wondering, 'How can we relate assemblage and the time image to generating space through mobile sections?' To do this, let's first look at Cassavetes' *Faces* to see more specifically what assemblage, broken sensori-motor schema and optical images are so we have a richer grasp of what leads to time images.

Cassavetes' *Faces*

Let's observe the process of assembling in a film where the characters' sensori-motor schema break down, perceptions no longer result in action and optical images form. Keep in mind the assemblage that we just explored in the linear and then crystalline assemblage of the frames and shots from your daily life. These crystalline assemblages help you to understand qualitative differences in time rather than seeing only the routine of automatic activities of everyday life. Let's look closely at both the type of shot produced with the hand-held camera and the organising of shots in the final sequence of Cassavetes' *Faces*. This analysis helps us to understand the **time image**, the subject of the last chapter. More immediately, it helps us to assemble moving drawings in ways that can hold attention, not because of some gimmick, but because there is really something in them worth looking at carefully – for instance, the space generated by qualitative change in duration.

At the beginning of this chapter we defined traditional assembling or montage in film as the piecing together of shots in a linear, causal succession so 'the shots describe sensori-motor connections between events'.[17] What results is 'an indirect image of time'.[18] We also generated spaces from examining intervals in the movements in space as any-instant-whatever. Initially, the clip from *Faces* seems to assemble shots by connecting them in a linear, causal succession. The shots describe a sequence of events, just as we did when we told our friend about our day – but in this case not a common everyday occurrence. When we view the opening of the scene, we are experiencing movement images from the organic regime because what the husband senses and his resulting bodily actions, recorded by a hand-held camera, dominate Cassavetes' organisation of the opening shots. The husband's motor responses are controlling the space: getting out of his car in front of his home, dancing into the house, running upstairs, standing momentarily just outside his bedroom door, running through his bedroom to look out of a window to discover an unknown man running over the roof of his house (shots 1, 2, 3, 4, 5). Up to this last shot (shot 5), the regulating idea of the clip is the movement of the husband's body in patterns that flow uninterruptedly from perception through affection to action. A hand-held camera kinesthetically records Cassavetes' body movements as he follows the husband. The principle that organises the shooting and the assembling of the opening shots is the husband's moving body, which expresses the interplay between his senses, feelings, and actions – his sensori-motor schema.

In chapter 1 *Framing*, we examined the framing of matter-flux in which Ozu kept his camera still on the floor for the full length of the shot. In chapter 3 *Shooting*, we examined the shooting of any-instant-whatever by Godard as slow, mechanical pans, tilts and tracks of the film camera with the exaggerated horizontal proportions of a cinemascope frame. In this chapter we are looking at John Cassavetes' film *Faces* (1968) in which he uses a hand-held camera. This allows the director to construct shots following the movements of actors rather than being restricted to the Cartesian geometries of the spaces in which they were filmed. The coordinated movement of actor and cameraman generate a topological relational space based on the interaction of two human bodies and a camera in space, rather than the more mechanical movement of tracking, panning and tilting in Godard or the strictly Euclidean geometrical frame of Ozu.

Exercise 5.4: *Experiment with filming people in motion and at rest with a constantly moving hand-held camera, getting as close to your subjects as possible. Shoot them from as many different angles as you can. See if you can imagine an invariant order to your shooting – one in which you move your camera along some constant variable such as sine curve or a parabola as seen in illustrations 5_15 and 5_23.*

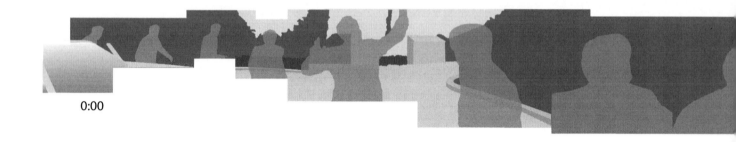

0:00

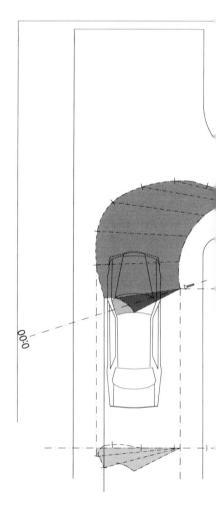

0:00

5_06 Shot 1 from *Faces* consists of a dance between the hand-held camera and the husband's dash from his car to the front door of the house. In grey is shown the space generated between the actor and the camera, in plan and side elevation. Dashed lines represent one second of duration.

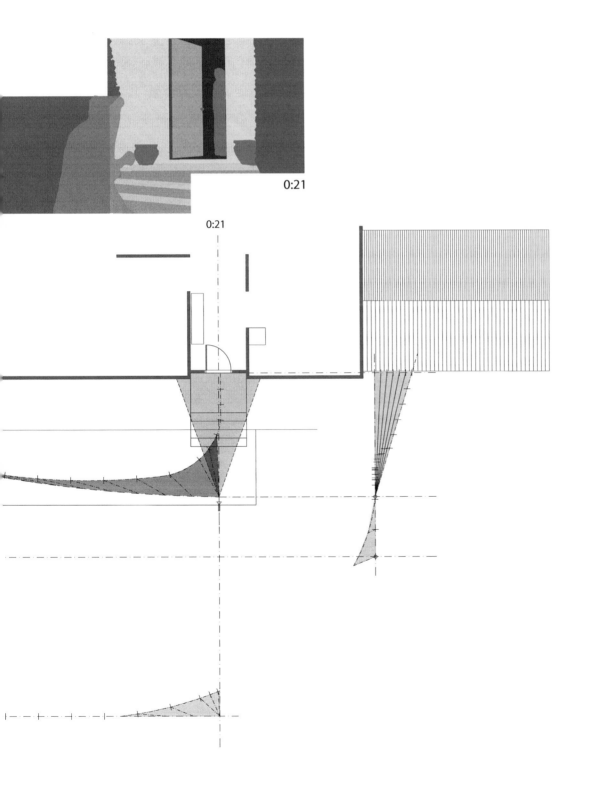

0:21

0:21

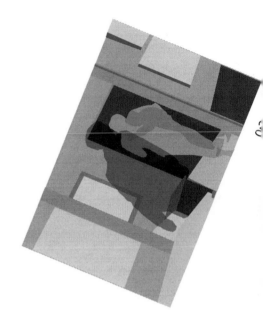

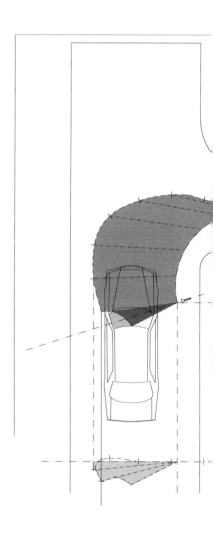

5_07 Shot 2 frames the entry vestibule from the living room as the husband jumps into the frame kicking, dancing, spinning, and looking around. He disappears down the hall as the camera unsteadily holds on the empty frame.

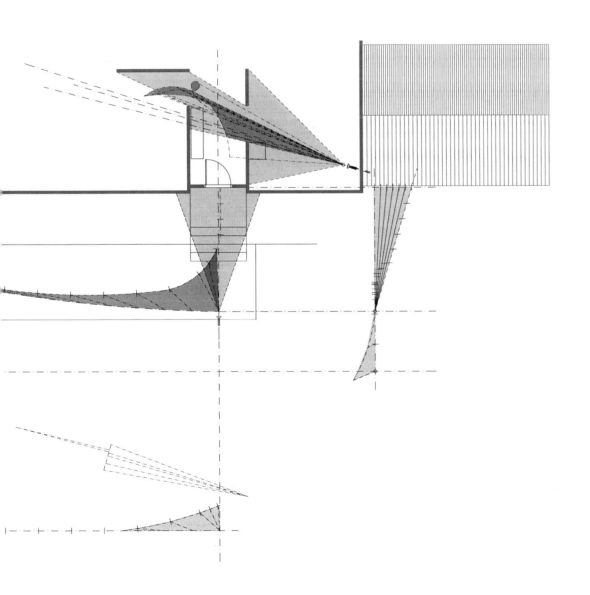

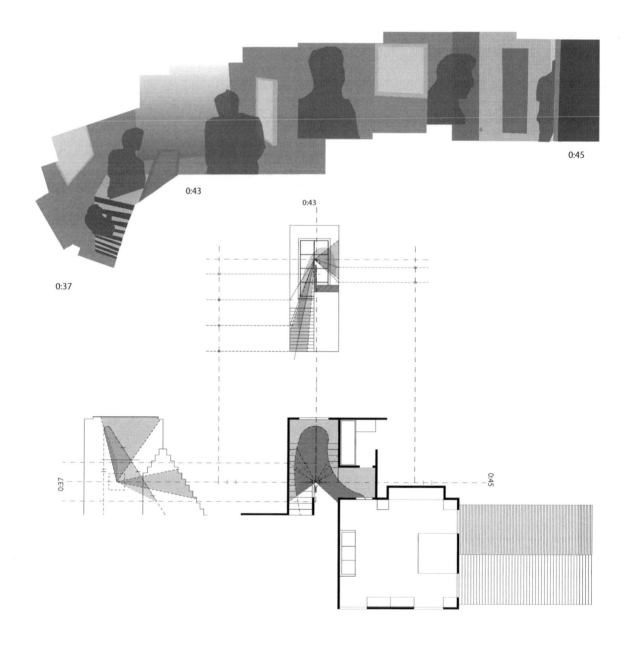

0:45

0:43

0:43

0:37

0:37

0:45

5_08 Shot 3 begins looking down at a stairway and holds as the husband appears at the bottom of the stairs. He runs up the stairs and the camera follows him spiralling up and to the right. He turns at the upstairs landing to camera level and the camera pans right in anticipation of his movement as he enters the vestibule to the right and holds as he pauses at the doorway to the bedroom.

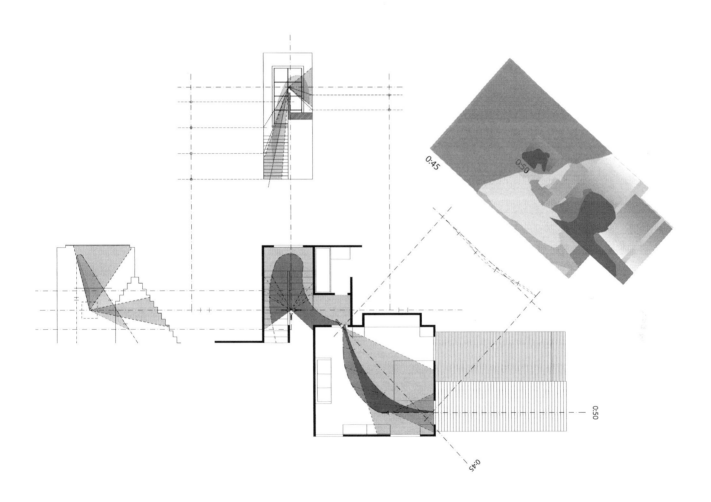

5_09 Shot 4 begins with an over-the-shoulder shot right behind the husband, looking into the bedroom with his head filling the screen and blocking the viewer from seeing into the room. He runs around the bed as the wife runs to the right and she exits the frame. The camera quickly follows him as he reaches an open window into the blinding light, in hot pursuit.

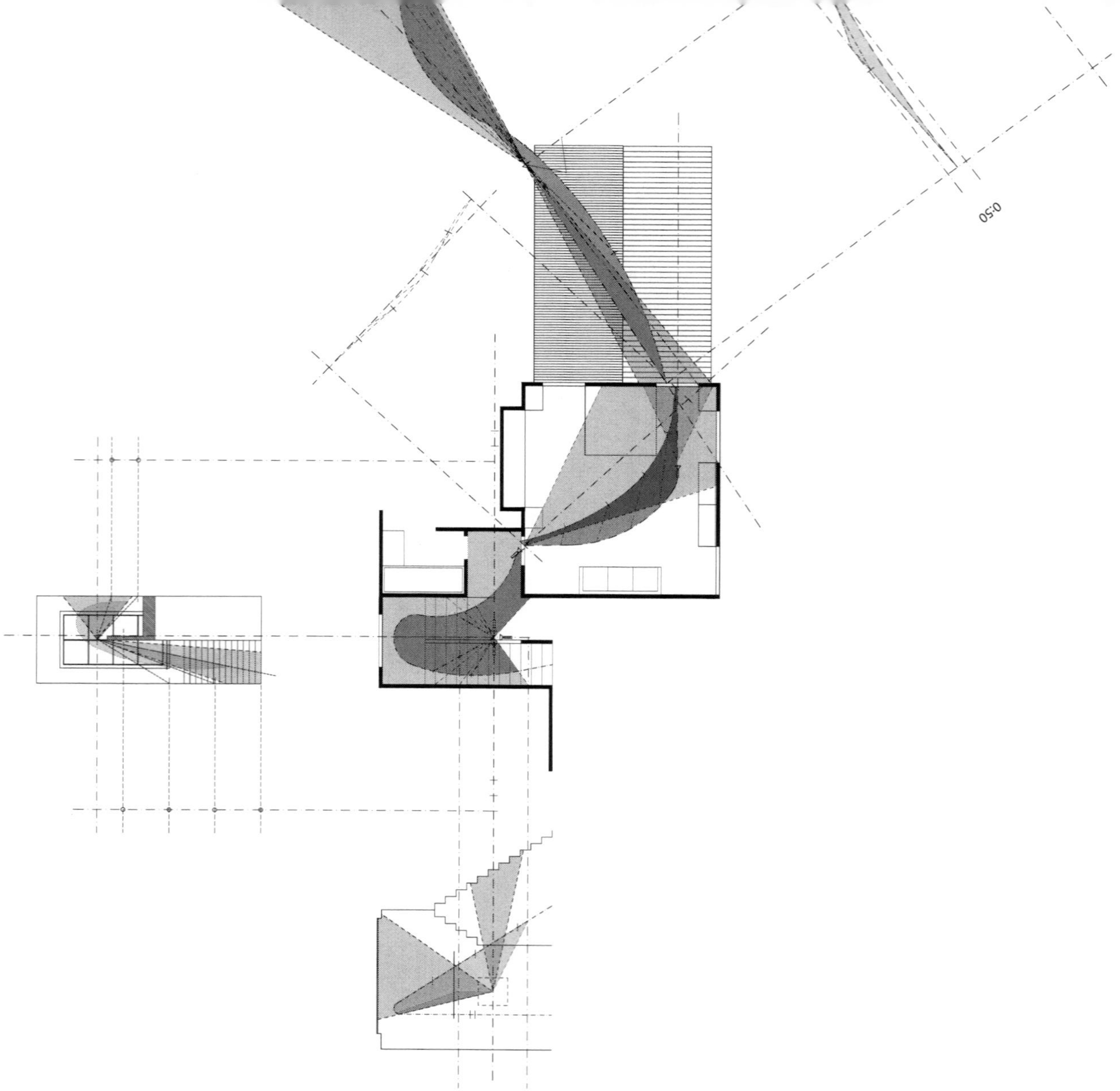

204

5_10 Shot 5 consists of a telephoto lens zooming out from outside the window, framing the husband looking out of the window. We first just see the leg of a man running away on the roof. The camera zooms back showing the length of the roof with the window rapidly diminished in size. We see a flash of body fragments of the running man up to chest height. The camera starts to pan left and down in anticipation of the man as he jumps down to the ground and runs off disappearing into the suburban streets. Shots 3, 4 and 5 are a rapid succession of **action images** following first the husband and then the interloper, escaping from the bedroom.

0.50

Let's return to the film clip: the unexpected discovery of his wife's infidelity breaks the husband's accustomed everyday reality. Her unfaithfulness is real, he has the evidence of his own eyes: a half-naked man fleeing over his rooftop, his dishevelled wife. Suddenly in shot 6, all his movements stop, he does not know how to react. Memory in the form of **automatic recognition,** which shapes habitual action, fails him. The action image of the fleeing man does not fit into a known pattern. He himself has just cheated on his wife. How to react? The cheating and cheated-on husband remains motionless at the window, his back to us (shot 6). The shot is held for an unbearably long time, framing just the back of his shoulder. The stillness and silence are excruciating. Slowly the husband straightens up from the window and finally glares at his wife. He has stopped acting and is perhaps beginning the process of **attentive recognition** in order to find a way to act in this new, unexpected situation.

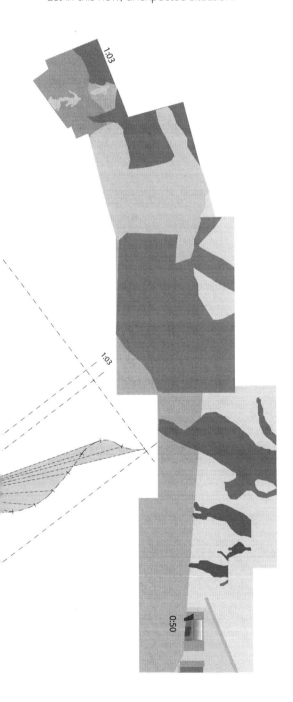

!:26

1:03

5_11 Shot 6 again begins over the husband's shoulder. The back of his bent head fills the frame in a gesture of heavy sadness. The camera holds for a very long time. He starts to slowly stand up straight and turn around to face the camera in a close-up – the **sensori-motor schema** is broken and now we are in a pure **optical image**. Shot 7 is a close-up zoom of the wife's face.

1:32   1:26

The assembling shifts to a close-up shot (shot 7) of the wife's face, smeared with streaked make-up, recalling the blurs of the husband's car windshield in the first shot of this clip – a similarity that perhaps suggests that neither husband nor wife sees their situation clearly. We then see the husband in an over-the-wife's-shoulder shot that frames him full figure as he stares at his wife, hands in pocket (shot 8). Their life together is not as transparent as they each believed. What is the reality of that moment? All is distorted and blurred. Nothing is as it once was.

By stopping the camera and his actors' physical movements, Cassavetes has created shots that are opimages. They mark the occurrence of 'something intolerable, unbearable', something 'too powerful that exceeds our sensori-motor capacities'.[19] In the shots that follow (shot 9, the opening half of shot 10), the husband wanders aimlessly in his own house, unable to get his bearings, perhaps looking for more evidence in order to reconstruct the events leading up to his wife's infidelity. He moves out of the bedroom, into the hall, then into the bathroom, looks around, picks up the pill bottle used in his wife's suicide attempt. He throws the empty bottle into a wastebasket without seeming to make any connection between the empty bottle, her dishevelled state, and the degree of her unhappiness. Abruptly, he moves out into the hall again, back toward the bedroom, and then down the stairs. **Attentive recognition** seems to fail him – he is unable to connect this new situation with his own memory of the events of his married life.

iVERPOOL JOHN MOORES UNIVERSITY
LEARNING SERVICES

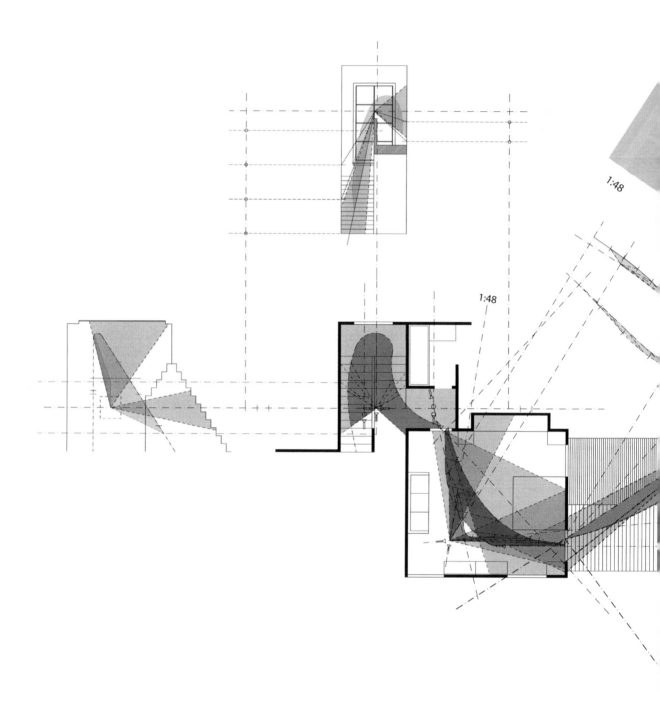

1:48

1:48

5_12 Shot 8 looks over the wife's shoulder framing the husband in full figure – hands in his pockets staring at her. He starts to move forward towards his wife. The camera tilts up to frame his upper torso and face. The camera holds and pans left as he slowly turns right and leaves the room.

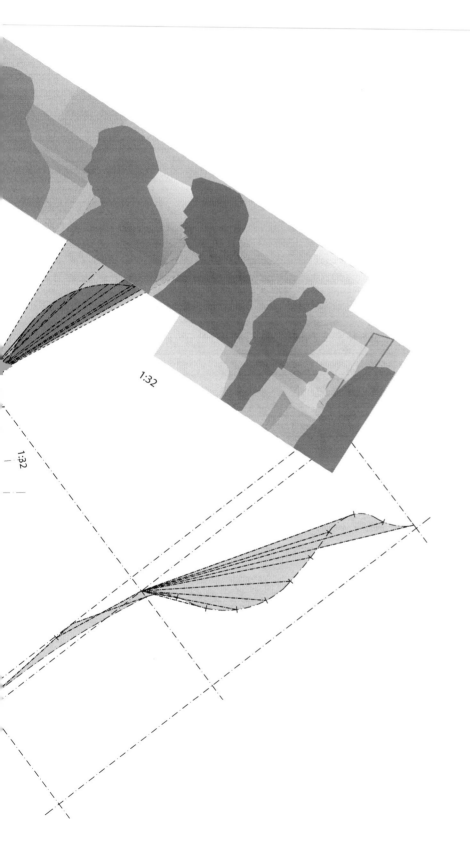

1:32

1:32

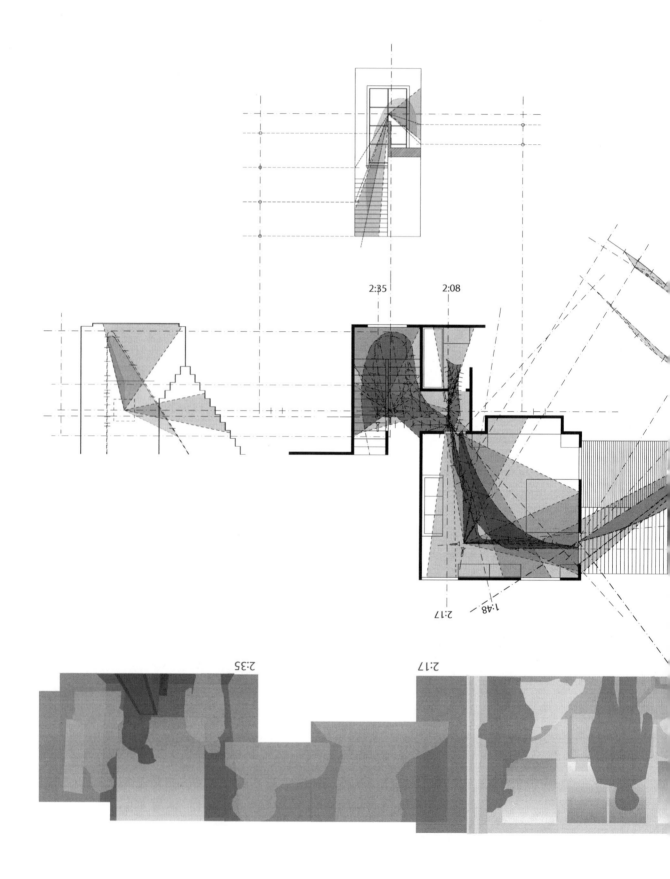

2:35

2:08

2:17

1:48

2:17

2:35

2:17

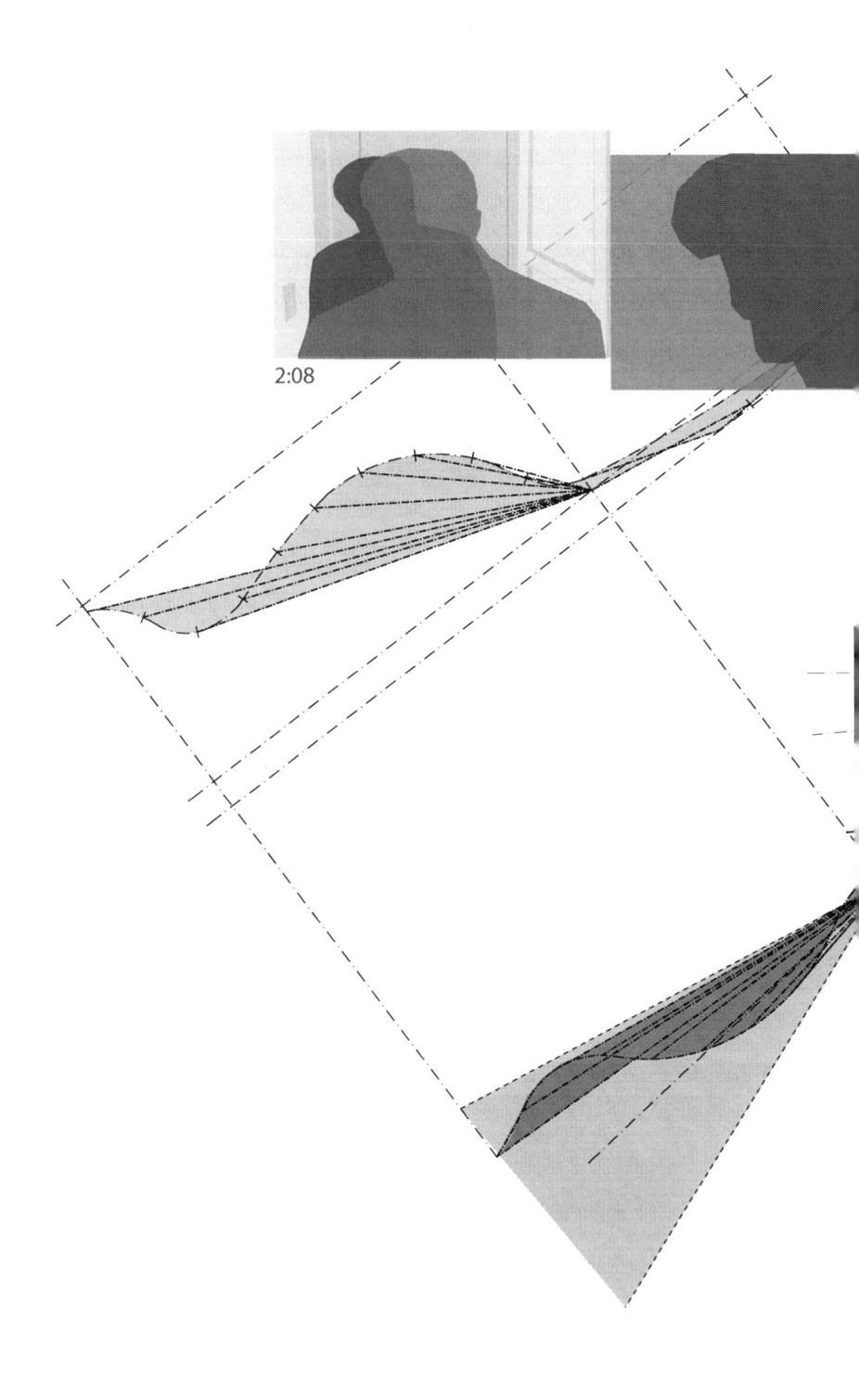

2:08

5_13 Shot 9 frames the bedroom from the vestibule threshold. The husband walks out towards the camera and the wife is seen behind him. The husband reaches the doorway and turns right, as the camera back pans left 90 degrees to follow him to the bathroom. The camera holds as he looks around, picks up a bottle of pills and throws it out. He walks out towards the camera. The camera spins 180 degrees as he passes it and walks back to the bedroom where she is leaning against the door. A shot over his shoulder contains the side of his head filling the frame as he points his finger at his wife. He moves forward still pointing his finger – the space of the frame is very crowded as the camera zooms into her as well. He turns to the right and the camera pans right 270 degrees, pirouetting around him as he turns to head down the stairs. The camera holds as he goes down to first the landing, and then it moves over the railing to tilt down to watch him go back down the stairs.

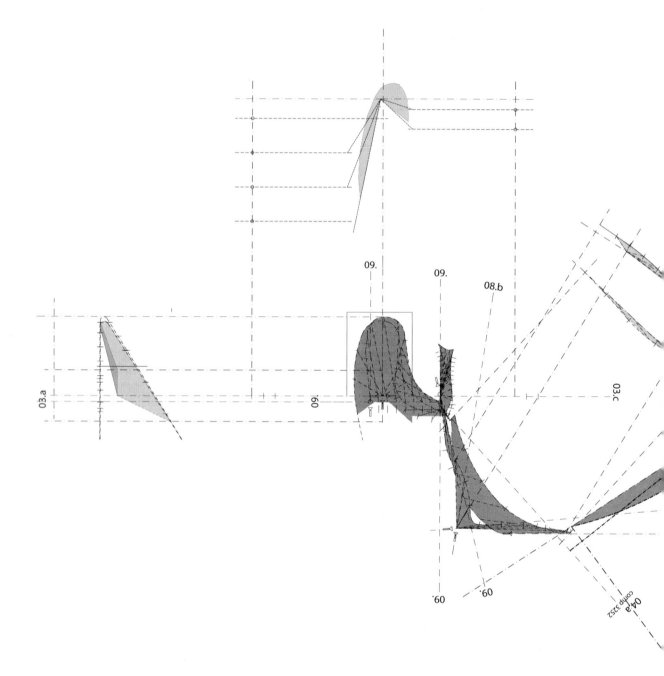

5_14 The space generated between the camera and the characters in shots 3 to 9.

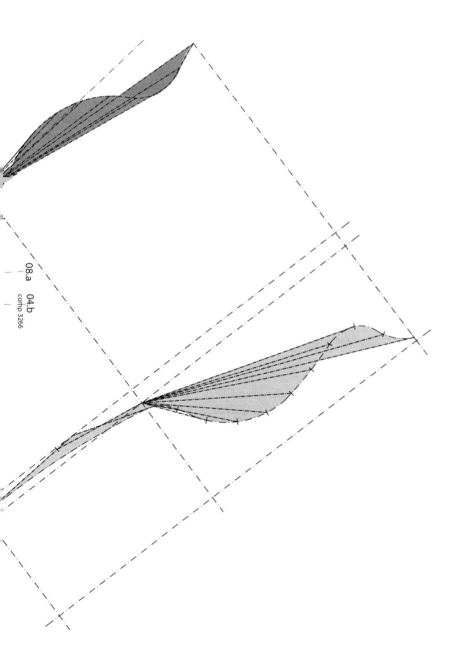

08.a

04.b
comp 3266

Caught in the disorientation of shot 9 and the opening half of shot 10, the husband works himself into a violent anger, which climaxes when he throws his wife against the wall at the top of the stairs, filmed as a spatially deep shot from the ground floor. She reacts by slapping him twice. In a series of rapid intercuts we see close-ups of both her face and his (the latter half of shot 10 through shot 16).

In shots 17 to 22, we witness the husband falling back into his habitual routine, unable to think about the rupture in his reality or react in new ways to it. He walks down the stairs again, enters the kitchen, takes a cigarette from a box on top of the refrigerator. He returns to the stairs and sits on them, lights a cigarette, throws the pack up to his wife who is now also sitting on the stairs, then tosses her his lighter. She is sitting in the same posture as her husband (shot 18, 4:50). She begins violently coughing, then he coughs. What follows is a sequence of movements in which husband and wife mirror each other. They have sunk back into habitual sensori-motor patterns that the realities of their simultaneous infidelities could not break. Their habitual movements underscore their futile attempts to break free and create something new.

At the end of the clip, we see the staircase where much of the action just described takes place. But now it is empty. Cassavetes holds the camera on the stairs, creating an optical image that lets us see starkly the stagnated emptiness of the couple's life together. Cassavetes creates an optical image in which he shows us that the husband and wife's habitual sensori-motor schema of relating to each other cannot cope with their reality. This opimage marks the occurrence of 'something intolerable, unbearable', something too powerful that exceeds their routine patterns of relating senses to actions.[20] We experience directly in this shot an answer to our opening question: "*What happens when the sensori-motor schema breaks down and perceptions no longer result in action?*" Numbness, bewilderment, resignation, an inability to think or act – these are some of the reactions we see in the *Faces* clip. Usually these kinds of feelings frighten us and we quickly avoid them and try to resume the normal narrative of our life. However, an opimage can form from the break in sensori-motor schema, which allows us to really see what is happening.

How can opimages be valuable in developing our architectural drawings or generating spaces? They can make accurate seeing of a problem in an expanded field of relations possible. Before we can begin thinking about a disturbing situation in meaningful ways, we need to see it as clearly as possible. What is wrong? Why the breakdown? No amount of thinking about a crisis in a time image will amount to anything if we don't truly understand the situation the crisis is immersed in – the situation that suspended our routine responses. We need to really look at the particulars of the breakdown and their relationships in a wider field in order to begin to comprehend what is going on.

For instance, we have seen in our three film examples the breakdown in social-spatial relations. Ozu's film is about the disruption of traditional domestic life by the new 'salaryman' professions. The commuting husband is quickly bored by the routine, misses an important ritual to honour his dead son, and carries on an affair with a co-worker. The couple is reconciled at the end of the film, but the last images are billowing smokestacks – symbols of the new industrial economy of post-war Japan. Godard's film, like many he made in the 1960s, is a critical take on the dominance of American culture and consumer values in post Second World War Europe. We witness the tyrannical rule of the vulgar Hollywood producer over the lives of the European characters within the ruins of a now dead classical European culture.

We have seen how Shigeru Ban confronted the challenges of creating a reclusive home and workplace in the heart of a dense contemporary metropolis. We also have explored how Curzio Malaparte created a completely original contemporary home from his own life experiences of Fascism, world war, and exile.

All three films also give us glimpses of today's ecological challenges. They depict modern modes of inhabiting and using land, especially in cities and suburbs. These interventions disturb in unprecedented ways our ecological relations as much as our social ones. Architecture can be a regenerative tool. But first we need to look closely at the ecological conditions our industrial habits have engendered to fully understand the possibilities for alternatives. Some of the disruptive conditions are shown in the films but not as opimages – the blighted areas in *Early Spring,* the intrusion of consumer values in the classical landscapes of *Contempt,* and the boredom of suburban life in *Faces.*

Before even beginning to think about how to address the cultural and ecological breakdowns in post-industrial Asian, European and US culture, we need to really look directly at the disruptions themselves, as we just did when we stared at the empty staircase in the last shot of *Faces.* We need to make opimages in our drawings, connecting them to an expanded field of relations through **attentive recognition**. Imagine showing your client, a community group, or a government agency a moving opimage created through attentive recognition of a qualitative change in relations that helps them grasp the challenges of contemporary society. No design solution forms part of an opimage. Something 'new' is called for but its exact nature is yet to be discovered. For now we need to look directly at our accustomed design procedures in which social relations and ecological systems are often not considered. Then, after making opimages that examine the breakdowns in these relations and systems, we can begin to put the spaces generated through the first four exercises into relations with them.

If we look at the durational reality of these social and ecological conditions today as opimages, then the possibility of drawing different worlds in the making begins to arise. The opimage can open the way to the **time Image** and the **crystalline regime,** where we can thoughtfully consider a problem that we have looked at carefully. In chapter 6 *Cybernetic Seeds,* we explore the time image and its relation to drawing an architecture responsive to the cultural and ecological conditions that have created a rupture in our accustomed responses.

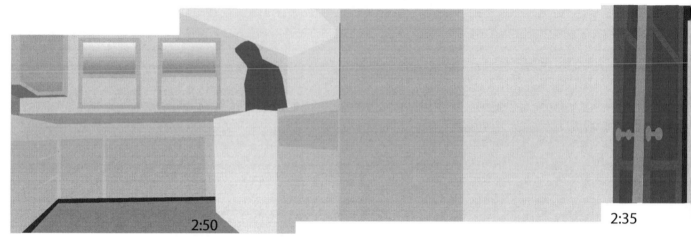

3:20

2:50

2:35

5_15 Shot 10 consists of a long shot framing the stairway from below. The husband slowly walks down and turns to his right, frame left into another off-screen space. The camera holds on the empty frame for a moment and then pans left framing a low angle shot of the kitchen. He enters the frame from the right. The camera holds as he pauses. The camera pans right as he disappears off screen to the right and reappears in the same frame of the stairway from below. He runs up the stairway and disappears off screen at the top of the stairs to the right. We see the wife thrown into the top of the frame on the stair landing, pushed by her husband. She leans against the wall as they argue at the top of the stairs.

3:34

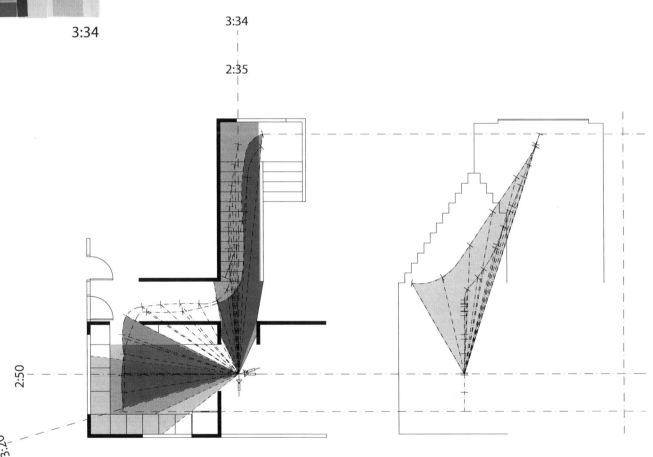

3:34

2:35

2:50

3:20

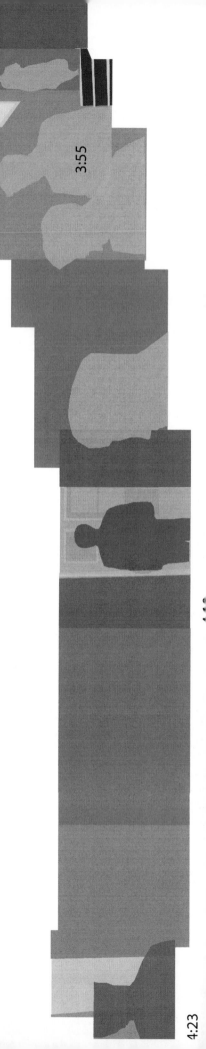

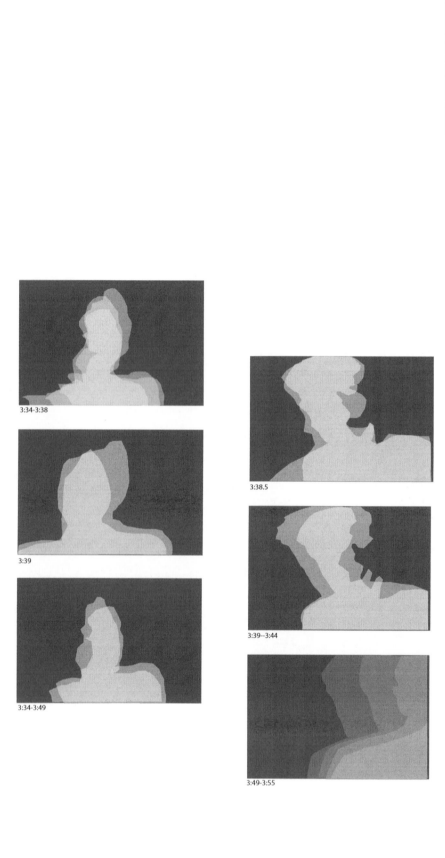

3:34-3:38

3:39

3:34-3:49

3:38.5

3:39–3:44

3:49-3:55

5_16 Shots 11, 12, 13, 14, 15, and 16 jump back and forth between close-ups of the couple as she slaps him twice in the face. He stares at her unflinching and finally walks out of the frame.

3:55

4:23

5_17 Shot 17 begins looking up from under the top flight of the stair, a chandelier dangles from the top of the frame. The husband slowly walks downstairs. The camera is still as he slowly walks down, hands in pockets. The camera pans left as he passes, following him as he turns right – with his back to the camera – walking down the hallway to the kitchen. The camera remains still as he slowly walks down the hallway and turns left into the kitchen off frame left. The camera slowly pans along the wall to the left. We see the wallpaper design like an animation with a crow pattern enlarging and disappearing off frame. The camera pauses at the threshold to the kitchen as he appears in the frame and grabs a box of cigarettes. The camera is still as he takes a cigarette out, puts it in his mouth and moves towards the threshold. The shot cuts as he seems to walk straight into the camera frame.

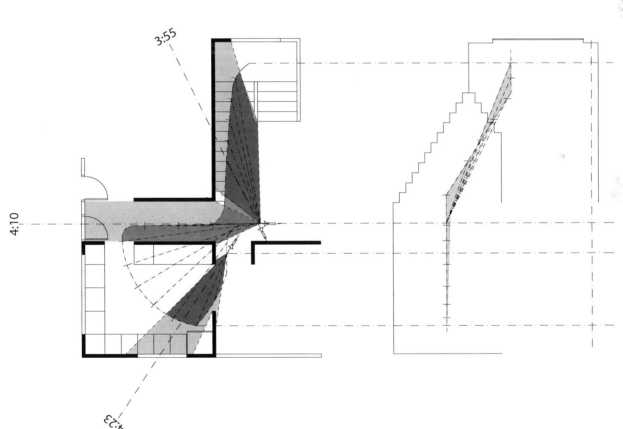

3:55

4:10

4:23

4:23-5:17

5:17

4:23

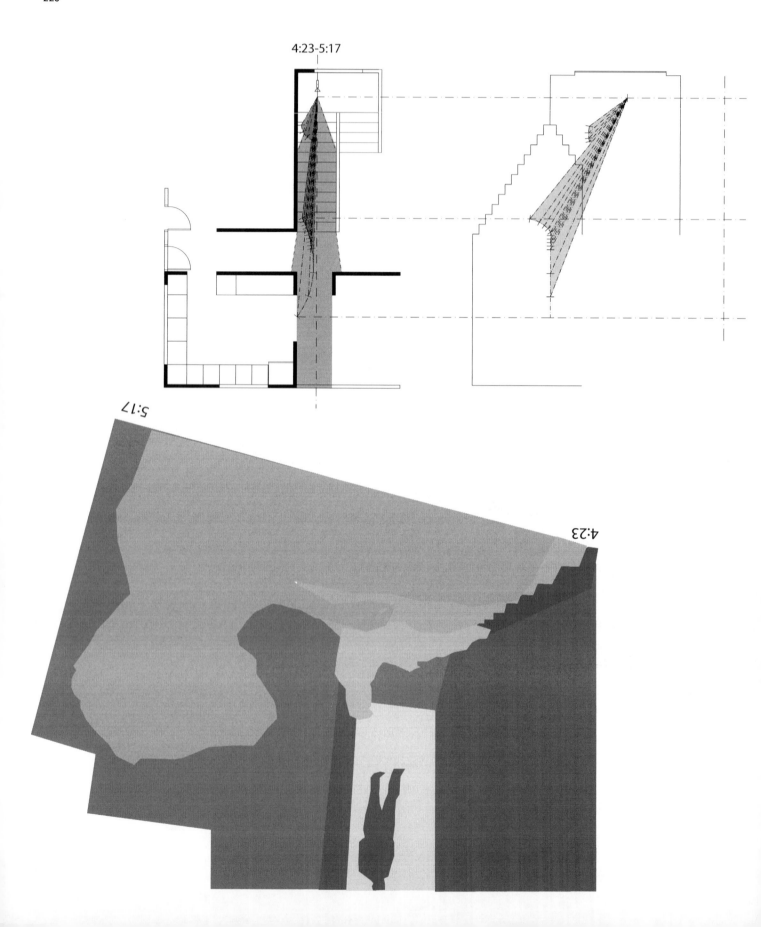

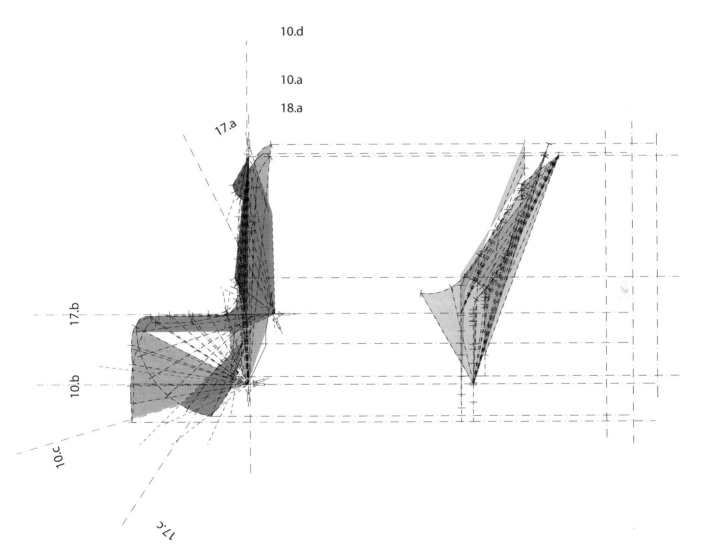

5_18 Shot 18 looks down the stairs from the landing. The wife is sitting at the top of the stairs in the foreground. Her husband is walking from the kitchen towards the stairs in the deep background. He sits on the bottom stair and throws a pack of cigarettes up to her. She reaches down to get a cigarette. She sits back up and leans against the same wall mirroring his posture. He throws up a lighter. She lights a cigarette and throws the lighter back down. She violently heaves with a fit of coughing.

5_20 Shots 10, 11 and 12 circuit around the constricted space of the stairway and kitchen. The expansive space generated from shots 3 to 9 (illus 5_15) has been compressed to the stairway at the core of the house.

5:17-5:27   5:32-5:42

5:27-5:42   5:42-5:45

5_20 Shot 19, the camera is on the floor looking up at the husband sitting on the bottom stair, with a short wall in the foreground. He is smoking, his hands and the smoke from his cigarette are the only movement in the shot. He coughs as well. Shot 20 is from the stairs looking up at the wife still coughing. Shot 21 he continues smoking and turns to look up at his wife. Shot 22 she has stopped coughing – her head is now in her hands.

5:45-7:16

5_21 Shot 23, the final shot, the camera looks up the stairs. The husband turns around and leans against the opposite wall. The wife does the same. He gets up, walks up the stairs stepping over her and disappears to the right at the top of the landing. She gets up, walks up the stairs and disappears to the right at the top of the landing. He crosses her path at the landing, then slowly walks down the stairs and sits down again. She appears at the top of the stairs, walks down and stops as his legs are blocking her way. He lowers his legs to let her pass. She walks straight into the camera frame and turns right, frame left, into the kitchen as he walks back upstairs. He disappears to the right at the top of the landing. The camera holds on the empty staircase.

224 Cassavetes' *Faces* has helped us demonstrate what assemblage, broken sensori-motor schema and optical images are. In the next chapter, we explore the relationship between assemblage and the time image in the generation of space.

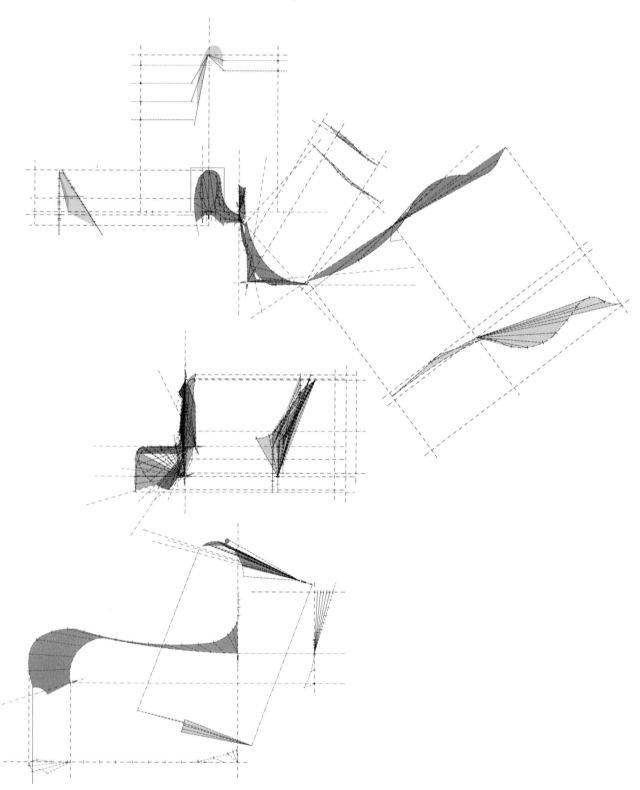

5_22 An **assemblage** of the spaces generated in all 23 shots of this sequence. The expansive space of the action image from car to roof top that opened the scene collapses to the singular affect image of the stairway as an any-space-whatever.

1 Bogue, *Deleuze on Cinema,* p 107.

2 D.N. Rodowick, *Gilles Deleuze's Time Machine,* Duke University Press (London), 1997, p 51.

3 D.N. Rodowick, *Gilles Deleuze's Time Machine,* p 81.

4 Bogue, *Deleuze on Cinema,* p 112.

5 Bergson, *Matter and Memory,* Zone Books (New York), 1988, p 104.

6 Bergson, *Matter and Memory,* p 105.

7 Bogue, pp 113, 112, 119.

8 *http://www.ark.fi/ark4_98/casa_ malaparte_e.html*

9 *http://www.ark.fi/ark4_98/casa_ malaparte_e.html*

10 Talamona, Marida, *Casa Malaparte,* trans Vittoria di Palma, Princeton Architectural Press (Princeton), 1996, pp 61–3.

11 Bogue, *Deleuze on Cinema,* p 136.

12 Bogue, *Deleuze on Cinema,* p 136.

13 Bogue, *Deleuze on Cinema,* p 136.

14 Bogue, *Deleuze on Cinema,* p 109.

15 Bogue, *Deleuze on Cinema,* pp 110, 111, 110.

16 Rodowick, *Gilles Deleuze's Time Machine,* p 80.

17 Rodowick, *Gilles Deleuze's Time Machine,* p 81.

18 Bogue, *Deleuze on Cinema,* p 107.

19 Bogue, *Deleuze on Cinema,* p 110.

20 Bogue, *Deleuze on Cinema,* p 110.

CHAPTER 6

CYBERNETIC SEEDS

How can we generate space as seeds of different worlds in the making?

In the previous chapter we discussed the emergence of the **opimage** when our **sensori-motor** reflexes break down and perceptions no longer result in action. Such a breakdown can lead to transformation because a qualitative movement within the open whole has occurred rather than a quantifiable movement across space. As a result, the **time image** can form in **crystalline states**. Breaks in the sensori-motor schema thus create an opportunity via the time image for new thoughts to develop because the boundaries of linear thinking dissolve. In this section of the book, we will explore how the time image can also lead to an architecture of cybernetic seeds for new social and ecological relations.

Words in bold are Keywords found on pages 260-265

The closing shot of Cassavetes' *Faces* - a deserted staircase - introduced us to the opimage that can arise when we realise that we no longer know how to act. The camera holds longer than we expect. We are forced to face the bleakness of the conflicted couple's lives. We just witnessed their aimless wandering around their home for the last five minutes of the film. Memory in the form of automatic recognition fails them. A question hangs in the air: can they face and act on the knowledge of their unhappiness? Memory in the form of **attentive recognition** also deserts them – they cannot confront creatively their mutual sensori-motor collapse. Like the husband's car windshield and the wife's make-up smeared face, what to do next is a blur. They abandon the stairway, the site of their inability to act, and resume their habitual, every-day routine. Cassavetes leaves us staring at an optical image that, in addition to seeing, we read.

When we are stuck in the inaction visualised by optical images is our only recourse a return to ineffective routines? Cassavetes doesn't answer this question in *Faces*. He abandons us in a state of pure seeing: the held image on the vacant stairs. The **affect image** of the empty-stairs – an **any-space-whatever** – has imperceptively become a pure optical image. We know from previous opimages in *Faces* that they don't lead to **movement images**. The connection between affect and action is severed. Instead, optical images emerge that can be read, but are not acted on, which opens up the possibility of time images arising.

To understand the emergence of the time image from a breakdown in the sensori-motor reflexes, let's see if you can think of a particularly dramatic situation in which your habitual pattern of sensing and acting broke down, leaving you suspended. Examples of changes within sensori-motor systems examined previously in this book may help you remember such a condition. In *Losing Perspective* we discussed architects' sensori-motor reactions when mechanical drawing tools replaced electronic ones. At first, people brought the **know-how** of the mechanical architect to the new electronic computer. This drafting board know-how was transferred as virtual drafting tools to computers without recognising that the computer was completely different from the drafting table. Eventually, some architects realised that when drawing left the drafting table, the know-how of architecture needed to change. They realised a rethinking of their skills was called for because their senses were responding to an entirely different tool context. Instead of continuing to automatically repeat the traditional production acts of architecture, they began to experiment with attentive recognition of this new electronic tool.

Exercise 1 in *Framing* - waking up and changing our routine through a recording process of attentive recognition – also marked a pause and then a shift in normal habits. In the pause-**interval**, we experienced **matter-flux** in order to begin understanding how we become **living images** when we frame sets of information as a basis for making perception, affect and action movement images. In *Immobile Cuts*, we used the five aspects of framing the three primary movement images as ways to construct **immobile cuts** through architecture as matter-flux - as pauses or **arrested images** within the open whole. In *Shooting*, we suspended the normal practice of seeing social situations as **privileged poses** and began shooting different kinds of movement images as **any-instant-whatever**. We also expanded our range of movement images and observed impulse, reflection, and relation images. In *Mobile Sections* we used the techniques of moving drawings to examine how we generate space in relation to 'what appears,' – a startling break from our accustomed habits of drawing conventional space. Finally, in *Assembling* we re-examined the suspension of our normal routine to explore how memory plays out in the gaps between sensing and acting. This suspension, by interrupting automatic sensing and acting, deepens our relation to the present and influences how we organise our moving drawings and the new kinds of spaces we generate. So, in the context of learning *Cinemetrics*, there have been repeated occasions to suspend habitual patterns in the ways we experience the world, in the ways we draw, and in the ways we generate space.

Now we will examine how the new ways of drawing and the new spaces we generate can be cybernetic seeds of new worlds in the making – by establishing within our process of drawing social and ecological feedbacks and circuits in time.

6_01 Site plan of the Raybould House showing the original salt-box house, barn, swimming pool and creek, as well as the proposed addition and structures designed for the garden.

The reason for suspending our normal habits as part of learning *Cinemetrics* is to develop new practices responsive not only to the changes in architectural **know-how** but also its **know-about**. Recognising these personal breaks supports your making design **assemblages** engaging the expanding field of relations affecting architecture. The unexpected processes provoking our personal sensori-motor reflexes or those of the film characters in *Early Spring, Contempt* and *Faces* are not the only disturbances currently erupting more and more frequently. Such disruptions are becoming common culturally and ecologically as we experience more and more bewildering events for which we have no frame of reference, such as the growing frequency of severe storms and sudden temperature extremes of climate change, environmental degradation, new diseases, religious and class tensions and aggressions. No wonder we often find ourselves unable to react, let alone know how these processes affect architecture.

Current ecological and cultural upheavals indicate we are witnessing not just a dramatic shift in our tools but also in our relationships to the world around us. We no longer look forward solely to the "goods" of industrialisation but anxiously grapple with its run-away feedbacks – the "bads". These changes, which some label the Second Modernity[1], are breaking our habitual sensori-motor patterns personally and professionally. They necessitate rethinking everything from social and ecological relations to building types and interior environmental systems. Being aware of breaks within our own experiences can guide us when we address the field of architectural concerns that is expanding in response to personal, cultural, and ecological disturbances - the know-about of architecture. The breaks help us understand how to generate drawings and spaces as cybernetic seeds that emotionally, factually and critically can guide clients and the general public to recognize cultural and ecological ruptures that impact not just architecture but also their lives.

6_02 Rendered view of the house and addition designed as an organic hybrid derived from the topologies of the roof of the original house and the contours of the sloping site, yet maintaining its own formal identity.

How? When the regulating idea that informs our **assemblage** of images emerges in part from our own experiences of the dramatic changes in the field of relations in which architecture participates, then our moving drawings and generated spaces are both more immediate. The challenge ahead is to communicate and connect our own autopoietic knowledge to the dynamics of the larger social and ecological processes that involve architecture through all its phases: imaging, material extraction and transport, construction, use, maintenance, retrofitting, adapting and recycling. Assembling time images of our generated spaces is a way to make that connection by creating scenarios of different possibilities.

So that's why we are asking you to be attentive of vivid suspensions of your sensori-motor reflexes beyond the examples in this book. Your experience and memory serve as references in drawing the architecture as cybernetic seeds for new worlds in the making.

The Raybould House

Exercise 6.1: *Recall a building or landscape that shocked you, causing a break in your sensori-motor reflexes. Can you draw its effect on you, paying particular attention to depicting the* **opimage** *that resulted from this* **affect image***?*

It looks like it's going to eat the house.

This has certain integrity to its globbiness.

So, we're discussing aesthetics. What makes a beautiful house?

I don't see why they should do all these shapes.

I would like to see nice shapes.

It raises all kinds of issues of whether or not it's beautiful.

It's pretending the earth is warping up to these forms, but in the end it's going to be a big aluminum thing parked on some grass.

But it has a client. It has a budget.

It's …a bit romantic about technology.

Why is this an inevitable challenge to domesticity?

It's actually a conventional house.[4]

These are not imagined words. They are comments from an awards jury for the magazine *Architecture*. This expert panel could not get their heads around, let alone agree about, what they were looking at: the addition to the Raybould House by architects Sulan Kolatan and William MacDonald (KolMac Studio 1998–99), this chapter's architectural example.

Exercise 6.2: *Assemble images and words about the selected building, space or event that broke your sensor-motor routine. Recognise that the words and images of the selected building are not the "truth" about its architecture. They are a fiction*

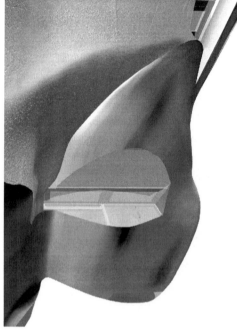

6_03 Site plan and four views looking at the front, back and side of the Raybould House. Starting at the top view and moving counter clockwise, view a is of a deck at the junction of the original house and the addition. View b is located at the lower level of the house addition. View c is looking at the side of the addition as it seems to flow down the slope towards the creek. View d is of the prow-like back of the house showing the detail of how standard operating doors and windows were designed as inverted bay windows to accommodate the geometrical difference between the shell of the house and standard window and door frames.

*or '**fabulation**' based on the limits of two-dimensional imagery as well as the limits of language. Here is a place to keep remembering that architecture is more than meets the eye! Keep relating your experience to what your body knows, using the techniques of **attentive recognition** and **sheets of the past** and **peaks of the present**. Now make a **time image** of your **assemblage**, which problemitises description, narration, interpretation, and even time itself.*

A building that physically surprises us has a very different impact if we only see it reproduced. One of the problems in understanding the Raybould House, and most examples of reproduced architecture, is that we, just like the *Architecture* design jury, often rely solely on pictures. We all know what we see in reproduction is not the whole story of a building even when it has not been built. Yet we often expect drawings to simulate what the actual physical building will be like! Their expectations from the simulations are not being met.

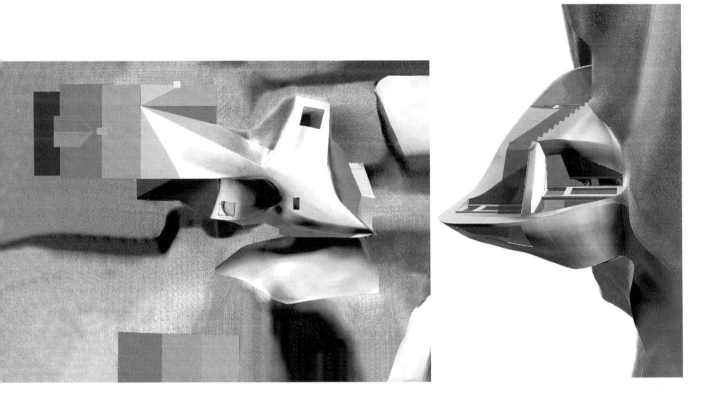

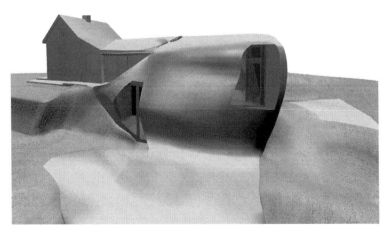

234   Architecture involves more than what meets the eyes. Our body experiences of it engage us through all our five exteroceptive senses, the multiple **proprioceptive** ones, and our memories. If we take the time to pause and pay attention to our body experiences of the world around us, as we did when we woke up, these experiences can expand what we know about our world, which is intricately woven into how we process **autopoietically** what we sense. Our knowing is multi-sensorial. When we pause to frame disruptive experiences in opimages, we consciously expand our world by looking directly at what is. Our body incorporates the world, creating patterns of responses that can guide us in unknown territory if we are attentive. These patterns can help us to meet the 'new' in reproduction and actuality. They can also help create moving drawings as seeds of different worlds in the making.

Below are questions and observations to help you think about the time images of powerful spaces you have experienced and generated as well as about the images of the Raybould House. Use these as a basis for drawing the moving time image for this exercise.

> *Why did the dramatic building stop your normal sensor-motor reflexes? Perhaps, it was the light that attracted you? No, it was the unfamiliar geometries. Wait, not the geometries, it was the materials – their strange colours and shapes. Wasn't that it? The feelings you had were so unexpected that now the details of the situation become unclear.*

> *As you describe your experience, the narrative of that day, not just the details, gets confusing. How can you feel exhilarated and frightened at the same time? What was the order of time that morning anyway? Now you are no longer thinking about what was real on that day and what was imaginary, but what is true and what is false. True and false have become 'undecidable.' You realise what you have been calling 'the past is not necessarily true.'* [5]

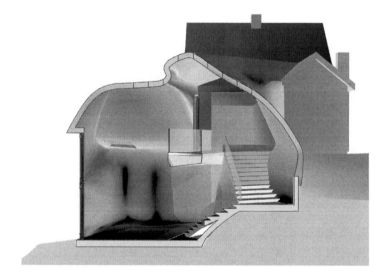

This confusion starts a questioning of time itself. How can you describe the event to anyone if the sequence of narration is unclear?... Whatever... you just keep narrating the incident even if the sequence of details is wrong or, miraculously —who knows— the description of the details might be right. The story becomes more compelling as more, possibly false, images join with the initial ones. You are enjoying the feeling of being a storyteller, of choosing between incongruous truths, creating different worlds that could not possibly co-exist. Storytelling is making the world a **fable**. And it has started you thinking about time itself. [6]

As you keep redrawing the story of being in a startling new space, those vague images of dissatisfaction with your future plans become more insistent. How to interpret the plans? They seem so conventional now that you relate them to the strange building. Are the plans merely a fulfillment of some long-ago decision, based on what now seems like a problematic judgment? Are your evaluations of the strange computer generated building also only habitual automatic reactions to what you don't understand – to the new?

Hey! Why not start **assembling** your thoughts in new combinations. Let the **intervals** between cuts get more and more non-linear by framing vastly different sets of seemingly unrelated information. After all, your sensori-motor system has broken done. You are no longer following a habitual routine. You are pausing and reconsidering. Why not take this opportunity to playfully imagine as you did when you created the secret shelter under the kitchen table? Why not draw freely assemblages of alternate worlds in the making? What happens if you assemble ecological and cultural research as part of the expanded field of different worlds in the making? You are now ready to make the time image for Exercise 6.2

6_04 Longitudinal and latitudinal sections through the house showing how the interior steps down the slope and a bridge is constructed between the original house and the master bedroom.

236　Let's look closely at the time image you have drawn. It metaphorically is a multifaceted **crystal**. It shows incongruent thoughts so different from each other they could not possibly co-exist, and yet they do! In the crystalline regime, which 'emerges out of the social, historical, and cultural context of postwar reconstruction,' [7] they co-exist. You have created something 'new'. It is based on looking carefully at 'what is' – at your opimage – and then thinking about what you have 'read' in that image, doing research provoked by that reading, and finally letting your thoughts free associate. For you, the very notion of what is true in our everyday commonsense world is in crisis; each image or statement you make is or could be true.　But suddenly, amidst uncertainty, a feeling of exhilaration arises. This process rendered your thoughts open-ended. In the interval between assembling **shots**, you have become free of past habits of thinking because your sensori-motor system has collapsed.[8] A crystallized time image, composed of parallel worlds in the making, emerged in the gap.

'The time-image wants to augment our powers of thought through assisting our knowledge of those powers.' Thought is a becoming. In the preceding exercise, you kept thought moving, not to a predetermined end, but to the new and unforeseen. You created moving drawings connected by nonlinear cuts involving all sorts of unpredictable scenarios about alternative worlds in the making.[9] Now, based on all these assemblages, you can decide which world to realise. You can re-assemble images in unconventional ways, opening up the possibility of participating creatively in your own and architecture's evolution.

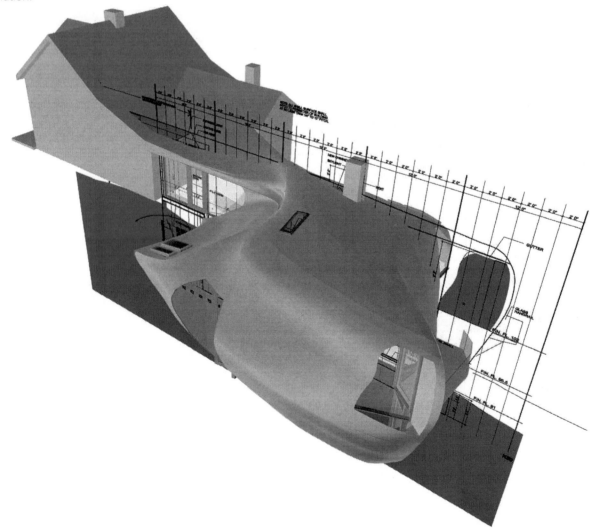

6_05 and 6_06 Views of the computer model of the house and the construction documents generated at critical sections through the shell of the house addition.

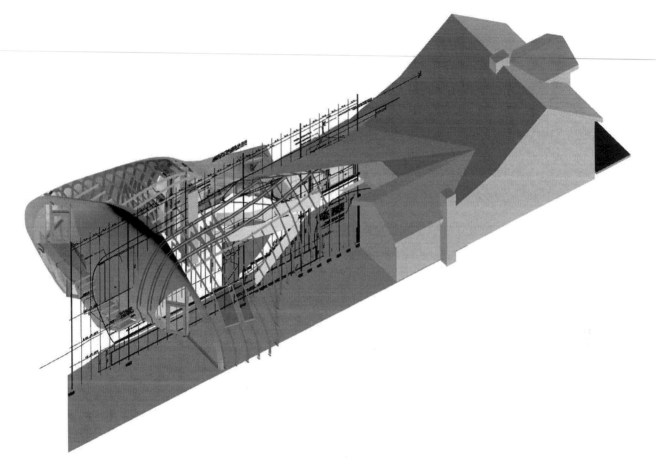

The Cybernetic Regime

Architectural drawing, as well as life, isn't only about thinking. When construction is the objective (illus 6_07–6_16), open-ended drawing of the time image eventually must feed back to an affect image that, instead of stopping action, can lead to building. This is a **cybernetic** process that unfolds in a manner similar to this:

Undergoing something that disturbs our routine – perhaps reading this book – can leave us suspended, unable to act. It can result in our staring at an opimage and thinking about a time image, both of which have emerged autopoietically from our experiences. It can leave us caught in a many-surfaced crystal. But even suspension in a gap between an affect image and an action image involves sensations, if only numbness from the shock. These sensations range from the paralysis of inaction through the excitement of thinking.

By being in **attentive recognition**, we realise that our body is always present while thinking. If we look at our own experiences, we also see that open-ended thinking in the time image feeds back cybernetically into what we do and how we sense and draw. The loop from initial action-stopping affect image to a time image of seeing, hearing, describing, narrating, and interpreting creates new emotions that feedback to the original affect images, changing them. The altered affect images differ from those that stopped us because they result from having thought about our experiences. They can help free us from our confusion and lead to action images in skeleton or respiration spaces.

Let's unpack the last paragraph to be sure the cybernetic dynamic is clear, as this process is operative in drawing and space generation as well. As feelings, spurred by thinking, loop back to the initial affect image that stopped action, they impact that

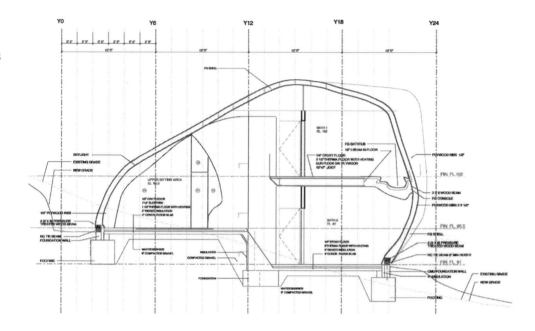

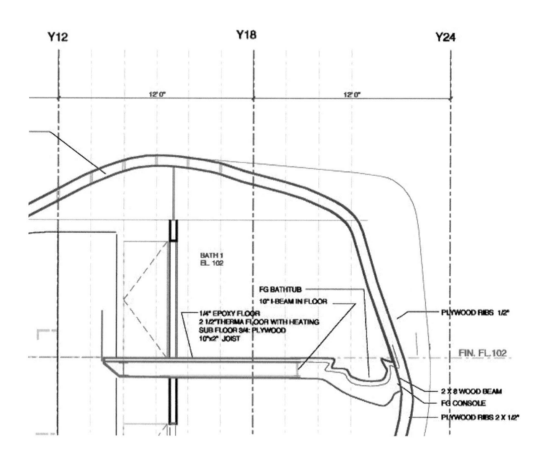

6_07 Construction document and detail showing how the floor and bath are constructed integrally with the shell of the house. On a windy day the water in the bath will respond to the swaying of the shell of the house.

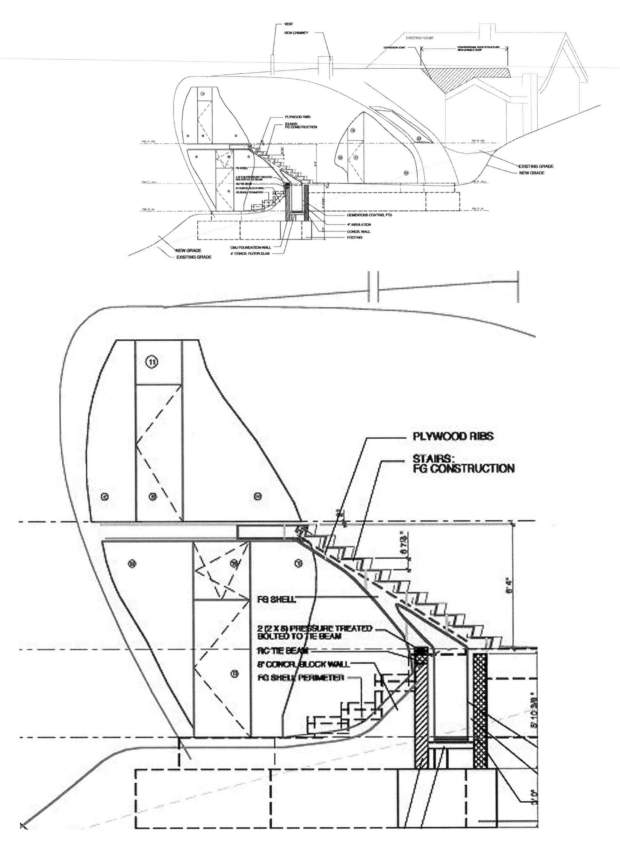

6_08 Angled elevation of the house showing operable windows and doors in relation to the house. The shell of the house is secured on a concrete foundation — the structural problem was not gravity, but counteracting the tendency of the form to levitate in strong winds.

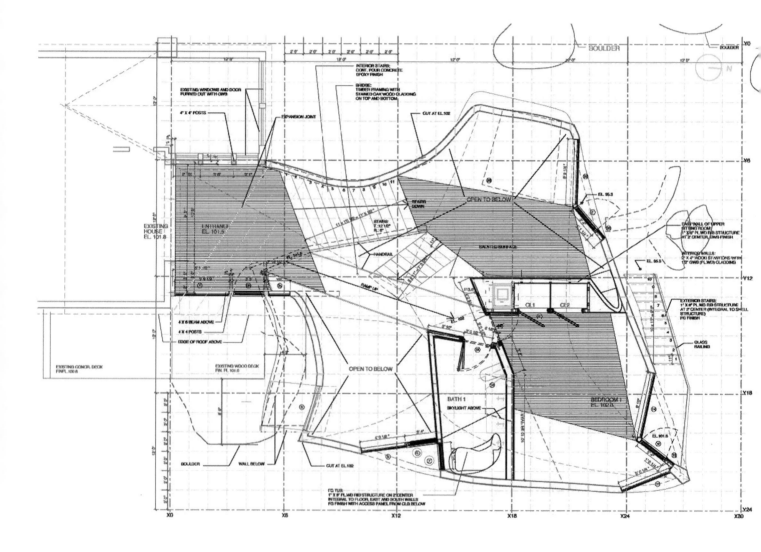

6_09 Upper level of the house showing the stair down to the living area, which serves as a piano performance space, and the bridge to the master bedroom.

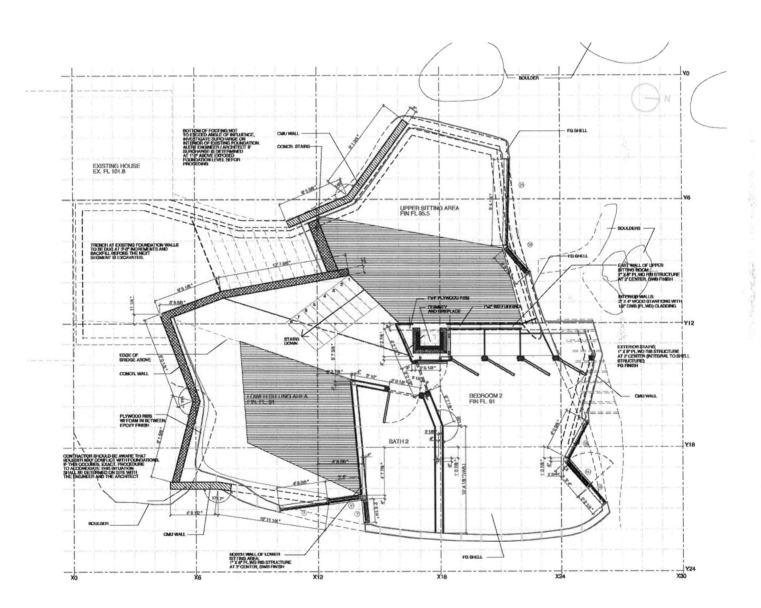

6_10 Lower level of the house showing the living area and the second bedroom.

242 image cybernetically. In other words, some features of the output – the original affect image – return to us in transformed ways that make a difference, changing us. As we examine our experiences, we can see that our sensations as well as impulses, actions, reflections and relations are actually caught up in multiple cybernetic relationships. Even though some images may be connected in what appears a linear manner, they eventually form a cybernetic circuit. These cybernetic relationships reveal alternate routes of becoming conscious, being a sign, making images, and drawing the spaces we generated in *Mobile Sections*. The resulting assemblages benefit from our thinking in the time image if we don't lose touch with their relation autopoietically to our body. They make possible our development of a regulating idea that permeates our moving drawings, enabling them to communicate, not a simulated reality, but a concept. *Cinemetric* drawing is a process, not of abstract replication, but of embodied thinking.relationships reveal alternate routes of becoming conscious, being a sign, making images, and drawing spaces that we generated in *Mobile Sections*. These assemblages benefit from our thinking in the time image if we don't lose touch with their relation autopoietically to our body. They make possible our development of a regulating idea that permeates our moving drawings, enabling them to communicate, not a simulated reality, but a concept. *Cinemetric* drawing is a process, not of abstract replication, but of embodied thinking.

The **fabulation** we explored in exercise 6.1 resulted in a multfaceted time image. The thinking you then did in the time image by assembling increasingly disjunctive image sequences fed back into your original shocked affect image that suspended action. The thinking changed the affect image. It opened up the possibility of a response. Understanding this cybernetic process is a fundamental feature of the cybernetic-organic architect in the process of making *Cinemetric* moving drawings. But, regardless of whether you are working on or off the computer, **attentive recognition** of your cybernetic processes can support your participating creatively in your own and architecture's evolution.

Let's use the Raybould House to exemplify this cybernetic process. As discussed in *Framing* and *Immobile Cuts*, the images we **frame** in everyday life, film and architecture are composed from the three basic categories of ' "direct appearances" as they pop into the mind'. [10] We make images as we scrutinise what appears, composing them within or across the three fundamental categories that Peirce described as **firstness, secondness**, and **thirdness**. When we scrutinise qualities of direct appearances, such as colour, texture, smell, we are in firstness. If we frame an image in this state, it is an affect image. When we scrutinise facts – the specifics of the physical world – we are in secondness. If we make an image when we are in secondness, the image is either a small form or a large form action image. When we scrutinise patterns and context, observing the whole, laws or theories, we move to thirdness, framing a relation image. We also discussed how the impulse image forms between an affect and an action image and reflection images form between action and relational images.

The Raybould House can illustrate these three basic categories of what appears so the above discussion is clear. Before doing Exercise 6:3, read again the comments of the architectural awards jurists. Are there any that spontaneously describe the KolMac addition? Spontaneous sensing involves awareness but with 'no definite linkage to an … object.' [11] This is the state of firstness - feeling while experiencing qualities without yet connecting specifically to the house itself. In this state, we are totally immersed in the present. We are senso-architects who draw architectural affect images in any-space-whatever. Many architectural drawings noted on scraps of paper are made in firstness. Let's use the three basic categories of 'direct experiences' in the next exercise to understand an architecture that seems strange to you. (You benefit from repeating this as well as all the exercises. Repeated practice is the basis of forming new sensori-motor responses.)

Exercise 6.3: In analysing a strange, uncanny or unfathomable space, such as the Raybould House, start at the most basic level, which is organising your analysis according to the three basic categories of qualities, facts and relations discussed above and in chapter 1 Framing. Frame the images of the house you researched as close-up **iconic** affect images in which the colour, texture, quality or shape of the form dominates rather than any identifiable normative feature. Gather all the factual or indexical information you found about the building, making **indexical** action images. And finally interrelate the various iconic qualities of the building's affect images with the building's indexes, developing a pattern about the architecture in a **symbolic** relation *image. Be sure the space you generate responds to specifics of construction, use, and larger socio-ecological forces, as well as historical memories of the context because these are all 'direct appearances' that need to be embodied in your moving drawings.*

The *Architecture* magazine jurists did not know how to respond to the affect images of the house they conjured from photographs. They stared at its shapes, even began obsessing about them. Optical and sonic images emerged as the words of the jury attest to. A time image, which questions description, narration, even thinking itself, can form at this point of confusion if we do not retreat to familiar habits. As we have experienced in the last exercise, the time image has transported us to the crystalline regime where the truth of what we experience and even the future of architecture are in crisis. Now what? How do we move from here so we can act?

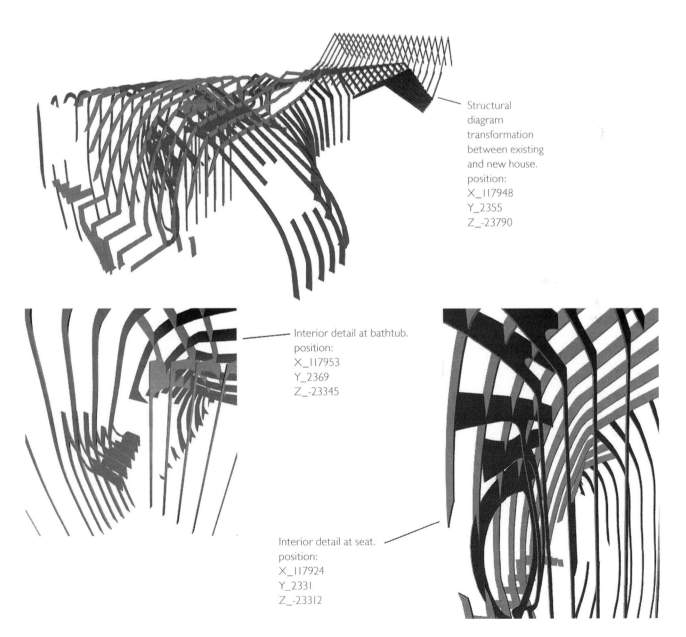

Structural
diagram
transformation
between existing
and new house.
position:
X_117948
Y_2355
Z_-23790

Interior detail at bathtub.
position:
X_117953
Y_2369
Z_-23345

Interior detail at seat.
position:
X_117924
Y_2331
Z_-23312

6_11 The shell of the house is constructed through computer numerically controlled (CNC) cut ribs from 1 inch plywood separated by standard 2 x 4s.

244   To free ourselves from being stuck in the unfamiliar images of the spaces we generate or in the strange images of the Raybould House, we can start re-assembling our moving drawings in unorthodox combinations of Peirce's three basic categories of 'direct appearances'. Then we can frame a new set of information, which enables us to act because we have re-formed cybernetically our original affect image of the building in firstness that left us suspended. This re-forming frees us from the **any-space-whatever** where our habitual response patterns first collapsed. Video artist Paul Ryan's diagram

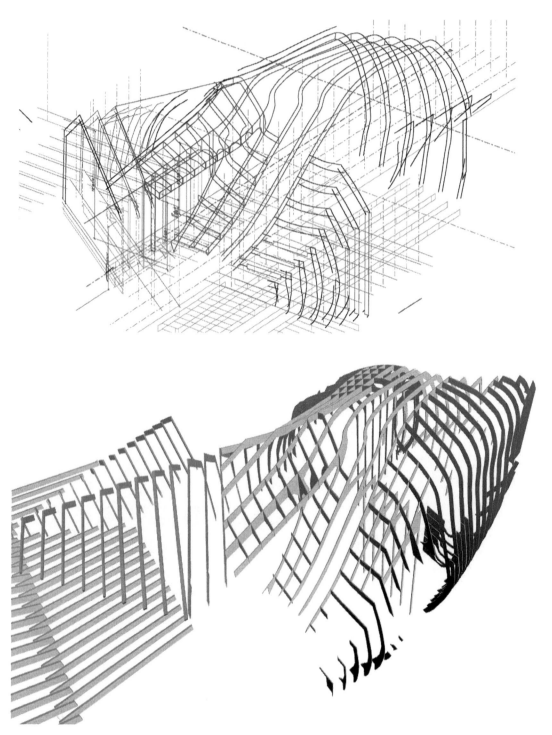

6_12 The shell of the house is constructed through computer numerically controlled (CNC) cut ribs from 1 inch plywood separated by standard 2 x 4s.

of the Relational Circuit (illus m), presented in *Losing Perspective,* demonstrates this cybernetic process. Both the Raybould House and the Relational Circuit developed using new **know-how** - cybernetics and topology – to develop a new **know-about** – how to respond to the Second Modernity**.** Let's use the house and the circuit as examples for how to develop design assemblages that can free us from inaction.

The Relational Circuit helps us think about the cybernetic interplay of the design process by diagramming relationships in the continuum of Peirce's three categories. The categories are not cuts: they form one open-ended whole. Keep in mind that cybernetics has to do with differences in relationships that make differences in other relationships that are all interconnected. Now, imagine yourself moving through the Relational Circuit in **attentive recognition**, activating your mind and your sensori-motor system. Differences in category/position within the circuit's continuum make differences in relationships to the other categories/positions. For instance, the middle diagram in the second column on the left in illus m shows how secondness contains firstness, which changes firstness because it has been affected by secondness. The third diagram shows how secondness is within thirdness, which changes both secondness and firstness.

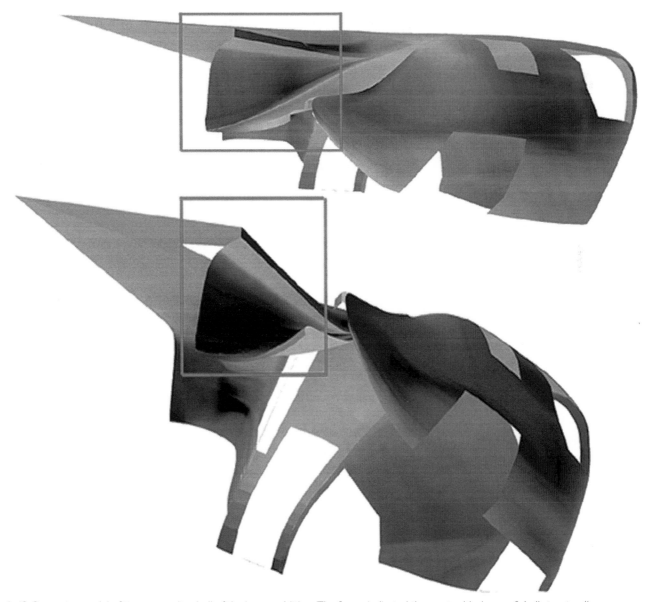

6_13 Computer model of the composite shell of the house addition. The frame indicated the most critical area of shell structurally.

6_14 and 6_15 Construction of critical area of composite shell structure.

Each of Peirce's categories and its corresponding position in the Relational Circuit also indicates a particular way of using your mind-body and generating space. In the category/position of firstness (second column on the left, first diagram in illus m), you simultaneously make and engage affect images, forming any-space-whatever. In the loop inbetween firstness and secondness you compose the impulse image and its originary world space (right column, first diagram). In the category/ position of secondness (second column on the left, second diagram), you form action images that contain affect and impulse but are primarily about action in either a skeleton or respiration space. In the position in-between secondness and thirdness (right column, middle diagram), you shape the reflective image and its transformative space. In the category/position of thirdness (second column on the left, bottom diagram) you contain affect, impulse, action and reflection in a relational image and a symbol space. There is no image in the loop between thirdness and firstness (right column, bottom diagram). In this empty position there is an opportunity to stop the generation of images and spaces before starting another round of movement. Here you can see in all directions at once. Because the circuit is intransitive, when you are in any of the six categories/positions, you can move in either direction, thus reassembling images and spaces as a result. Changes in any category/position make cybernetic changes in every other category/position. In the loop between thirdness and firstness, you not only can change direction but also reconsider the whole of your movement.

Relate the images of the Raybould House or the images you made for exercise 6.3 to categories/positions in the Relational Circuit. What results is a diagram of the cybernetic interconnections between the images. Did your **indexical** images (**secondness**) contain the feelings triggered by the **iconic** affect images (**firstness**) as well as traces of impulses? What

6_16 Laboratory testing of structural failure of composite shell. Sensors indicate the structural limits of this untested construction technique.

feedback loops can be found in your final **symbolic** relational moving drawings (**thirdness**)? How is your understanding of the relational images of the Raybould House changed by considering and incorporating the cybernetics of their formation?

Now let's connect the three categories of the Raybould analysis to the signs of ourselves and to the images we make and their spaces in order to fully understand your role in this process. When architects observe what appears to them in the state of firstness, they form signs of themselves as senso-architects and make affect images with any-spaces-whatever (illus. 6_22). In-between firstness and secondness, they are impulse architects and form impulse images and originary spaces (illus. 6_02). In secondness they form signs of themselves as either detail architects (illus 6_08, 6_10) or large scale architects or both. In these signs they make action images in skeleton and/or respiration spaces. In between secondness and thirdness

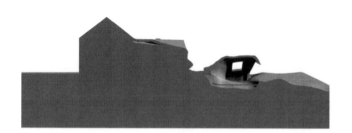

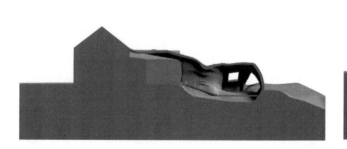
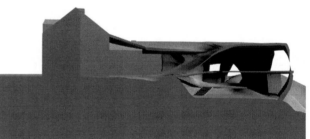

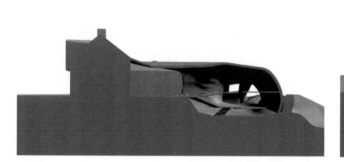
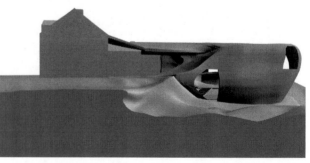

they are change-reflector architects and/or architects in an expanded field, making reflection images in transformation spaces. In thirdness, they are artist-, critic-, and cybernetic architects (Illus. 6_01) and make corresponding relation images and symbol spaces. These signs should ring a bell. In *Mobile Sections* we analysed your walk outside and also the Casa Malaparte clip to identify the signs of ourselves in an ordinary everyday activity. Again we find direct links between what we know from everyday life and architectural drawing.

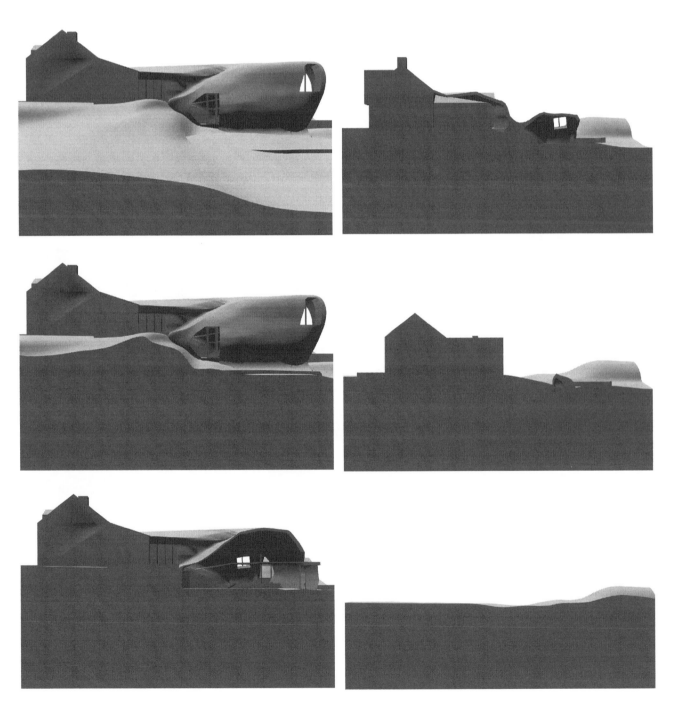

6_17 and 6_18 **Mobile section** through the side of the house showing how the space of the house is generated between the profile of the roof of the original house and the contour geometries of the site.

Finally, let's consider how you can begin to act again by moving from time images to action ones in conscious cybernetic awareness. Also, let's be sure you understand how your new sensori-motor schema now differs from the one that got your stuck in the first place. To move cybernetically entails alertness and constant awareness in order to make choices. Our new sensori-motor schema is not automatic. Instead, the new sensori-motor system of the cybernetic architect involves constantly making selections and being persistently attentive. Our new habits demand **attentive recognition** as part of

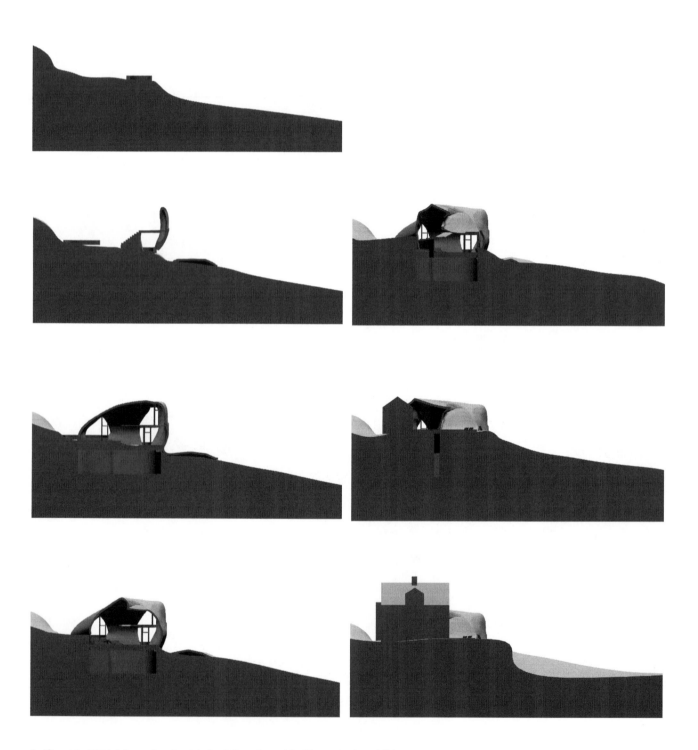

6_19 and 6_20 Mobile section front to back from the original house to the addition.

our new sensori-motor system.[12] We thus can consciously relate what we draw to direct experiences, rather than being 251 **servo-mechanisms** to our computers by only interacting robotically with electronic signals, creating images with no relation to life. Cybernetic-organic architects, working autopoietically within the expanded field of architecture, consciously take part in evolution.

De-generation of the 'New'

How can *Cinemetrics* help us understand the cybernetic process for designing moving drawings of possible worlds in the making, such as the Raybould House? Perhaps we can uncover an affect image underlying a design embodying the 'new', such as the Raybould House, that can help us understand a specific cybernetic process that generated a cybernetic architectural seed in relation to the expanded field of cultural and ecological relations.

Exercise 6.4: *How can Cinemetrics help us understand the cybernetic process for designing moving drawings of possible worlds in the making, such as the Raybould House? Let's deconstruct the Raybould House, starting with our initial reaction to it, to see what affect image may have helped lead the architects to something so 'new' – to different worlds in the making.*

What in the world is this? (illus 6_01) I see all sorts of wiggly dynamic shapes. They look like play dough floating around in something. But I see what might be a road leading to a rectangular shape, with another rectangle off to the right. Let me enlarge one of these rectangles for a closer look? (illus 6_03a) I don't believe my eyes. The shape on the left looks like an aerial view of a house roof! So what's that thing to the right of it that looks like it might eat the house?

By putting ourselves in the position of the *Architecture* awards jury, we can look at the Raybould House with fresh eyes. We'll start our **semiotic** de-generation with the fully developed proposal (illus 6_03), which is a **relation image** in a symbol space, **framed** by KolMac, cybernetic architects. What we are looking at is an addition to a traditional salt–box house. The drawing also shows existing features of the site, such as a stream flowing across the land; a kidney shaped swimming pool as well as a barn.

We de-generate from the relation image of the Raybould House to earlier drawings to help us understand how the architects assembled illus 6_01. We will analyse the relation image of the house by following two possible paths of de-generation so you can see the relational possibilities for your own drawing system. These de-generating assemblages are the reverse of the signs we combined for the walk in *Mobile Sections*.

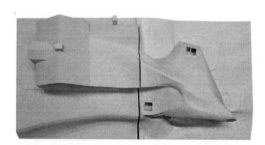
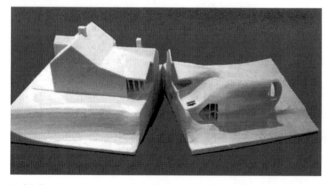
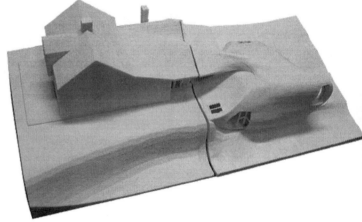

6_21 Computer-generated physical model of the house rendered in a homogeneous material.

In the **relation image**, the architects factored in their intentions as critic architects. We see these intentions in illus 6_01. They generated the patterns for the addition by hybridising the '...contour line traces at different angles through the existing house and landscape...' using various parameters. The result is a house that is '...a system of planar surfaces with ridges, peaks and valleys. Not so dissimilar to a landscape that can be defined as a system of surfaces of variable curvature with ridges, peaks and valleys.' [13]

The de-generating route from the critical drawings bifurcates. One pathway leads to a **reflection image** of the house in a transformation space in which the architects have considered how the house is in an expanded field of relations (illus 6_02). These images reveal the architects' struggle with the demands of the local ecology, the restrictions of local construction practices and the desires of the clients. The architects not only created an opimage but they also figured out how to construct the house using the computer. By generating the form of the house from the contours of the existing roof and site, they generated a space which is part of the watershed of rainwater catchments of the site, potentially bringing the house back to the close relation it had with water, soil and nutrient cycles when it was a farm house. The existing kidney shaped swimming pool is a sign that at some point in its history the use of the property changed from a farm to an urban weekend retreat, thereby losing this soil-based link to the ecological processes of the site.

From the reflection image the drawing unfolds to the house in a respiration space in which the architects are large-scale actors. We see this large-form action image in the same drawings that reveal the reflection image (illus 6_03). The architects developed their drawings by exploring the larger situation of the expanded field of architecture, which then changed their drawing actions. 'In addition to ... cross-categorical transformations (evident when we look at the reflection image), cross-scalar transformations are introduced... Considered in this way, the hierarchical interrelation of scales yield to one that is networked between scales.' [14]

The drawings in Illus 6_05 and 06 also evocate possible impulses of originary spaces the architects might have experienced while working. The interior spaces of the house addition suggest the primal shelters of cave or womb. Having merged the addition with the existing landforms, the interior feels as if it is sheltered within the earth itself.

The architects not only had to grapple with a real client and budget for the house, they had to devise a system to build the house with local contractors. They developed a controlled numerical computer cutting system of ribs, which could be easily constructed. A foam-like substance was planned to construct the shell of the house, and a lawn mower-like machine would have been used to shape its form (illus 6_11-6_13).

From here we de-generate to the illustration of vehicles (illus 6_22), which the architects made as senso-architects. The vehicles are uncannily familiar forms, which we cannot exactly place. Is that a phone or a soap dish? In fact these sculptural objects are all derived from hand-held tactile objects from everyday life that have been hybridised to create chimera-like forms.

We can follow another combination of signs through the drawings, which reveal the architects' work as artists and change-reflectors. From the critical drawings, instead of moving to reflecting on expanded fields, we go to Illus 6_05 and 06 where they studied, as change-reflector architects, the relationships between the functions accommodated in the existing house and the addition. From here we follow the path described above from drawings 6_05 and 06, showing possible impulses of originary spaces the architects might have experienced while working. We move from here to the vehicles, made as senso-architects. Either route leads to the same response to our bewildered question:

"What in the world is this?"

It is a house that has evolved from the affect image formed by the architects' tactile explorations. We have found what we were looking for. We have uncovered an affect image underlying a design embodying the 'new'! No wonder the Raybould House looks like something I could hold in my hands. It is a cybernetic seed for new worlds in the making that emerged **autopoietically** from identifiable body experiences.

The methodology of *Cinemetrics* detailed in this chapter and in previous ones can help us generate new architectures that, like the Raybould House, begin to address the cultural, ecological and material conditions of the Second Modernity. In particular, in this chapter we have explored how multifaceted time images; engendered when our sensori-motor reflexes break down, give us the opportunity to imagine different worlds in the making. These alternatives, when we realise they are embodied autopoietically in ourselves, create new feelings that can feed back to the affect images that stopped us in our tracks, changing them and releasing us from the grip of inaction. New sensori-motor schema begin to develop that enable us to draw *cinemetrically* in an expanded field of considerations that responds cybernetically to both the new **know-how** of electronic computers and the new **know-about** of architecture in the Second Modernity.

You are now a cybernetic architect, ready to generate new spaces as seeds of different worlds in the making.

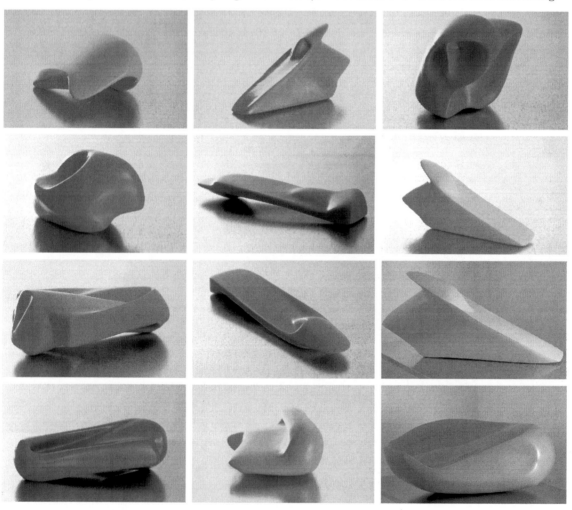

6_22 KolMac's vehicles were their first exercise in exploring 'organic' rather than 'mechanical' hybrid forms derived from familiar hand-held objects such as telephones and bottles.

1 Ulrich Beck, *Risk Society: Towards a New Modernity,* Sage Publications (London), 1992.

2 Deleuze, *Cinema 2,* pp 272, 273.

3 Rodowick, *Gilles Deleuze's Time Machine,* p 80.

4 'Raybould House', *Architecture,* Vol 90, #4 April 2001, pp 108–9.

5 Deleuze, *Cinema 2,* p 274.

6 Deleuze, *Cinema 2,* p 275.

Rodowick, *Gilles Deleuze's Time Machine,* pp 97, 83.

7 Rodowick, *Gilles Deleuze's Time Machine,* p 13.

8 Deleuze, *Cinema 2,* p 277.

9 Rodowick, *Gilles Deleuze's Time Machine,* pp 84, 86, 85.

10 Merrell, 'Thought-signs, sign-events', p 3.

11 Merrell, 'Thought-signs, sign-events',

p 20.

12 Paul Ryan, 'From Video Feedback to the Relational Circuit to Threeing', *Leonardo,* and 'A Sign of Itself', *On Semiotic Modeling,* eds F. Merrell and M. Anderson, Mouton de Gruyter (Berlin/New York), 1991.

13 GA Houses, 59, pp.105-106.

14 GA Houses, 59, pp.105-106.

PROLOGUE TO WHAT IS POSSIBLE[1]

Where to now?

The Raybould House is just one of many indications that we are experiencing a fundamental shift as architectural drawing moves from the drafting board to the computer screen. We argue that this shift is as radical as the 15th century Florentine change from a handcrafted to a mechanical culture, where perspective signalled a new way to understand and represent the world. Contemporary science and philosophy can help us frame and understand the consequences of today's paradigm shift for ourselves, for architecture and for our world, but nothing can replace direct experience. Our own personal sensori-motor experiences of this shift ultimately ground and guide us in coming to terms with our unfamiliar world.

In the course of exploring *Cinemetrics,* you were continually asked to check our words with your own experiences: **framing** matter-flux as a thought-experiment as you woke up in the morning, and then as a method of selecting computer generated images of architecture as **immobile cuts** or intervals in flowing matter-flux; **shooting** any-instant-whatever rather than privileged poses as a way of understanding duration as continual change and understanding **mobile sections** as a way of generating architectural space in expanded social and environmental relationships; and **assembling** time images in non-chronological ways. The last step was checking our words with your own direct experiences of disturbing affect images as the basis for a new sensori-motor system with which you can generate spaces and design assemblages that are **cybernetic seeds** of different worlds in the making.

The digitisation of cinema has supported developing the methodology and tools of *Cinemetrics* which examines the shift in the sensori-motor schema of the mechanical to the cybernetic architect. The digitisation allows us to more closely note the kinds of movement and time images produced in films – something we are better able to understand through repeat viewings – by isolating frames, slowing down shots, identifying the six kinds of movement images, and experimenting with different modes of assembling images. The *Cinemetric* methodology and tools also help us to create computer generated drawing systems based on cybernetic recombinations and feedback loops rather than static picture making. *Cinemetrics* promotes the simultaneous development of a new know-about architecture and ourselves along with the new know-how of digital tools.

Your new *Cinemetric* knowledge of how images are framed, shot and assembled will make you not only alert to how your own sensori-motor system behaves, but also to how our media-saturated environment preys on people's emotions. *Cinemetrics* is more than a preserve of complex concepts. It is a method of turning everyday image making towards the pressing issues and challenges of today – where architecture can play a significant role.

The pages of a book tend to form linear arguments, but we continually encouraged you to skip ahead and go backwards in the text. The illustrations ask you to occasionally turn the book around side-ways and upside down as well. This is by design, to encourage you to make sense of this material in your own time and in your own way, and to realise that it is not a recipe or formula, but the framework of a cybernetic system for making architectural drawings that *move.*

We are just at the beginning of something new. Your personal development of *Cinemetric* tools is just the first step – and why we consider it a seed of worlds in the making. The ultimate development of a more detailed drawing system linking design, social and cultural participation and communication, building production and performance evaluation, and ecology is ultimately a collective endeavor. The grand figure of the professional architect that the mechanical draftsman supported is being replaced by networked cybernetic-organic architects – a collective body joined through computer-generated drawing and communication. Collaborative work will continue to be more and more important in the practice of architecture. This is where the power of cinema to *move* people is the ultimate lesson for the **Cybernetic Architect** making architectural drawings that *move.*

The essence of a thing never appears at the outset, but in the middle, in the course of its development, when its strength is assured.[4]

1 Wallace Stevens, 'Prologues to
  What Is Possible', 'The Rock',
  The Collected Poems of Wallace
  Stevens, Alfred A. Knopf (New
  York), 1977.
2 GA Houses, 59, pp 105–6.
3 GA Houses, 59, pp 105–6.
4 Deleuze, Cinema 1, p 3.

KEYWORDS

Keywords link bold words in the text to concepts derived from Gilles Deleuze, Charles Sanders Peirce and Henri Bergson as well as define unfamiliar terms as an aid for further study.

action image: see **movement image**

affect image: see **movement image**

angle of framing: the geometric point of view of the camera frame in relation to the geometry of the set of information.

any-instant-whatever: '… cinema is the system which reproduces movement as a function of any-instant-whatever that is, as a function of equidistant instants, selected so as to create an impression of continuity.' (Deleuze, *Cinema I*, p 5.) For more information, see '**newness**'.

any-space-whatever: 'a perfectly singular space, which has merely lost its homogeneity, that is, the principle of its metric relations or the connection of its proper parts, so that the linkages can be made in an infinite number of ways. It is a space of virtual conjunction, grasped as pure locus of the possible.' (Deleuze, *Cinema I*, p 109.)

arrested image: the term Robin Evans uses for perspective projection to distinguish it from the active experience of space by a mobile viewer. See **immobile cut**.

aspect ratio: the proportional relationship between the width of the picture and the height of the picture.

assemblage: 'More than style of cutting, montage expresses a logic of composition – a concept or a regulating Idea in the philosophical sense – that informs the system of the film globally and in each of its parts. Montage indicates a particular organising principle or *agencement* of images in the form of Ideas.' (D.N. Rodowick, *Gilles Deleuze's Time Machine*, p 51.)

attentive recognition: increasingly larger circuits of memory projected on an object. (Bogue, *Deleuze on Cinema*, p 111–17.)

automatic recognition: immediate perception-memory inseparable from the object itself. (Bogue, *Deleuze on Cinema*, p 111–17.)

autopoiesis: 'literally means "auto (self)-creation" … and expresses a fundamental complementarity between structure and function. The term was originally introduced by Chilean biologists Francisco Varela and Humberto Maturana in 1973. (*Autopoiesis and Cognition: the Realization of the Living*, Robert S Cohen and Marx W Wartofsky (Eds), Boston Studies in the Philosophy of Science 42. Dordrecht: D Reidel Publishing Co.' (Wikipedia.)

blocks or frames of space-time: see **frame**

centre of indeterminacy: an interval or gap in the universal interaction of matter-flows, called also a living image. (Bogue, *Deleuze on Cinema*, p 35.) See **interval**.

closed system/set: 'includes everything which is present in the image – sets, characters, props'. (Deleuze, *Cinema I*, p 12); '"immobile sections + abstract time" refers to closed sets whose parts are in fact immobile sections, and whose successive states are calculated on an abstract time'. (Deleuze, *Cinema I*, p 11.)

coordinates of **Euclidean geometry**: see **Euclidean geometry**

crystalline regime: 'Crystalline states … reveal different ways in which the whole of that great ocean of the virtual past may be related to the ongoing actualization of time in a present moving towards the future.' (Bogue, *Deleuze on Cinema*, p 126.)
'emerges out of the social, historical, and cultural context of postwar reconstruction'. (Rodowick, p 13.)

cybernetics: the study of communication in organisms, organic processes, and mechanical systems.

duration: '[Bergson's] notion of *duree* as the time-space flux of a vibrational whole informs Deleuze's entire conception of cinema …' *Duree* is 'the dynamic movement of passing yet continuing time'. *Duree* is 'time that makes a difference, each moment bringing forth something qualitatively new.' (Bogue, *Deleuze on Cinema*, pp 3, 12, 14.)

Euclidean geometry: 'Euclidean geometry is a mathematical system due to the Greek mathematician Euclid of Alexandria … Euclid believed that his axioms were self-evident statements about physical reality. However, Einstein's theory of general relativity shows that the true geometry of spacetime is non-Euclidean … Until the 20th century, there was no technology capable [of] detecting the deviations from Euclidean geometry, but Einstein predicted that such deviations would exist. They were later verified by observations such as the observation of the slight bending of starlight by a solar eclipse in 1919.' (Wikipedia.)

fabrication/fabulation: 'The power of the false is a generative force … self-invention and the invention of [a] … story are metamorphic processes, becomings that produce a reality rather than represent it.' (Bogue, *Cinema I*, p 154.)

firstness: Charles Sanders Peirce argued that when we scrutinise qualities of direct appearances, such as colour, texture, smell, we are in **firstness**. (Merrell, 'Thought-signs, sign-events', p 3.)

frame: 'We will call *the determination of a … relatively closed system which includes everything which is present in the image – sets, characters and props – framing.*' (Deleuze, *Cinema I*, p 12.) The five aspects of framing are derived from Deleuze's discussion of framing in *Cinema I*, pp 12–18.

icon: 'possesses the character that renders it significant, even though its object has no existence.' (Charles Sanders Peirce)

image: 'Matter, in our view, is an aggregate of "images." And by "image" we mean a certain existence which is more than that which the idealist calls a *representation*, but less than that which the realist calls a *thing* – an existence placed halfway between the "thing" and the "representation."' (Bergson, *Matter and Memory*, pp 9–10.)

immobile cut or **section**: a closed system/set. See **any-instant-whatever**. (Deleuze, *Cinema I*, p 8.)

index: 'would lose the character which makes it a sign if its object were removed, but would not lose that character if there were no interpretant.' (Charles Sanders Peirce)

impulse image: see **movement image**

interval: is 'the "center of indetermination" of a living image, an *interval* or gap in the universal interaction of matter-flows.'
(Bogue, *Deleuze on Cinema*, p 35.)

know-how and **know-about**: American philosopher, psychologist, and educational reformer John Dewey distinguished between skills, or *know-how*, and concepts, or what we are calling *know-about*, in his book on the role of habit in human behaviour, *Human Nature and Conduct* (1922). 'We may be said to know how by means of our habits … We walk and read aloud, we get off and on street cars, we dress and undress, and do a thousand useful acts without thinking of them. We know something, namely, how to do them … [If] we choose to call [this] knowledge … then other things also called knowledge, knowledge of and about things, knowledge that things are thus and so, knowledge that involved reflection and conscious appreciation, remains of a different sort.' Also found in John Dewey's *Experience and Nature*, Open Court Publishing Co (Chicago), 1925.

living image: see interval

matter-flux: see **whole**

mobile section: movement is a **mobile** section of duration, that is, of the Whole. (Deleuze, *Cinema 1*, p 8.)
A computer-generated animation that does not take on the role of a virtual human eye in a simulated architectural space, but mobilises conventional architectural representations which cut and slice through buildings showing interior, exterior and membrane construction.

movement image: according to Deleuze, Henri Bergson in *Matter and Memory* (1896) diagnosed 'a crisis in psychology. Movement as physical reality in the external world, and the image, as psychic reality in consciousness, could no longer be opposed'. In his Glossary, Deleuze defines movement image as 'the acentred set of variable elements which act and react on each other'. (Deleuze, *Cinema 1*, p 217.) There are six types of movement images:

> **perception image**: 'set … of elements which act on a centre, and which vary in relation to it'. (Deleuze, *Cinema 1*, p 217.) A gaseous, liquid or solid-object space 'curves around' the perception image.
> **affection image**: 'that which occupies the gap between an action and a reaction, that which absorbs an external action and reacts on the inside'. (Deleuze, *Cinema 1*, p 217.) An any-space-whatever 'curves around' the affection image.
> **action image**: 'reaction of the centre to the set'. (Deleuze, *Cinema 1*, p 217.) A zig-zag sketelon space 'curves around' the small form action image. A respiration space curves around the large form action image.
> **impulse image**: 'the energy which seizes fragments in the originary world'. (Deleuze, *Cinema 1*, p 124.) An originary world space 'curves around' an impulse image.
> **reflection image**: '… deformations, transformations or transmutations … which go beyond the question of the action-image …' by reflecting on it. (Deleuze, *Cinema 1*, p 178.) A transformation space 'curves around' the reflection image.
> **relation image**: 'an image which takes as objects of thought, objects which have their own existence outside thought, just as the objects of perception have their own existence outside thought. It is an image that takes as its object, relations, symbolic acts, intellectual feelings'. (Deleuze, *Cinema 1*, p 198.) A symbol space 'curves around' a relation image.

Movement images are either **objective** or **subjective.** Objective perception is provisionally defined as a point of view from outside the framed set, while subjective perception is defined as a point of view from within the framed set. (Deleuze, *Cinema 1*, pp 71–6.)

newness: Deleuze notes that Bergson 'transformed philosophy by posing the question of the "new" instead of that of eternity'. (Deleuze, *Cinema I*, p 3.) Newness as any-instant-whatever is '… the production and confrontation of the singular points which are immanent to movement. Now this production of the singularities (the qualitative leap) is achieved by the accumulation of banalities (quantitative process), so that the singular is taken from the any-whatever, and is itself an any-whatever which is simply non-ordinary and non-regular.' (Deleuze, *Cinema I*, p 6.)

objective image: see **movement image**

open whole: see **whole**

optical images: 'Opsigns mark the occurrence of "something intolerable, unbearable," something "too powerful" … that exceeds our sensori-motor capacities.' (Bogue, *Deleuze on Cinema*, p 110.)

peaks or **points of the present**: The heightened experience of the present moment as the continually passing of the present into an always unreachable future. (Bogue, *Deleuze on Cinema*, pp 136–40.)

perception image: see **movement image**

privileged instant/pose: a character or figure in a unique moment. (Deleuze, *Cinema I*, p 5.)

proprioception: 'is the sense of the relative position of neighbouring parts of the body. Unlike the six exteroception human senses (sight, taste, smell, touch, hearing, and balance), by which we perceive the outside world, proprioception is an interoception sense that provides feedback solely on the status of the body internally. It is the sense that indicates whether your body is moving with required effort, as well as where the various parts of the body are located in relation to each other'. (Wikipedia.) Brian Massumi notes in *Parables for the Virtual: Movement, Affect and Sensation* that the proprioceptive sense registers stimuli before they are perceived cognitively. Deleuze is perhaps describing this sense when he writes: '[The cinema] … gives an intermediate image, to which movement is not appended or added: the movement on the contrary belongs to the intermediate image as immediate given. It might be said that the position of natural perception is the same. But there [in natural perception] the illusion [of movement] is corrected "above" perception by the conditions which make perception possible in the subject.' (Deleuze, *Cinema I*, p 2.)

reflection image: see **movement image**

relation image: see **movement image**

secondness: according to Charles Sanders Peirce, when we scrutinise facts – the specifics we are up against in the physical world – we are in **secondness**. (Merrell, 'Thought-signs, sign-events', p 3.)

semiosis: 'the process of signs becoming other signs.' (Merrell, 'Thought-signs, sign-events', p 1.)

sensori-motor schema/reflexes/system: Bergson states in *Creative Evolution* that '"the sensori-motor system" [is] the cerebro-spinal nervous system together with the sensorial apparatus in which it is prolonged and the locomotor muscles it controls,' (p 124). 'A "sensori-motor schema" organizes and coordinates the perceptions, affections, and actions of each living image, and from this schema issues a particular configuration of the world …'. (Bogue, *Deleuze on Cinema*, p 4.)

servo-mechanism: from Marshall McLuhan, *Understanding Media*, p 46: 'An Indian is the servo-mechanism of his canoe, as the cowboy of his horse or the executive of his clock.'

set of information: a way of looking at an image, not as a picture, but as a set of elements in relation to each other which give you a limited frame of the open whole.

shot: 'intermediary between the frame and montage, each shot framing a limited set of entities and at the same time suggesting the relations beyond itself that may guide its assembly in a montage sequence'. (Bogue, *Deleuze on Cinema*, p 3.) Of particular interest to the field of architecture is the fact that the French word for 'shot' is 'plan'. (Deleuze, *Cinema I*, p xii.)

symbol: is a sign, 'which would lose the character that renders it a sign if there were no interpretant.' 'A symbol has general meaning and cannot indicate any particular thing; it denotes a kind of thing. Not only that, but it is itself a kind and not a single thing.' (Charles Sanders Peirce)

tabula rasa: 'in architecture signifies the utopian blank slate on which a new building is conceived, free of compromise or complication after the demolition of what previously stood on the site.' The term originates with John Locke.(Wikipedia)

signaletic matter: a way of looking at cinema or architecture as the continual presentation of material signs to the sensate and mobile observer.

subjective image: see **movement image**

thirdness: according to Charles Sanders Peirce, when we scrutinise patterns and context, observing the whole, laws or theories, we are in thirdness. (Merrell, 'Thought-signs, sign-events', p 3.)

time crystals: '… refracting, filtering, and reflecting surfaces in which virtual and actual are made visible and rendered indiscernible as they pass into each other in circuits of exchange.' (Bogue, *Deleuze on Cinema*, p 6.)

time image: 'a direct manifestation of time'. (Bogue, *Deleuze on Cinema*, p 107.)

topology/topological invariants:
Topology. A branch of mathematics that deals with those properties of figures and surfaces which are independent of size and shape and are unchanged by any deformation that is continuous, and with those of abstract spaces that are invariant under homeomorphic transformations.
Invariant. A function of the coefficients in an expression such that, if that expression is linearly transformed, the same function of the new coefficients is equal to the first function multiplied by some power of a constant pertaining to the transformation. Any quantity or expression which is invariant under a specified transformation or operation.' *(Oxford English Dictionary.)*

'Architectural topology means the dynamic variation of form facilitated by computer-based technologies, computer-assisted design and animation software.' (Giuseppa Di Cristina [ed], *Architecture and Science*, Wiley-Academy [London], 2001, p 8.)

whole: 'Bergson's conclusion …: if the whole is not giveable … it is because it is the Open, and because its nature is to change constantly, or to give rise to something new, in short, to endure. "The duration of the universe must therefore be one with the latitude of creation which can find place in it".' (Deleuze, *Cinema I*, p 9.) '"The real whole might well be … an invisible continuity".' (Deleuze, *Cinema I*, p 10.)

BIBLIOGRAPHY

Books

Bateson, Gregory, *Steps to an Ecology of Mind: A Revolutionary Approach to Man's Understanding of Himself,* Ballantine Books (New York), 1972

Beck, Ulrich, *Risk Society: Towards a New Modernity,* Sage Publications (London), 1992

Bergson, Henri, *Creative Evolution,* trans Arthur Mitchell, University Press of America (Lanham, MD), 1983 (originally published in 1907)

Bergson, Henri, *Matter and Memory,* trans NM Paul and WS Palmer, Zone Books (New York), 1991 (originally published in 1896)

Bogue, Ronald, *Deleuze on Cinema,* Routledge (New York), 2003

Bordwell, David, *Ozu and the Poetics of Cinema,* Princeton University Press (Princeton), 1988

Capra, Fritjof, *The Web of Life: A New Scientific Understanding of Living Systems,* Anchor Books, Doubleday (New York), 1996

Carney, Ray, *The Films of John Cassavetes: Pragmatism, Modernism, and the Movies,* Cambridge University Press (Cambridge), 1994

268   Carringer, Robert L, *The Making of Citizen Kane,* University of California Press (Berkeley), 1996

Crary, Jonathan, *Techniques of the Observer: On Vision and Modernity in the Nineteenth Century,* An October Book, MIT Press (Cambridge, MA), 1990

Deleuze, Gilles, *Cinema 1: the Movement Image,* trans Hugh Tomlinson and Barbara Habberjam, University of Minnesota Press (Minneapolis, MN), 1986. *Cinema 2: the Time-Image,* trans Hugh Tomlinson and Robert Galeta, University of Minnesota Press (Minneapolis, MN), 1989

Dewey, John, *Experience and Nature,* Open Court Publishing Co (Chicago), 1925

Dewey, John, *Human Nature and Conduct: An Introduction to Social Psychology,* G Allen & Unwin (London), 1922

Di Cristina, Giuseppa (ed), *Architecture and Science, AD,* Wiley-Academy, 2001

Dubery, Fred and John Willats, *Perspective and other Drawing Systems,* Van Nostrand Reinhold Company (New York), 1972

Evans, Robin, *The Projective Cast: Architecture and Its Three Geometries,* MIT Press (Cambridge, MA), 1995

Hansen, Mark BN, *New Philosophy for New Media,* MIT Press (Cambridge, MA), 2006

Hensel, Mark, Menges, Achim, Weinstock, Michael (ed*),* *Techniques and Technologies in Morphogenetic Design, AD,* Wiley-Academy, March/April 2006

Hockney, David, *Photographs,* International Exhibitions Foundation (Washington, DC), 1986

Kepes, Gyorgy, *Language of Vision,* Paul Theobald (Chicago), 1951

Martin, Leslie C, *Design Graphics,* The Macmillan Company (New York), 1968

Massumi, Brian, *Parables for the Virtual: Movement, Affect and Sensation,* Duke University Press (Durham, North Carolina), 2002

Maturana, Humberto and Varela, Francisco, *The Tree of Knowledge: The Biological Roots of Human Understanding,* Shambhala Publications (Boston, MA), 1987

McLuhan, Marshall, *Understanding Media: The Extensions of Man,* Signet Book, New American Library (New York), 1964

Peirce, Charles Sanders, *The Essential Peirce: Selected Philosophical Writings,* Vol 2 (1893–1913), ed by The Peirce Edition Project, Indiana University Press (Bloomington, Indiana), 1998

Rodowick, D.N., *Gilles Deleuze's Time Machine,* Duke University Press (Durham, North Carolina), 1997

Ryan, Paul, 'A Sign of Itself', *Video Mind, Earth Mind: Art, Communication and Ecology,* Peter Lang (New York), 1993

Silverman, Kaja and Harun Farocki, *Speaking about Godard,* New York University Press (New York), 1998

Talamona, Marida, *Casa Malaparte*, trans Vittoria di Palma, Princeton Architectural Press (Princeton), 1996

Ware, William, *Modern Perspective: A Treatise upon the Principles and Practice of Plane and Cylindrical Perspective,* The MacMillan Company (New York), 1905

Journal Articles

Kolatan, Sulan and William J MacDonald, 'Raybould House, Fairfield, Connecticut; Architects: Kolatan & MacDonald Studio', *Domus* #822, January 2000, pp 14–19

Merrell, Floyd, 'Thought-signs, sign-events', *Semiotica: Journal of the International Association for Semiotic Studies,* Vols 87–112, pp 1–57, 1991

'Raybould House and Garden, Connecticut; Architects: Kolatan MacDonald Studio', *GA Houses,* no 59, February 1999, pp 106–7

'Raybould House', *Architecture* Vol 90, #4 April 2001, pp 108–13

Ryan, Paul, 'From Video Feedback to the Relational Circuit to Threeing', *Leonardo*, Vol 39, No 3, pp. 199–203, 2006

INDEX

Sulan Kolatan, Max Fisher Visiting Professor at University of Michigan and Partner in KOL/MAC LLC and William Mac Donald, Professor and Chair of Graduate Architecture and Urban Design at School of Architecture, Pratt Institute, and Partner in KOL/MAC LLC:

'By progressively positioning their architectural research on "digital drawing" as contemporary cultural practice, Brian McGrath and Jean Gardner demonstrate not only a unique lateral intelligence but – to paraphrase George Lang's declaration that tradition is a conspiracy often used to keep the future from happening – ensure that the future is happening now. This daringly analytical book precisely and effectively delineates heretofore hidden systems of emergent relations between ideology, methodology, representation and production.'

Joan Ockman, Director of the Temple Hoyne Buell Center for the Study of American Architecture, Graduate School of Architecture, Planning and Preservation, Columbia University:

'With this engaging, mind-expanding and original guide to contemporary modalities of visualizing and representing architecture, the authors usher the not-yet-initiated into the digital design age.'

Mark Robbins, Dean and Professor, Syracuse University School of Architecture

'Cinemetrics extends the parameters of representation by drawing on aspects of media, film and video. This book is an addition to the lineage of expanding the pictorial field – the Nude Descending a Staircase meeting the battleship Potempkin. The digital drawing methodology produces an explosive shattering of architectural space and reflects the understanding of multiple vantage points and the simultaneity of events in the manner of postmodern literature and filmmakers such as Godard. These drawings have the power to communicate as seductively as the moving image how architecture, space, inhabitation, perception and experience unfold over time. The book offers new ways to analyze space and more importantly new ways of generating it.'

Professor Neil Spiller, Professor of Architecture and Digital Theory, Vice Dean, Bartlett School of Architecture, University College London:

'In a world of change, fluctuating points of view, duration and virtuality, it is vital for designers to reassess the representation of their work in new and non-orthogonal ways. This book addresses this most fundamental of design questions and explains various representational protocols for the designer at the cusp of the twenty-first century. A must have book.'

Susan S Szenasy, Editor in Chief, *Metropolis Magazine*:

'A new generation of architects and designers has turned from the drafting table to computer drafting and design, seemingly seamlessly and without much turmoil. But, in reality, a whole new way of thinking about architecture has developed – the computer is changing way designers see the physical world. *Cinemetrics: Architectural Drawing* Today discusses the theory and practice of design in the digital age.

Karen Van Lengen, Dean and Edward E Elson Professor of School of Architecture, University of Virginia:

'This is a serious and timely book that proposes new methods of representation for designers working in the digital age. The "moving drawing system" celebrates the designer as a multidimensional thinker, a networked thinker, a flux conductor in search of new relationships and possibilities for cultural and environmental design. This book, with its stunning and sophisticated visual documentation, is destined to be an essential resource for the next generation of designers.'

Michael Weinstock, Academic Head and Master of Technical Studies, Architectural Association School of Architecture:

'The presentation of a drawing system based on a cinematic understanding of the dynamics of architectural space is admirably clear, and the system has the potential to generate new spaces.'

Kim Tanzer, Association of Collegiate Schools of Architecture (ACSA) President 2007-08, Professor of Architecture, University of Florida:

'Five hundred years from now architects may look at Cinemetrics the way today's architects look at Alberti's *On Painting* – as a critical point of disciplinary redirection. In fact, if architecture is still being built 500 years from now it may well be as a result of the cognitive shift McGrath and Gardner propose, asking us to "lose perspective and find duration." In the process of laying out a concrete set of design strategies, this book makes original connections between theory and ecology, science and art, technology and touch.'

Printed and bound in the UK by
CPI Antony Rowe, Eastbourne